Database Dreaming

Volume II

Relational Writings Revised

and Revived

C. J. Date

Published by:

115 Linda Vista, Sedona, AZ 86336 USA
https://www.TechnicsPub.com

Cover design by Lorena Molinari

First Printing 2022

Printed in the United States of America.

ISBN, print ed.	9781634629881
ISBN, Kindle ed.	9781634629898
ISBN, ePub ed.	9781634629904
ISBN, PDF ed.	9781634629911

Library of Congress Control Number: 2021953505

You see things, and you say, "Why?"
But I dream things that never were, and I say "Why not?"
—George Bernard Shaw:
Back to Methuselah (1921)

I suspect that there are more things in heaven and earth
than are dreamed of, or can be dreamed of,
in any philosophy.
—J. B. S. Haldane:
Possible Worlds (1927)

Many's the long night I've dreamed of cheese—
toasted, mostly.
—Robert Louis Stevenson:
Treasure Island (1883)

[There] is no scorn more profound, or on the whole more justifiable,
than that of the men who make for the men who explain.
Exposition, criticism, appreciation, is work for second-rate minds.
—G. H. Hardy:
A Mathematician's Apology (1940)

——— ♦♦♦♦♦ ———

***To all my old friends and colleagues at LEO—
stars and pioneers***

About the Author

C. J. Date is an independent author, lecturer, researcher, and consultant, specializing in relational database technology. He is best known for his book *An Introduction to Database Systems* (8th edition, Addison-Wesley, 2004), which has sold some 900,000 copies at the time of writing and is used by several hundred colleges and universities worldwide. He is also the author of numerous other books on database management, including most recently:

- From Morgan Kaufmann: *Time and Relational Theory: Temporal Databases in the Relational Model and SQL* (with Hugh Darwen and Nikos A. Lorentzos, 2014)

- From O'Reilly: *Relational Theory for Computer Professionals: What Relational Databases Are Really All About* (2013); *View Updating and Relational Theory: Solving the View Update Problem* (2013); *SQL and Relational Theory: How to Write Accurate SQL Code* (3rd edition, 2015); *The New Relational Database Dictionary* (2016); *Type Inheritance and Relational Theory: Subtypes, Supertypes, and Substitutability* (2016)

- From Apress: *Database Design and Relational Theory: Normal Forms and All That Jazz* (2nd edition, 2019)

- From Technics: *Logic and Relational Theory: Thoughts and Essays on Database Matters* (2020); *Fifty Years of Relational, and Other Database Writings: More Thoughts and Essays on Database Matters* (2020); *Stating the Obvious, and Other Database Writings: Still More Thoughts and Essays on Database Matters* (2020); *E. F. Codd and Relational Theory, Revised Edition: A Detailed Review and Analysis of Codd's Major Database Writings* (2021); *Database Dreamings Volume I: Relational Writings Revised and Revived* (2022)

Mr Date was inducted into the Computing Industry Hall of Fame in 2004. He enjoys a reputation that is second to none for his ability to explain complex technical subjects in a clear and understandable fashion.

Contents

Preface

The title of this book is, of course, Database Dreamings Volume II. The preface that follows consists of a lightly and appropriately edited version of the preface from the book's predecessor, Volume I.

A little while ago I gave an online presentation with the title "My Life as a Writer." During the discussion that followed, one of the attendees raised the point that many of the shorter pieces I'd written over the years, ones I'd touched on in my presentation, were now quite hard to find. And it's true: Despite the fact that most of the pieces in question have been collected and published in various "Relational Writings" books over the years, most of those books now seem to be out of print. The attendee went on to suggest that I might want to do something about this state of affairs. He was right, and I did, and—together with its predecessor, Volume I—this book is the result. To be specific, what I did was the following: I went back and reviewed all of those "Writings" books, looking for pieces that seemed to be worth reviving (or, rather, revising and reviving) at this time. Of course, some of them definitely weren't! However, out of a total of around 130 original papers, I did find some 20 or so that (a) seemed to me worth preserving and (b) hadn't already been incorporated in, or superseded by, more recent books of mine. So I tracked down the original versions of those 20 plus papers and set to work. When I was done, though, I found I had somewhere in excess of 600 pages on my hands—too much, in my view, for just one book, and so I split the pieces across two separate volumes.

Let me say a word about my title, *Database Dreaming*. It's meant primarily as a respectful nod to the culture and belief system of the Aboriginal peoples of Australia (though it does also reflect my own personal dreams in this connection). One of the simplest and best introductions I know to Aboriginal Dreamings and the Dreamtime is in Bruce Chatwin's beautiful book *The Songlines*. Here are a few quotes:

> In Genesis, God first created the "living things" and then fashioned Father Adam from clay ... [In the Dreamtime] the Ancestors created themselves from clay, hundreds and thousands of them, one for each totemic species.

Any species ... can be a Dreaming. A virus can be a Dreaming. You can have a chickenpox Dreaming, a rain Dreaming, a desert-orange Dreaming, a lice dreaming. In the Kimberleys they've now got a money dreaming.

Aboriginals [believe] that all the living things had been made in secret beneath the earth's crust, as well as all the white man's gear – his aeroplanes, his guns, his Toyota Land Cruisers – and every invention that will ever be invented; slumbering below the surface, waiting their turn to be called.

Structure of the Book

Actually there isn't much (structure, that is)—most of the chapters were originally written to stand alone and are thus, for the most part, independent of all the others. However, I've tried to arrange them in such a way that if you do want to read them in sequence, then there is a kind of flow to them. I've also done my best to edit out the worst of the overlaps and inconsistencies among them, though to what extent I've succeeded in that effort I'll let you be the judge.

Technical Background

My target audience is database professionals; thus, I assume you're reasonably familiar with both the relational model and the SQL language. However, there are a few technical terms that (a) are appealed to repeatedly and (b) might not be as familiar to you as all that, so I thought it would be a good idea to define and explain them here, in the preface. The terms in question are *relvar*, **Tutorial D**, and *commalist*.

Relvar: "Relvar" is short for *relation variable*. What all too many people still call just "relations" (meaning constructs in the database, that is) are indeed really variables; after all, their value does change over time as INSERT, DELETE, and UPDATE operations are performed, and "changing over time" is exactly what makes them variable. In fact, *not* distinguishing clearly between relation values and relation variables—or table values and table variables, in SQL—has led to an immense amount of confusion in the past, and indeed continues to do so to this day. In our work on *The Third Manifesto*, therefore, Hugh Darwen and I decided to face up to this problem right from the outset. To be specific, in that *Manifesto* we framed all of our remarks in terms of relation values when it really was relation values that we meant, and in terms of relation variables when it really was relation variables that we meant, and we abided by this discipline rigorously (indeed, one hundred percent). However, we also introduced two abbreviations: We allowed "relation value" to be abbreviated to just *relation* (exactly as we allow, e.g., "integer value" to be abbreviated to just *integer*), and we allowed "relation variable" to be abbreviated to *relvar*.

Tutorial D*:* I mentioned *The Third Manifesto* in the previous paragraph. Now, *The Third Manifesto* (the *Manifesto* for short) isn't a language definition; rather, it's a prescription for the functionality that its authors, Hugh Darwen and myself, claim a language must provide in order to be considered truly relational. But we did need a way of referring generically to any such language within our *Manifesto*, and we used the name **D** for that purpose. Note carefully, therefore, that **D** isn't a language as such, it's a family of languages; there could be any number of individual languages all qualifying as a valid member of that family. **Tutorial D** is one such.[1] **Tutorial D** is based on the relational algebra; it's defined more or less formally in the *Manifesto* book,[2] and it's used throughout that book and elsewhere—the present book included—as a basis for examples. In fact, I and others have been using that language for such purposes in books and presentations for many years now, and I think our experience in that regard has shown that it's both well designed and fairly self-explanatory.

Note that the names **D** and **Tutorial D** are always set in boldface as shown.

Commalist: This term is used heavily in syntax definitions and the like. It's short for "comma separated list." It can be defined as follows: Let *xyz* be some syntactic construct (for example, "attribute name"); then the term *xyz commalist* denotes a sequence of zero or more *xyz*'s in which each pair of adjacent *xyz*'s is separated by a comma. Within a given commalist, spaces appearing immediately before the first item or any comma, or immediately after the last item or any comma, are ignored. For example, if *A*, *B*, and *C* are attribute names, then the following are all attribute name commalists:

---

[1] By contrast, SQL isn't.

[2] *Databases, Types, and the Relational Model: The Third Manifesto*, by Hugh Darwen and myself (3rd edition, Addison-Wesley, 2007). *Note:* We've made a number of improvements to the language since that book was published, however. Those changes, along with much other relevant material, can be found on the website *www.thethirdmanifesto.com*.

```
A , B , C

C , A , B

B

A , C
```

So too is the empty sequence of attribute names.

Suppliers and parts: Many of the examples in this book makes use of the familiar suppliers-and-parts database. Here's the usual sample value:

S

SNO	SNAME	STATUS	CITY
S1	Smith	20	London
S2	Jones	10	Paris
S3	Blake	30	Paris
S4	Clark	20	London
S5	Adams	30	Athens

SP

SNO	PNO	QTY
S1	P1	300
S1	P2	200
S1	P3	400
S1	P4	200
S1	P5	100
S1	P6	100
S2	P1	300
S2	P2	400
S3	P2	200
S4	P2	200
S4	P4	300
S4	P5	400

P

PNO	PNAME	COLOR	WEIGHT	CITY
P1	Nut	Red	12.0	London
P2	Bolt	Green	17.0	Paris
P3	Screw	Blue	17.0	Oslo
P4	Screw	Red	14.0	London
P5	Cam	Blue	12.0	Paris
P6	Cog	Red	19.0	London

And here are definitions, expressed in **Tutorial D**, of the three relvars in this database:

```
VAR S BASE RELATION    /* suppliers */
  { SNO    SNO ,
    SNAME  NAME ,
    STATUS INTEGER ,
    CITY   CHAR }
  KEY { SNO } ;
```

```
VAR P BASE RELATION     /* parts */
  { PNO     PNO ,
    PNAME   NAME ,
    COLOR   COLOR ,
    WEIGHT  RATIONAL ,
    CITY    CHAR }
  KEY { PNO } ;

VAR SP BASE RELATION    /* shipments */
  { SNO     SNO ,
    PNO     PNO ,
    QTY     INTEGER }
  KEY { SNO , PNO }
  FOREIGN KEY { SNO }
          REFERENCES S
  FOREIGN KEY { PNO }
          REFERENCES P ;
```

Note: I've made a few small changes to the foregoing definitions for the purposes of this volume. To be specific, in Volume I attributes SNO, PNO, SNAME, PNAME, and COLOR were all defined to be of type CHAR; here they're of various user defined types instead—SNO is of a user defined type also called SNO; PNO is of a user defined type also called PNO; SNAME and PNAME are both of a user defined type called NAME; and COLOR is of a user defined type also called COLOR.

Now read on ...

C. J. Date
Morristown, Vermont
2022

Chapter 1

Much Ado about Nothing

Part 1

In December 1992 and January 1993 I published a pair of articles with the titles "Why Three-Valued Logic Is a Mistake" and "Nothing in Excess," respectively. The articles in question—a combined and edited version of which appears as an appendix to Chapter 2—were consecutive installments in the regular series I was doing at the time for the magazine Database Programming & Design ("DBP&D" for short), and what they did was briefly review a few of the things that I believe are wrong with the idea of using nulls and three-valued logic (3VL) as a basis for handling missing information. Among the letters I received after the articles appeared was one from Ted Codd, who—unsurprisingly, since he was responsible for proposing that idea in the first place—didn't agree with my criticisms at all. His letter, together with my response to it, grew into a somewhat lengthy debate that subsequently appeared as an article in its own right in a later issue of DBP&D. Of course, it goes without saying that the debate didn't lead to any kind of resolution or agreement between us; however, I still think it's useful, inasmuch as it does at least air many of the arguments on both sides of the issue. So what follows is an updated version of that original debate.

Publishing history: This is a considerably revised version of, and supersedes, a published debate between Ted Codd and myself[1] that first appeared in Database Programming & Design 6, No. 10 (October 1993) and was later republished in my book Relational Database Writings 1991-1994 (Addison-Wesley, 1995). I've divided this revised version into two parts to make it a little more

---

[1] It goes without saying that in the case of Codd's remarks the revisions are cosmetic only—I haven't changed the meaning of those remarks in any way.

*digestible—the first part contains the debate as such, the second
contains some further thoughts and technical correspondence. This
version (both parts) copyright © C. J. Date 2022.*

It's convenient to begin with a lightly edited version of *DBP&D*'s own
introduction to the original published version of the debate:

> A point / counterpoint on the tough issue of missing values ... E. F. Codd and
> C. J. Date are two of the best known figures in the history, development, and
> exposition of what was a breakthrough concept in database technology: the
> relational model. Ever since the model was first defined by Codd in 1970, in his
> famous paper "A Relational Model of Data for Large Shared Data Banks,"[2] we've
> been reading, listening to, and interpreting their commentaries on it. While Codd
> and Date have agreed upon much during the course of the relational model's
> evolution and implementation, on some issues they definitely don't agree. One
> important disagreement—and the topic of this special article—centers on the issue
> of nulls and missing values, and the underlying theoretical problems of three- and
> four-valued logic.
>
> Both have written extensively on these topics, as is clear from the
> "References" section in what follows.[3] The [criticisms] presented here were
> sparked by Date's columns in *DBP&D* last December and January, when he
> discussed the three-valued logic approach to missing information. Codd then sent
> us his criticisms of Date's columns; [those criticisms] are presented here. Date
> then provided a series of rebuttals to specific points of Codd's, which follow
> Codd's remarks. Finally, we gave Codd a chance to rebut Date's rebuttal.
>
> For the reader's convenience, we've kept Codd's [criticisms] together, so
> they can be read as a whole. We've noted throughout, however, where Date's
> specific rebuttals apply, and should be read. This way, the reader can follow
> Codd's [criticisms] all the way through, and then return to his essay, reading
> Date's rebuttals as appropriate.[4]

---

[2] Actually Codd first described his model in 1969, not 1970, in an IBM Research Report with the title
"Derivability, Redundancy, and Consistency of Relations Stored in Large Data Banks" (IBM Research
Report RJ599, August 19th, 1969). The much better known 1970 paper consisted essentially of a somewhat
revised version of that 1969 paper. *Note:* The original 1969 version was quite hard to find until it was
eventually republished in *ACM SIGMOD Record 38*, No. 1 (May 2009).

[3] That section appears in the next chapter.

[4] I have to say I don't quite follow this sentence. I'm glad it wasn't me who wrote it. *Note added later:*
Perhaps it means "return and read Codd's criticisms again, but this time reading Date's rebuttals at the
appropriate points."

At first, the issues might seem arcane and theoretical, but most developers and DBAs know they're clearly not, and merit serious debate. Missing values remain one of the toughest—and potentially most dangerous—problems in database technology.

CODD'S COMMENTS

Although Date has been a strong supporter of the relational approach to database management for over 20 years,[5] from time to time I have found that his criticisms of the relational model have been incorrect. I do agree with many of his criticisms of SQL; however, he often fails to make a clear distinction between SQL and the relational model. SQL came after the relational model was described; it was invented by a small IBM group in the Yorktown Heights (N.Y.) Research Laboratory. In my book, *The Relational Model for Database Management: Version 2* [4], I make it clear what semantic properties a relational language should have if it is to conform to the model, and label such a language *RL*. I also describe three major shortcomings of SQL (there are, of course, numerous others [4]):

- As a user option, SQL permits rows to occur within a single relation that are complete duplicates of each other. I call this a *tabular error* because it is based on two misconceptions:

    1. That relations and tables are in one to one correspondence, and

    2. That duplicate rows are essential to some applications.

- Full support of first order predicate logic is sacrificed in the name of user friendliness. I call this a *pyschological mixup*: A logically sound language is absolutely necessary as a foundation. Any useful "user friendly" features should be grafted as a layer on top, along with rigorously defined translation between layers.

- The treatment of missing information is wrong for two reasons:

---

[5] That was in 1993. Now it's over 50 years.

1. Support in the language for multivalued logic is grossly inadequate, and

2. A user is permitted to designate a value that is acceptable to a column specifically to indicate the fact that some value is missing from that column. I call this latter error one of *missing value misrepresentation*.

Date has criticized the multivalued logic approach to missing values in the relational model, claiming it can lead to catastrophic errors. He has advocated the missing value misrepresentation approach, which he calls the *default value* approach. In 1986, when Date had his original paper [5] reprinted in the U.S., I prepared a technical response [3].[6]

The ideas behind Date's default value approach came completely from prerelational products that used single record at a time processing. The default value approach appealed to RDBMS vendors because it placed all of the responsibility for the representation and handling of missing values in a relational database completely on the users. However, I think it is best described as a nonsolution to the problem, and a complete evasion of the issue. The approach contains no clear description of how missing values in a column are to be treated. That means that the treatment will often be invented by application programmers and buried in their programs. It also means that there are likely to be many different treatments buried in numerous programs.

Now that we are dealing with RDBMSs that employ multiple record at a time processing, this default value approach is unacceptable for the following reasons:

1. The *meaning* of the fact that a value is missing from some part or column of a relational database is quite different from the meaning of a value that is legitimate within that part or column.

2. A single relational request can touch many different columns in a relational database, and therefore it is intolerable that in conceiving such a request the

---

[6] The history isn't quite as Codd describes it here. It's true that I published a paper called "Null Values in Database Management"—an invited paper, incidentally—in the proceedings of a U.K. conference in 1982; it's also true that in that paper I criticized nulls and sketched what I called a "less ambitious" alternative approach, based on default values; and finally it's also true that I republished that paper in my book *Relational Database: Selected Writings* (Addison-Wesley) in 1986. But the paper in question was just an expanded version of something I originally wrote in 1980 or 1981 at the very latest [5], something that I'd shown to Codd *and discussed with him, at length, in his office at IBM, at the time*. So he shouldn't be claiming as he seems to be doing here that he didn't became aware of that paper until 1986.

user should have to understand and cope with as many different representations and treatments of missing values as the columns that are touched. In a relational database, both the representation and treatment of missing values *must* be uniform across the entire database.

```
┌─────────────────────────────┐
│   See Date's Rebuttal I     │
└─────────────────────────────┘
```

Date and other critics of multivalued logic claim that serious errors are inevitable if a multivalued logic is made available to users. However, such critics have failed to provide a single example of a *severely wrong* answer being delivered as a result of a multivalued logic. A result is severely incorrect if the logical expression is evaluated by the DBMS to be

- *True* when it is actually *false* or *unknown*, or

- *False* when it is actually *true* or *unknown*.

A result is *mildly incorrect* if the DBMS evaluates an expression as *unknown* when it is actually either *true* or *false*. In the paper in which I introduced three-valued logic (3VL) [2], I cited an example of a request *mildly mishandled* by 3VL: For some requests the condition would be evaluated as *unknown* when the correct answer was *true* or *false*, if the DBMS were unable to recognize tautologies. This example shows that simple 3VL should be augmented by some inferential capability. An example would be the following: Suppose that the birth year is recorded for most employees, but is missing from the database for a few. Now, consider the request: Retrieve the serial numbers and names of employees for each of whom

1. The birth year is 1960, or

2. The birth year is earlier than 1960, or

3. The birth year is later than 1960.

Suppose the DBMS does NOT have the capability of recognizing that the whole condition must be *true* for every employee, whether the birth year happens to be missing or not. That is, it is unable to detect tautologies or contradictions.

Then for those employees whose birth year is unknown, the DBMS comes up with *unknown* for each of the three subconditions. And, using the rule that for truth values *unknown* OR *unknown* is *unknown*, it evaluates the whole condition to be *unknown*. This is an example of a mild error. This kind of error is just as likely to occur (and other kinds much more likely) if the responsibility for handling missing information is placed totally on the users.

```
See Date's Rebuttal II
```

Now, an obvious cure for [this kind of mild error] is to equip the DBMS not only with 3VL, but also with the capability of recognizing for any whole condition whether it is a tautology. This would be easy if only propositional logic were being supported. However, the relational model requires the more powerful predicate logic to be supported in specifying the condition part of a request. It is well known that it is a logically undecidable problem to determine whether an arbitrary formula in predicate logic is a tautology or a contradiction.

Therefore, it is pointless to search for an allegedly universal algorithm for detecting all possible tautologies and all possible contradictions. A reasonably good algorithm can be developed that will take care of at least all of the simple cases that will be encountered in commercial activities, and this algorithm should be incorporated into every RDBMS product. The RDBMS will then make mild errors only when a most unusual request is made. An RDBMS must admit its inability to deduce a sound response to a user request whenever this is impossible because of missing values. Also, present treatment by SQL of missing values is, in my opinion, totally unsatisfactory. For a more complete treatment of missing values and a refutation of Date's criticisms, refer to my book [4].

```
See Date's Rebuttal III
```

Date's argument that *true* and *false* are the only truth values, and that, therefore, *unknown* cannot be treated as a logical value makes no sense to me. After all, it is very common in mathematics to label unknown values by letters such as m, n, x, y, z. The fact that the letters m, n do not "look like" any of the integers does not prevent them from actually having integer values in an expression such as $m + n$, $m - n$, or an assertion that $m \times m = n$. In any event, when dealing with missing values, an RDBMS must be able to determine whether [each of] NOT A,

A OR B, and A AND B is *true, false*, or *unknown* when A, or B, or both are *unknown*.

Date's argument that the number of distinct functions from truth values to truth values is very large, and that fact makes 3VL and four-valued logic (4VL) unusable is ridiculous. After all, the number of distinct functions from integers to integers is infinite, because the number of distinct integers is infinite. However, no one in his right mind would use that as an argument that integers are unusable.

Taking the whole of Date's article into consideration, I completely reject Date's claims:[7]

- To have inserted "more nails into the 3VL coffin";

- That it is time to drop the pretense that 3VL is a good thing.

| See Date's Rebuttal IV |

DATE'S REBUTTAL I

Let me begin by making one thing crystal clear: My quarrel isn't with the relational model. On the contrary, I felt at the time when it was first introduced, and I still feel now, that the original model was a work of genius. All of us owe Dr Codd a huge debt of gratitude for his major contribution. And, as the originator and "elder statesman" of relational theory, Codd always deserves the courtesy of very close attention to his remarks on relational matters.

Actually there's something else I'd like to make "crystal clear" as well. In his remarks, Codd accuses me of "often failing to make a clear distinction between SQL and the relational model." I utterly deny this charge![8] In fact I'm rather amazed that anyone, let alone Codd himself, would even consider making it, given my well known and well documented criticisms of SQL as such— especially since those criticisms are directed in very large part at, specifically,

---

[7] These "claims" (characterized as such by Codd, not me) are paraphrased versions of remarks I made in the second of my *DBP&D* articles [8].

[8] Especially since, with respect to the present debate specifically, I went out of my way in the first of the two *DBP&D* articles that triggered that debate [7] to say this: "Let me make it quite clear that my argument here is not so much with SQL per se; rather, it's with the underlying theory, namely 3VL, on which SQL is based." (As you'll see from the appendix to the next chapter, this is a direct quote.)

SQL's failure to serve as a good realization in concrete terms of the abstract concepts of the relational model. What's more, many of those documented criticisms appeared in the public domain well before 1993, the date of this debate. Some of them were even published under the auspices of our own consulting company!—the company, that is (Codd & Date International), of which Codd and I were principals and founding members.

So, to say it again, my quarrel isn't with the relational model, but rather with nulls and three-valued logic (3VL), which were first discussed by Codd in detail in a database context in 1979 [2].[9] It's true that Codd now regards 3VL as an integral part of the relational model, but I don't (and I'm not alone in taking this position). Indeed, the whole question of how to handle missing information is largely independent of whether the underlying model is relational or something else. Thus, I'd like to distinguish very carefully between what we might call "RM" (the original model, with two-valued logic) and "RM+3VL" (Codd's version, with three-valued logic). My quarrel, to repeat, is with the "3VL" portion of "RM+3VL."

Now, regarding Codd's first point (viz., that default values misrepresent the fact that information is missing): I don't dispute this! However, I'd like to make two points:

1. It's default values, not nulls, that we use in the real world, as I pointed out in reference [7].

2. Nulls misrepresent the semantics too (see below). In other words, I don't think we yet know how *not* to misrepresent the semantics; and given that this is so, I take the position that we shouldn't undermine the solid foundation of the relational model with something as suspect as 3VL, when it demonstrably doesn't solve the problem anyway.[10]

Note: When I talk about "undermining the foundations of the relational model," what I mean is that a "relation" that contains nulls, whatever else it might be, *isn't a relation.* As a consequence, the entire foundation crumbles; we can't be sure any longer of *any* aspect of the underlying theory, and all bets are

---

[9] Actually Codd did include a kind of passing reference to such matters in reference [1], which was published in 1971—but reference [2] was the first publication in which he discussed the ideas in any depth.

[10] In other words, I think we should apply *The Principle of Cautious Design* [13].

off. I find it hard to believe that Codd really wants to destroy the entire edifice that he has so painstakingly constructed over the years.

Let me elaborate briefly on the foregoing paragraph. I said that a "relation" that contains a null isn't a relation, and that's true. In fact, a "type" (or "domain") that contains a null isn't a type, and a "tuple" that contains a null isn't a tuple, either. The point is, types and tuples and relations all (by definition) contain *values*, and the one thing that everyone agrees on—well, Codd and I agree on, at any rate—in connection with this topic is that nulls, whatever else they might be, certainly aren't values.[11] Thus, I repeat: If nulls are involved, then all bets are off.

As for nulls also misrepresenting the semantics, consider the following two points:

■   A (Codd-style) 3VL system supports just one kind of null, viz., "value unknown." Thus, there's a strong likelihood that users will use that null for purposes for which it's not appropriate. For example, suppose employee Joe isn't a salesperson and so doesn't qualify for a commission. Then Joe's commission is quite likely to be misrepresented as "value unknown" (it should of course be "value doesn't apply"). One simple consequence of this misrepresentation error is that Joe's total compensation (salary plus commission) will incorrectly be considered to be "unknown" instead of just the salary value.

What's more, an analogous argument will continue to apply so long as the system supports fewer kinds of nulls than are logically necessary. In other words, simply adding support for a "value doesn't apply" null might solve the specific problem mentioned in the previous paragraph, but it doesn't solve the general problem. Thus, a system that supports fewer types of null than are logically necessary is just as open to misuse—perhaps even more so—than a system that doesn't support nulls at all.

■   Now suppose the system supports two kinds of nulls, "value unknown" and "value doesn't apply" and *four*-valued logic (4VL)—which Codd in fact advocates—and suppose employee Joe's job is unknown. What then do we do about Joe's commission? It surely must be null—the information is surely missing—but we don't know whether that null should be "value

---

[11] I say this despite my unfortunate choice of title for both my 1982 U.K. paper as such and the section in reference [5] on which that paper was based, viz., "Null Values [*sic*] in Database Management." I do now regret that title.

unknown" or "value doesn't apply." Perhaps we need another kind of null, and *five*-valued logic (the new null meaning we don't know which of the first two is appropriate) ... This argument clearly goes on for ever, leading to an apparent requirement for *an infinite number of kinds of nulls*. What do we conclude from this state of affairs?

Next, regarding Codd's allegation that the default values approach lacks a "clear description of how [such] values are to be treated": Well, I've published several such descriptions over the years, the first in 1982, a more extensive one in 1992, and others since then (see the annotation to reference [5]).

Of course, Codd is quite right to warn of the dangers of *undisciplined* use of default values. That's why I've consistently advocated a *disciplined* approach. One aspect of the discipline I have in mind is that users never need to know what the default values actually are—instead, they can refer to the default value that applies to some specific column *C* by means of an operator invocation of the form DEFAULT (*C*). Thus, I reject Codd's argument that "the user [will] have to understand and cope with as many different representations and treatments of missing values as the columns that are touched" (i.e., in some given relational expression).

By the way, a system that supports nulls can still be used in an undisciplined way, as I've already shown. In fact, an argument can be made that such a system is *more* susceptible to lack of discipline, partly (a) because of the false sense of security provided by the fact that nulls are supported ("Missing information? Don't worry about it—the system can handle it"), and partly (b) because

1. The system designers assume that users are going to use nulls, and so

2. They typically don't provide explicit support for defaults, and so

3. Users who have made the (in my opinion, very sensible) decision to avoid nulls are on their own—the system doesn't help; in fact, it positively hinders.

Finally, I categorically reject Codd's allegation that the default values idea comes from prerelational systems. On the contrary, it comes from the real world, as I've already said. Indeed, let me point out that examples *in Codd's own book* [4] all use values (e.g., dashes, question marks), not nulls as such, to represent missing information! *Question*: In the real world, when we fill out an application form or something of that nature, what do we do if some piece of information is missing? *Answer:* We leave the position blank, or we put a dash, or a question mark, or N/A, or something along those lines—and those blanks and dashes and the rest are all very definitely values. What we don't do is put a null (or "mark") in that position! There's no such thing as a null in the real world. So all the default values scheme does is this: It makes the database system behave the same way the real world behaves. That's all.

I also reject Codd's allegation that the default values scheme has anything to do with "record at a time" thinking. How we deal with missing information has nothing to do with whether the operators are record or set at a time. And on behalf of the DBMS vendors, I reject the allegation that default values appealed to them "because it placed all of the responsibility on the users." Might it not have been that the vendors had their own misgivings concerning 3VL? In any case, I know of no vendor that actually supported a proper default values scheme prior to supporting 3VL. Moreover, a proper default values scheme does *not* "place all of the responsibility on the users." To contend otherwise is to misrepresent the semantics of the default values scheme.[12]

DATE'S REBUTTAL II

First, a small point regarding Codd's claim that a certain "mild error" (as he calls it) "is just as likely to occur (and other kinds [are] much more likely)" in a default values scheme: It seems to me that there's all the difference in the world between

a. On the one hand, building a system—i.e., one based on 3VL—in which we *know* errors will occur, because the system has logical flaws in it, and

---

[12] Mind you, I don't want to "come on too strong" regarding default values. That is, I don't mean to suggest that default values are the perfect solution to the missing information problem, because they're most certainly and obviously not. I just think that (a) in some cases, possibly only rather simple cases, they can be made to work, and (b) in all cases, they're better than nulls. I do think we need to do everything we can to avoid nulls and 3VL—and the great thing about defaults is that they do keep us firmly in the realm of 2VL. At the same time, I think there are other approaches to the missing information problem than can and sometimes should be used that are better than defaults (see, e.g., reference [11]).

b. On the other hand, building a system that's at least logically correct but is open to misuse. *Any* system is open to misuse. That's why we have to have discipline.

Second, and more important: Contrary to Codd's claim that I've "failed to provide a single example of a severely wrong answer," I gave such an example in 1989 [6]—i.e., several years before we engaged in the present debate— and repeated it in 1992 [7], and I repeat it again now. We're given a database (DB1) as shown in Fig. 1 (the question marks represent a "value unknown" null):

```
DEPT            EMP

 ┌──────┐        ┌──────┬──────┐
 │ DNO  │        │ ENO  │ DNO  │
 ├──────┤        ├──────┼──────┤
 │ D2   │        │ E1   │ ???  │
 └──────┘        └──────┴──────┘
```

Fig. 1: Example database DB1

Now consider the following SQL expression:

```
SELECT  ENO
FROM    DEPT , EMP
WHERE   NOT ( DEPT.DNO = EMP.DNO AND EMP.DNO = 'D1' )
```

Let's focus for a moment on the boolean expression ("*exp1*") in parentheses:

```
DEPT.DNO = EMP.DNO AND EMP.DNO = 'D1'
```

For the only data we have in the database, this expression becomes *unknown* AND *unknown* and thus evaluates to *unknown* overall. It follows that the original SELECT – FROM – WHERE expression returns an empty result, and thus in particular a result that doesn't contain the employee number E1. *But observe now that since employee E1 does have **some** (unknown) department, the question marks stand for some real value, say d.*[13] Now, either *d* is D1 or it isn't:

■ If it is D1, then expression *exp1* evaluates to *false,* because the term DEPT.DNO = EMP.DNO evaluates to *false.*

---

[13] In other words, we can think of that null as just a placemarker for some unknown but real value *d*.

- Alternatively, if *d* isn't D1, expression *exp1* also evaluates to *false*, because the term EMP.DNO = 'D1' evaluates to *false*.

In other words, expression *exp1* is always *false* in the real world, *regardless of what real value the question marks stand for*. Hence NOT (*exp1*) is *true* in the real world, and the right answer to the query in the real world should contain E1 (only).

What do we learn from this example? Well, the basic point is that the expression in the WHERE clause is "actually *unknown*" (Codd's phraseology) but is treated as *false*, with the result that—as we've seen—employee number E1 isn't returned but should be. That's a severe error by Codd's definition.

Another way to put it is: The answers that 3VL says are correct aren't always the answers that are correct in the real world. In other words, 3VL doesn't behave in accordance with the way the real world behaves; that is, it doesn't have a sensible *interpretation*.

Please note too that the error the example demonstrates isn't just an SQL error—it's intrinsic to the 3VL scheme. In fact, on page 183 of Codd's own book [4] we find the following (slightly paraphrased here):

> Executing a query delivers only those cases in which the condition part evaluates to *true*.

But this is tantamount to treating *unknown* as *false*—which is, again, a severe error by Codd's own definition.

In case you're still not convinced, let me give another example. Consider the database (DB2) shown in Fig. 2 and the query "Does anyone in department D1 earn a salary of 100K?" This query will involve a test to see whether the literal row (D1,100K) appears in the projection of EMP on DNO and SAL. In forming that projection, however, the row (D1,???) will be thrown out as a duplicate ([*sic!*]—see Codd's book [4], pages 189-190).[14] Result: The 3VL answer to the query is *false*; the real world answer, by contrast, is *unknown*. This is surely also a severe error by Codd's definition.

---

[14] Actually, a literal reading of the text on those pages would allow the row (D1,50K) to be thrown out instead. I'll leave you to think about that.

EMP

ENO	DNO	SAL
E1	D1	50K
E2	D1	???

Fig. 2: Example database DB2

Third and last (and much more important still): The whole business of "severe" vs. "mild" errors in any case is surely nonsense. It seems to me that it's nothing more than a rearguard attempt to shore up an already suspect position. After all, if we were talking about integers instead of truth values, what would we think of a system that occasionally produced the answer 2 when the correct answer was 1 or 3? And in what sense could this be any more acceptable than one that occasionally produced 1 or 3 when the correct answer was 2?

Suppose the DBMS says it *doesn't know* whether Country X is developing a nuclear weapon, whereas in fact Country X is *not* doing so; and suppose Country Y therefore decides to bomb Country X "back to the Stone Age," just in case. The error here can hardly be said to be mild. *Note:* This example is certainly not to my taste; I choose it deliberately for its shock value.

DATE'S REBUTTAL III

Here I'd just like to ask a few questions.

1. What evidence is there that "a reasonably good algorithm can be developed"?

2. Is there a precise definition of the "simple cases" that such an algorithm will handle?

3. If there is, is that definition intuitively understandable? In other words, will the user be able to predict with any confidence whether or not the DBMS is going to give the right answer to a given query?

4. If the answer to the previous question is no, then why would anyone ever use the system for any purpose at all?

5. In fact, Codd is requiring the DBMS itself to "admit its inability to deduce a sound response to a user request" whenever applicable. In other words, he's asking for a *decision procedure*—a procedure, that is, regarding the decidability of formulas in three-valued logic. What evidence is there that such a procedure exists?

6. What fraction of real world queries that are "encountered in commercial activities" are "simple" in the foregoing sense?

7. What evidence exists to support the answer to the previous question?

8. If we're limited to using such "simple" queries only, exactly what incremental value is the "RM+3VL" system providing over a prerelational, record at a time system?

9. What exactly does "commercial activities" include?

I think it's time to quote Wittgenstein again: *All logical differences are big differences.* (To my regret, I don't know the source of this quote. I'd be grateful to any reader who could help.)[15]

Turning now to Codd's discussion of missing values in his book, and refutation of my views therein: Codd claims that his book "refutes my criticisms in detail." I don't think it does. The two major criticisms dealt with in his book are (1) "the alleged counterintuitive nature" (i.e., of nulls and 3VL) and (2) "the alleged breakdown of normalization."

■ Regarding (1), Codd doesn't actually address the counterintuitive nature of 3VL at all, but simply claims that default values are counterintuitive too.[16] In doing so, incidentally, he confuses the semantics of the two very different expressions "not known" and "known not"—a trap that's all too easy to fall into, of course (indeed, this confusion is precisely one of the

---

[15] I'm delighted to be able to report that after I first raised this question, a reader did come through with the answer. The source is P. T. Geach, "History of the Corruptions of Logic," in his book *Logic Matters* (Basil Blackwell, 1972). The complete quote is: "As I once heard Wittgenstein say, all logical differences are big differences; in logic we are not making *subtle* distinctions, as it were between flavours that pass over into one another by delicate gradations." (See Chapter 4, footnote 1, for further specifics.)

[16] I'm not sure how valid this claim can be, given that (as I've already said) default values are what we use to represent missing information in the real world. However, I'm prepared to let the point go for the sake of the discussion.

reasons why I claim that 3VL is counterintuitive). In reference [12] I give an example of a (very simple!) query involving 3VL that Codd and I *both* seriously misinterpreted when we first discussed it (after a somewhat lengthy discussion too, I might add). The cause of the misinterpretation was, precisely, confusion over the distinction between "not known" and "known not." I stand by my contention that 3VL is difficult to deal with on an intuitive level.

■ Regarding (2), I originally claimed that "the fundamental theorem of normalization" breaks down in the presence of nulls [5], and so it does.[17] Codd's counterargument is unconvincing. Here for the record is that counterargument in its entirety (reference [4], pages 200-201):

It should be clear that because nulls—or, as they are now called, marks—are *not* database values, the rules of [normalization] do not apply to them. Instead, they apply to all unmarked [database] values.

In any case, I have several other serious criticisms of 3VL that Codd's book doesn't address at all. They include (and this isn't an exhaustive list):

■ The fact that we apparently need an infinite number of kinds of nulls

■ The semantic overloading or "misrepresentation" that occurs if some kinds of nulls aren't supported (which is bound to be the case, given the previous point, and quite obviously is the case in SQL)

■ The lack of any convincing justification for the difference in treatment between (a) equality of nulls in comparisons and (b) equality of nulls in duplicate elimination

■ The fact that the (admittedly informal) argument in support of the entity integrity rule ("primary keys in base relations don't permit nulls") quite obviously extends to *every column in the database*—implying that nulls should be inadmissible *everywhere*

---

[17] The theorem in question is Heath's Theorem, which can be stated thus: Let relation r have heading H and let X, Y, and Z be such that their union is equal to H (so X, Y, and Z are all subsets of H); let XY denote the union of X and Y, and similarly for XZ; if r satisfies the FD $X \rightarrow Y$, then r is equal to the join of its projections on XY and XZ. This theorem breaks down if X can be null.

■ If TABLE_DUM corresponds to *false* and TABLE_DEE corresponds to *true*—see reference [9]—then what corresponds to *unknown*?[18]

DATE'S REBUTTAL IV

Regarding my argument that there are only two truth values: Codd's counterargument here makes no sense to me. Is he suggesting that *unknown* isn't a truth value after all, but just a variable whose actual value at any given time is either *true* or *false*? So we aren't really dealing with 3VL after all?

The only way I might make sense of Codd's position here is to interpret his remarks as actually *agreeing* with what I said in reference [8], which I'm sure wasn't what he intended. Here's what I said in that reference:

> How many truth values are there? The answer, of course, is two: namely, *true* and *false*. Now, we might *say* that *unknown* is a third truth value, but that doesn't make it one. After all, I might *say* that oggle-poggle is another integer, but that doesn't make it one; it has absolutely no effect on the set of all integers. Likewise, the set of all truth values just *is* the set {*true, false*}, and there's nothing more to be said.
>
> If we're given some proposition, say the proposition "Employee E1 works in department D1," then that proposition is either *true* or *false*. Of course, I might not know which it is, but it *is* one of the two (if it isn't, it isn't a proposition). Let's assume that I don't know which it is. Then I certainly might say, informally, that the truth value of the proposition is unknown to me; but that "unknown" is a very different kind of object from the truth values *true* and *false* themselves. And pretending that it's the same kind of object—in other words, pretending that we have three truth values—is bound to lead to problems of interpretation, and so of course it does.

Of course, I understand that we're free to define a purely *formal* system in which there are as many "truth values" as we like. But that possibility doesn't alter the fact that, in the real world, the values *true* and *false* (on the one hand) and *unknown* (on the other) are totally different kinds of things.[19]

---

[18] Chapter 2 has more to say regarding this particular question.

[19] To spell the point out: *True* and *false* refer to actual states of affairs in the real world; *unknown* refers to someone's knowledge (or some DBMS's knowledge) of those states of affairs in the real world. They have to do with two different realms. Confusing those realms is what causes the muddle.

Finally, regarding my argument concerning truth valued functions (actually I prefer the term *operators* in this context): Here Codd both misrepresents my position and misses the point. My argument wasn't that because there were so many operators, we shouldn't support 3VL; rather, it was that if we want to support 3VL, we should be sure that we support all possible 3VL operators. Now, in the case of integers, it's true that the total number of operators is infinite—but it's also true that any such operator is expressible in terms of a small number of primitives, so all we have to do is support those primitives properly. Likewise, in two-valued logic (2VL), we know that all 2VL operators can be expressed in terms of a small (very small!) number of primitives, and so again all we have to do is support those primitives properly.

For 3VL, therefore, I was asking, first, for a suitable set of primitives that would guarantee that all 19,710 monadic and dyadic operators were supported.[20] (Indeed, if any of them aren't supported, then it can't reasonably be claimed that the system we're dealing with is 3VL.) Second, I was also asking for a suitable set of *useful* operators (not necessarily the same thing as primitive operators). I was also asking for a proof of completeness. I was also raising questions of testing, debugging, and usability. And then I was asking the analogous questions all over again for 4VL, where there are over *four billion* such operators. I believe these are serious questions that I've never seen 3VL and 4VL advocates even raise, let alone answer—and yet I believe those advocates are morally obliged to address them.[21]

Taking the whole of Codd's comments into consideration, I stand more firmly than ever by my original position.

REBUTTING THE REBUTTALS

(To close out this debate, Dr Codd offers the following comments on Date's rebuttals.)

Just about every database contains missing values scattered over numerous parts of the database. For example, an employee's birthdate might have to be marked

---

[20] In case you're wondering where that figure of 19,710 comes from, it's explained in Chapter 18 ("Why Three- and Four-Valued Logic Don't Work") of my book *Date on Database: Writings 2000-2006* (Apress, 2006).

[21] By "advocates" here, I mean people who advocate the use of 3VL or 4VL as a basis for dealing with missing information, of course.

"missing but applicable," because it is at present unknown. Or the employee's year to date commission might have to be marked as missing and inapplicable because he or she is not a salesperson.

Database management would be simpler if missing values didn't exist.[22] Unfortunately, for a variety of reasons, they do occur and need to be managed. Date's assertion that a relation containing missing values is not a relation is unacceptable. While relations that contain missing values [*sic!*] are not normally encountered in mathematics, the same operators in the relational model continue to be applicable. Requests expressed in a relational language must be able to cope with missing values, without resorting to guessing.

With Date's default value approach, both the representation and treatment of missing values can be peculiar to the columns in which missing values are permitted. This might be acceptable in a single record at a time DBMS; it is clearly *not* in a multiple record at a time DBMS. The principal reason for adopting an approach that is *uniform across the entire database* is that a single relational request may involve data from numerous distinct columns of the database, and many of these columns are likely to be permitted to have missing values. Imagine a request that deals with 12 or more such columns: A significant part of formulating this request would involve detailed knowledge of the 12 or more representations and treatments of missing values, if the default value scheme were adopted.

For uniformity, one might look to support in hardware. Today's memory technology, however, can't distinguish between values to be taken seriously and those that are not—such as those left in some condition by some previous activity. Once a disk is formatted, the computer regards every bit as part of the value of something. In my relational model version 2 (RM/V2), any column in which missing values are permitted is assigned one extra byte to indicate, for each row, whether the associated value is:

1. To be treated seriously, or

2. Missing and applicable, or

3. Missing and inapplicable.

IBM's DB2 partially supports this representation.

---

[22] This remark is priceless.

A basic ground rule in the relational model is that *the DBMS must NOT provide a definite response to a query when it is not certain about the response because values are missing.* [23] I remember well when I first arrived in New York City to reside in the U.S. It was the fall of 1948 and I was looking vigorously for a job. Often I would have to ask people on the street how to get to specific parts of the city. I received detailed directions, but almost invariably these directions were wrong. I stopped asking and used street maps instead. Similarly, people who use a DBMS that *guesses* the answer to a query but delivers it as if it were not guessing are likely to abandon its use.

Re: Date's Rebuttal I

In Date's Rebuttal I, he decries the inadequacies of three-valued logic (3VL), which I first discussed in 1979. In 1986, I proposed a significant improvement [3], which distinguished between two categories of missing database values:

1. Temporarily unknown;

2. Inapplicable, and hence unknowable.

Semantics make this distinction necessary. I also proposed four-valued logic (4VL) and *additional general purpose functions* to permit adequate handling of missing information. Date, in many of his examples, ignores both. This double oversight makes his examples merely cases of the incorrect use of the missing value machinery in RM/V2 [4].

In his Rebuttal I, Date asserts: "It is default values, not nulls, that we use in the real world." Arguments of this type can, and have, been used [*sic*] to delay every technical or scientific step forward. It could have been used to argue against the introduction of computers: "It is mental arithmetic that we use in the real world, not machines." The phrase "real world" is a serious trap, because what is real is continually changing.

Let's take one of Date's examples: A user enters data with an element missing, and he or she does not know whether the element is applicable or

---

[23] But that's *exactly* what Codd's "RM+3VL" does! And it's exactly what SQL does, too. Here's one specific illustration of the point (out of a literally infinite number of possibilities): Suppose we ask what the average salary of employees is, and suppose at least one employee is shown in the database as having a null salary. Then SQL simply ignores such employees and returns the average salary of the rest!—instead of responding "I don't know," which would be more honest. (It does admittedly return a warning code also, but there's no way to force the user to check for that code.)

inapplicable. Date would claim that, as a consequence, we need a third kind of missing value. In his rebuttal, he goes on to say that we need more and more distinct types of missing values.

I reject this sequence of arguments. In RM/V2, I discontinued using "null" because the term has been so often misinterpreted. As I pointed out earlier,[24] missing values are either *A-marked* (applicable, presently unknown) or *I-marked* (inapplicable, hence unknowable). Let's assume we have an RDBMS that is faithful to RM/V2. As background, remember that:[25]

■ For each column other than a primary key column, the DBA may declare that A-marks be permitted or prohibited.

■ For each column other than a primary or foreign key column, the DBA can declare that I-marks be permitted or prohibited.

■ A-marks are weaker and more flexible than I-marks [4].

■ A-marks likely occur more often than I-marks in a relational database that is in conceptual normal form (p) because p is the maximum percentage of I-marked values in any column, and p is normally set by the DBA to be considerably less than 1.

■ Whenever a tuple is entered with a missing value, this value is A-marked in the database, unless an integrity constraint exists that clearly indicates an I-mark must be recorded.

In this [*Date's?*] example, we must assume that both types of marking are permitted in the pertinent column, and that no declared integrity constraint resolves the issue of whether an A-mark or I-mark should be used. Then RM/V2 marks the missing value as applicable.[26] Later, if it is discovered that the value

---

[24] I presume this is a reference to the opening paragraph of the present section (?), though actually the terms *A-marked* and *I-marked* haven't previously been mentioned at all.

[25] This instruction from Codd to the reader strikes this particular reader as more than a little unfair, since *none* of the items in the subsequent bullet list has previously been discussed, or even mentioned.

[26] But how can it marked at all if it's missing (i.e., not there)? Please understand that this isn't a frivolous question—I believe it strikes at the very heart of Codd's entire scheme. What it leads to, it seems to me, is the need to draw a distinction between values as such, on the one hand, and storage positions or locations that hold such values, on the other—a distinction that didn't previously exist in the relational model at all.

should have been I-marked, not A-marked, then the DBA or someone with suitable authorization changes the marking on this missing value. Thus, I fail to see the need for more than two kinds of markings.

Date also asserts that multivalued logic destroys the foundation upon which the Relational Model is built. I do not agree. There is no theoretical impairment and no loss of usability, whereas both scope and usability are lost if the default value scheme advocated by Date is adopted.

Date also asserts that normalization becomes invalid when multivalued logic is introduced. This is false, providing that this logic is introduced correctly (few RDBMSs do this today) and care is taken with its use. For example, if the RDBMS supported DBA-defined requests (few do), the DBA could define integrity constraints that will be stored in the catalog to enable the RDBMS to enforce the functional, multivalued, and inclusion dependencies discovered at database design time. However, the RDBMS must withhold the enforcement of these constraints from the *missing* tuple components until they are replaced by actual values. This enforcement should occur at the time of attempted replacement.

Finally, I oppose the use of default values only if it's done to represent that a value is missing. Default values might be useful in other contexts. For example, a bank teller shouldn't be required to re-enter his or her terminal identifier every time he or she enters a customer transaction. The terminal should handle this itself.

(DBP&D gave me the opportunity to reply to Codd's additional comments, but it seemed to me that no further reply was warranted.)

To be continued.

Chapter 2

Much Ado about Nothing

Part 2

For a description of the background to this chapter, please see the preamble to Chapter 1. This version copyright © 2022 C. J. Date.

TECHNICAL CORRESPONDENCE

When it first appeared, the debate between Codd and myself led, perhaps not surprisingly, to a large number of letters from readers. In fact, several readers wrote in with attempts to salvage the idea that "automatic" null support might be provided *without* having to stray beyond the boundaries of conventional two-valued logic (2VL). Well, it's my loss, perhaps, but I have to say I found those attempts less than convincing, and I choose not to discuss them here.

Ceuan Clement-Davies from Frankfurt, West Germany, offered the following comment, which I can't do better than quote verbatim:

> One thing struck me forcibly ... [Codd's] remarks on tautologies seemed a significant admission. Since the example he gives [*regarding birth years*] isn't a tautology in Łukasiewicz's system (and any system of three-valued logic in which this was made to be a tautology would show unfortunate effects elsewhere), it isn't at all clear to me whether Codd is suggesting that a RDBMS should use two-valued logic to detect tautologies, and three-valued logic for everything else. This would be a curious mixture.

> To elaborate briefly:

■ Codd's birth year example had to do (in effect) with an expression of the following form:

```
x < 1960 OR x = 1960 OR x > 1960
```

If *x* is null, this expression evaluates to *unknown* OR *unknown* OR *unknown*, which reduces to *unknown*, and so the expression isn't a tautology in 3VL.

■ In case you're not familiar with the concept of a tautology, let me say a little more. Briefly, a tautology in logic is an expression that always evaluates to *true*, regardless of the values of any variables involved. For example, if *p* is an arbitrary boolean expression,, then the following is a tautology in 2VL:

```
p OR NOT ( p )
```

But it's not a tautology in 3VL—in Łukasiewicz's version of 3VL, at any rate—because it reduces to *unknown*, not true, if *p* is *unknown*. The 3VL counterpart to this 2VL tautology is:

```
p OR NOT ( p ) OR MAYBE ( p )
```

(The expression MAYBE (*p*) here is defined to evaluate to *true* if *p* is *unknown*, and *false* otherwise.)

■ But Codd's expression

```
x < 1960 OR x = 1960 OR x > 1960
```

isn't of the foregoing tautological form. Now, if Codd had written the following expression instead—

```
( x = 1960 ) OR NOT ( x = 1960 ) OR MAYBE ( x = 1960 )
```

(which evaluates to *unknown* OR *unknown* OR *true*, or in other words to *true*)—then he would have obtained the answer he wanted. But note very carefully that *if he'd done that, then he would have been asking a logically different question.* And all logical differences are big differences.

——— ♦ ♦ ♦ ♦ ♦ ———

Stephen Ferg of the U.S. Department of Labor (Bureau of Labor Statistics) wrote claiming that:

1. The concept of null is deeply embedded in the relational model, and probably can't be removed from it.

2. Nulls often, and in some cases must, have no semantic content whatever: They simply mean there's no value in a given column of a given row.

And he went on to say the following (this is an edited extract from his letter):

<quote>

Consider an EMP table with columns ENO, ETYPE, and TOTSALES. ETYPE indicates whether the employee in question is a member of the sales staff ... TOTSALES indicates the total number of sales the employee has made since the beginning of the year ... For an employee not on the sales staff, TOTSALES will be null. For a sales employee, TOTSALES may be null until the employee files his or her first sales report (until then, the number is applicable, but unknown).
    It's this kind of example that both Codd and Date seemed to have in mind during their debate. But there's another use for null that's far more important. Suppose we have two entities, EMP and DEPT, and a relationship, ASSIGNED, with the constraint that (at any given time) each employee is assigned to at most one department. There are two employees (E1, E2) and two departments (D1, D2). E1 is assigned to D1, but E2 isn't currently assigned to any department (E2 is on leave of absence and will be assigned to a department when [he or she] returns from that leave). A logically ideal implementation of this situation is shown in Fig. 1:

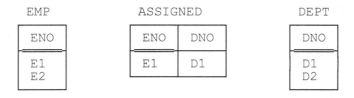

Fig. 1: The departments-and-employees database (first version)

Because ASSIGNED is a many to one relationship, however, the ASSIGNED table and the EMP table have the same primary key. This permits the schema to be "optimized" by merging the two tables, so that ASSIGNED.DNO becomes a foreign key in the EMP table, producing the structure shown in Fig. 2:[1]

```
EMP                        DEPT

┌───────┬───────┐          ┌───────┐
│  ENO  │  DNO  │          │  DNO  │
├───────┼───────┤          ├───────┤
│  E1   │  D1   │          │  D1   │
│  E2   │  ??   │          │  D2   │
└───────┴───────┘          └───────┘
```

Fig. 2: The departments-and-employees database (second version)

There are three things worth noting about Fig. 2:

1. First, such a design is extremely common—so common that many database designers think of it as the ideal relational implementation of such a situation, rather than as an optimized implementation one step removed from the ideal implementation.

2. Second, such a design requires the use of nulls in foreign keys.

3. Third, in such a design a null has no semantic content whatever: It exists only because of optimization and implementation considerations ... It's not the case that E2 can't be assigned to a department, and it's not true that E2's department number is "missing" or "unknown" (as if such a number really existed but we just don't know what it is). So we have a third kind of null: It doesn't mean "inapplicable" and it doesn't mean "unknown"—it simply means the column [position within that row] has no value.

Note that the design of Fig. 1 doesn't avoid the need for a "simply no value" null: If we do a left outer join of the EMP and ASSIGNED tables in that figure, we will produce a result table that's exactly the same as the EMP table in Fig. 2. An outer join produces nulls because we ask the DBMS to show us data

---

[1] As in Chapter 1, I use question marks to denote nulls in figures like Fig. 2.

from one table even when no matching data can be found in another table. Such nulls have no meaning, no semantic content.

My conclusions:

1. Despite the difficulties with null that Date points out, we can't have a relational model that's altogether free of null, so we'd better learn to live with it.

2. Despite Codd's impulse to distinguish different kinds of null on semantic grounds, it's probably better just to let null mean "no value here" [in order to avoid] the unmanageable complexities of 3-valued, 4-valued, ..., *n*-valued logic.

</quote>

My reactions to Ferg's letter are as follows.

First of all, I agree with Ferg that—precisely because it avoids nulls—the design of Fig. 1 is preferable to that of Fig. 2. However, Ferg claims that nulls are "deeply embedded in the relational model and probably can't be removed from it." But he provides no proof of this claim, and I couldn't possibly disagree with it more. (After all, the model survived very well without nulls for some ten years!) In fact, I challenge him to produce an example of a problem that appears to need nulls for its solution that can't also be solved without them.[2]

Ferg goes on to claim that nulls "often ... have no semantic content whatever," but subsequently contradicts himself on this very point. In the example he uses to support his claim, the null department number in the EMP row (E2,??) certainly does have "semantic content"—it means, loosely, "not yet assigned," i.e., that the employee will be assigned to a department when [he or she] returns from leave of absence (Ferg's own words).

Later Ferg says that the nulls that appear in the result of an outer join also "have no meaning, no semantic content." Again I disagree. The point isn't that those nulls have no meaning, but rather that different nulls in the same result can have many different meanings, as I've shown elsewhere [12].

In any case, "Do nulls have semantic content?" is the wrong question to ask. The point is, if we allow nulls, then operators (logical, computational, relational, or whatever) have to be defined to deal with them *somehow*. And it's

---

[2] It probably goes without saying that neither Ferg nor anybody else has ever produced such an example, so far as I'm aware. Nor do I think they can.

the behavior of those operators that, in effect, *defines* the semantics of nulls. In other words, nulls must always—necessarily—have *some* "semantic content." Ferg's suggestion that we should just let nulls mean "there's no value here" thus really makes no sense.

To pursue the point a moment longer: A large part of my objection to nulls is based on the fact that the particular "semantic content" defined by the operators of three-valued logic is of no practical value for the purpose at hand, because that "semantic content" doesn't mimic the way the real world works. To repeat something I said in the previous chapter, the answers that 3VL says are correct are often not the answers that are correct in the real world.

One last point: Ferg also proposes an example in which the TOTSALES figure for a sales employee who hasn't yet filed a sales report is given as null. It should of course be zero! This is another illustration of the kinds of mistakes that people are likely to make in a system that supports nulls. Indeed, SQL itself makes the same mistake when it defines the sum of an empty set to be null [10].

——— ♦ ♦ ♦ ♦ ♦ ———

Another correspondent, Martin H. Rusoff of Banc One Financial Card Services in Columbus, Ohio, wrote as follows (again this is an edited extract):

<quote>

It seems to me that the entire discussion is slightly off target ... There are usually several alternatives to handling [missing information]. These can range from ignoring it up to taking exceptional measures to discover the missing data. Any of these could be automated, but it requires knowledge of what the data *means* and possibly *why it's missing* to decide the correct response. While this might be decided in the data model, more often it depends on the use to which the data will be put—i.e., on the *application*.

By way of illustration, suppose we're given table EMP with a row as shown in Fig. 3, and we need to calculate the total amount needed to meet payroll. Then there are a number of possible responses:

EMP

ENO	ENAME	GRADE	SALARY	COMMISSION
E1	Smith	T4	??????	??????????

Fig. 3: Sample EMP row

- I don't know.

- Use the top and bottom figures for the salary for grade T4 to compute maximum and minimum amounts (a similar technique could be used to determine the commission, based on whether grade T4 is eligible for commission or not, and then looking at the maximum and minimum values in the database).

- Use a default of some kind, possibly calculated based on the maximums and minimums computed above.

- Ignore this employee.

- Use statistical data stored elsewhere to come up with probable amounts and then calculate a confidence [rating] for the entire result.

- Initiate exception processing to determine the answer, possibly then continuing to calculate the result ignoring the missing values.

Depending on the situation, any of these might be acceptable. However, an accountant would probably calculate the maximums after determining if a commission might apply and attach a note saying that the data was missing for certain listed individuals. I don't see how a database engine could decide this.

I fully agree that the current treatment [*of missing information*] is error prone ... [However,] I'm not sure that legislating 3VL, fuzzy logic (with ranges or probabilities), or using defaults is the right answer ... In the end, it might be appropriate to always generate an error whenever a null is located and permit an application to rerun the query using additional qualifiers telling the database engine how to process the nulls.

Instead of debates of this kind, I'd like to see an explanation of how the existing facilities can be used correctly to handle missing data.[3]

</quote>

I responded to these comments as follows.

I completely agree with Martin Rusoff that it'll usually be the case that only the application can decide what to do when nulls are encountered. His example makes the point admirably. But I don't agree that "the entire discussion is slightly off target." To be candid, I do admit to a sneaking sympathy with this position—I know the debate must have seemed somewhat academic and not too relevant to the rough and tumble of day to day operations—but the fact is that such a perception is sadly mistaken.

First of all (as I've observed many times, in the pages of *DBP&D* and elsewhere), **theory is practical!** That is, the theory on which a given DBMS is based necessarily has very practical consequences for the user of that DBMS. And if that theory is bad, the consequences will be bad too.

To see that this is so, it's sufficient to realize that it'll often be the DBMS, not the application, that has to "decide what to do when nulls are encountered." (I have argued this point before for the particular case of the optimizer component—see reference [7].) Note, moreover, that not all nulls "preexist" in base tables: Some are generated dynamically (i.e., in the middle of evaluating some expression). As a result, it's a virtual certainty that it'll be the DBMS, not the application, that has to decide how to deal with them. And the DBMS will typically not have the application-specific knowledge to enable it to make the correct application-specific decisions. Consequence: Wrong answers!

Also, of course, there's the point—admittedly only a psychological point, not a logical one, but one that's very much a practical consideration—that users will be lulled into a false sense of security by the fact that the system can "handle" missing information. That is, applications often do *not* include the necessary logic to deal with nulls, even when they should, because the user was under the misapprehension that the system has taken that burden off the user's shoulders.

———— ◆ ◆ ◆ ◆ ◆ ————

---

[3] So would I.

Finally, James R. Alexander of the Goochland-Powhatan Community Services Board, Goochland, Virginia, wrote as follows:

<quote>

If I don't know the gender of Person A and I'm asked *Is Person A female?*, I respond *I don't know.* However, if I'm asked *Do you know if Person A is female?*, I respond *No.* The first question concerns Person A's gender, the second question concerns my knowledge of Person A's gender. A query of a database is certainly a question of the second type ...

I have developed and been using for over three years a data collection engine which is the front-end for a database ... This engine understands that every attribute has, in addition to its explicit domain, an implicit domain ... composed of unknown, not applicable, and not represented (i.e., other), which are consistently represented by ?, !, and NO, respectively. The human services organization I work for uses this data collection engine to maintain data for many typical business applications ... We use various off-the-shelf reporting [programs], which employ two-valued logic, and we get correct results.

</quote>

I couldn't agree more with Mr Alexander. I said much the same thing in reference [12]. To quote:

> [We] obviously can't ask the system questions about the real world, we can only ask it about its knowledge of the real world, as represented by the data in the database.

The critical point, as Mr. Alexander observes, is to stay within two-valued logic. I'm glad to hear he has been using his technique successfully for several years.

REFERENCES

1. E. F. Codd: "A Data Base Sublanguage Founded on the Relational Calculus," IBM Research Report RJ893 (July 26th, 1971); republished in Proc. 1971 ACM SIGFIDET Workshop on Data Description, Access and Control, San Diego, Calif. (November 1971).

2. E. F. Codd: "Extending the Database Relational Model to Capture More Meaning," *ACM TODS 4*, No. 4 (September 1979).

3. E. F. Codd: "Missing Information (Applicable and Inapplicable) in Relational Databases," *ACM SIGMOD Record 15*, No. 4 (1986); "More Commentary on Missing Information," *ACM SIGMOD Record 15*, No. 5 (1986).

4. E. F. Codd: *The Relational Model for Database Management Version 2* (Addison-Wesley, 1990).

> Chapters 8 ("Missing Information" and 9 ("Response to Technical Criticisms Regarding Missing Information") of this reference discuss missing information. The two kinds of missing values are discussed on page 191. Chapter 9 in particular is where, according to Codd, "Date's criticisms are refuted in detail."
>
> *Note:* Codd adds: "Unfortunately, in the first printing, two errors appeared in the truth table for logical OR on pages 182 and 236. These have been corrected." Well, that's as may be (I choose my words carefully). For further discussion of these errors and their alleged correction, I refer you to Chapter 18 ("Why Three- and Four-Valued Logic Don't Work") of my book *Date on Database: Writings 2000-2006* (Apress, 2006).
>
> I note too that, in addition to the foregoing, Chapter 23 ("Serious Flaws in SQL") of this same reference [4] discusses among other things SQL's "[failure] to provide adequate support for the use of either three-valued or four-valued logic," and suggests
>
> a. "Steps that vendors should take to remedy [this problem],"
>
> b. "Precautionary steps that users can take to avoid severe difficulties before vendors take action," and
>
> c. "Steps to avoid compatibility problems when vendors make the necessary changes in SQL."

5. C. J. Date: *An Introduction to Database Systems: Volume II* (Addison-Wesley, 1982).

Section 5.5 ("Null Values") of this book includes a very brief overview of the default values scheme (see also the appendix to Chapter 13 in the companion to the present book *Database Dreamings: Volume I* (Technics Publications, 2022). A more detailed treatment can be found in Chapter 21 ("The Default Values Approach to Missing Information") in my book *Relational Database Writings 1989-1991* (Addison-Wesley, 1992).

    Note: As mentioned in Chapter 1, footnote 10, I'm somewhat embarrassed by the title of that Section 5.5, since the whole point about nulls is that they're not values, and the phrase "null value"—encountered all too frequently in SQL contexts in particular—is nothing but a contradiction in terms. I know better now.

6. C. J. Date: "Three-Valued Logic and the Real World," *InfoDB 4*, No. 4 (Winter 1989). Republished in my book *Relational Database Writings 1989-1991* (Addison-Wesley, 1990).

7. C. J. Date: "Why Three-Valued Logic Is a Mistake," *DBP&D 5*, No. 12 (December 1992)—originally published under the title "Why Accept Wrong Answers?" Republished in my book *Relational Database Writings 1991-1994* (Addison-Wesley, 1995). See also the appendix to the present chapter.

8. C. J. Date: "Nothing in Excess" *DBP&D 6*, No. 1 (January 1993). Republished in my book *Relational Database Writings 1991-1994* (Addison-Wesley, 1995). See also the appendix to the present chapter.

9. C. J. Date: "Tables with No Columns," *DBP&D 6*, No. 3 (March 1993). Republished in my book *Relational Database Writings 1991-1994* (Addison-Wesley, 1995). See also Chapter 3 of the present book.

10. C. J. Date: "Empty Bags and Identity Crises" *DBP&D 6*, No. 4 (April 1993). Republished in my book *Relational Database Writings 1991-1994* (Addison-Wesley, 1995).

11. C. J. Date: "Fifty Years of Relational: A Personal View Part II," in my book *Fifty Years of Relational, and Other Database Writings* (Technics Publications, 2021).

12. C. J. Date: "NOT Is Not 'Not'!" (in two parts), Chapters 12-13 of the companion volume to the present book.

13. C. J. Date: *The Principle of Cautious Design,* Chapter 2 of the companion volume to the present book.

APPENDIX

This appendix consists of a series of edited extracts from references [7] and [8]. The extracts in question deal with various aspects of nulls and 3VL that weren't addressed in the original debate, nor in the subsequent correspondence. Here first is the overall introduction to reference [7]:

> "Everyone knows" that SQL's approach to the problem of missing information is based on 3-valued logic (3VL). Many people also know that I'm opposed to that approach. And out of all the many reasons for my opposition, the most important is *wrong answers*. It bothers me a great deal—and it should bother you too—that we're getting wrong answers out of our SQL systems. Furthermore, the problem isn't fixable!—so long as we stay with 3VL, we'll keep on getting wrong answers.
>
> Before I go any further, let me make it quite clear that my argument here is not so much with SQL per se; rather, it's with the underlying theory, namely 3VL, on which SQL is based. Does 3VL therefore constitute an exception to my often repeated claim that "theory is practical"?
>
> Well, of course the theory in question has to be *good* theory! "Good" here means the theory must have a sensible *interpretation*; that is, there must exist some sensible and generally accepted correspondence between the specifics of the theory in question and phenomena in the real world. And it's my contention that 3VL does not possess any such interpretation.

Wrong Answers of the First Kind

"Wrong answer" queries come in many shapes and forms. One of the simplest and best known is illustrated by the following example:

```
SELECT ENO
FROM   EMP
WHERE  JOB = 'Clerk'
OR NOT JOB = 'Clerk'
```

The real world answer to this query is surely "all employee numbers" (it's surely true of every employee that he or she either is or isn't a clerk). In 3VL, however, we won't get the employee number for any employee whose job "is null." Thus, the answer that 3VL says is correct isn't the answer that's correct in the real world.[4]

Now, this example is so simple, and so familiar, that it's easy to overlook the seriousness of the error. A typical reaction on the part of 3VL proponents is "Well, of course, if you really wanted all of the employees, you should have added OR JOB IS NULL." I'll return to this point in a moment.

Wrong Answers of the Second Kind

The general point illustrated by the foregoing example is that the truth valued expression *p* OR NOT *p*, which is identically true in two-valued logic (2VL), is *not* identically true in 3VL. And, of course, there are numerous other examples of expressions that are identically true in 2VL but not in 3VL.[5] Here are a few more:

- $x = x$

- $x > y$ AND $y > z$ implies $x > z$

- T JOIN $T = T$

- If T and U have the same heading, then T INTERSECT $U = T$ JOIN U

Now, when 3VL proponents are shown such a list, their typical reaction is "So what? I'm never going to write a query that says WHERE $x = x$, or that joins a table to itself over all of its columns (etc., etc.). So who cares?" Needless to say, this is the *wrong reaction!* The point is, simple identities such as those above lie at the heart of the various *laws of transformation* that are used to convert queries into some more efficient form—laws, be it noted, that are used both by the system (when doing optimization) and by users (when choosing the "best" way to state the query). And if the identities don't work, then the laws

---

[4] Of course, this first example is basically just Codd's "birth year" example in different words. I apologize for the repetition, but I have my reasons for it.

[5] In other words, tautologies in 2VL aren't necessarily tautologies in 3VL, as we already know.

don't work. And if the laws don't work, then the transformations don't work. And if the transformations don't work, then accidents will happen.

What do I mean, "accidents"? I mean that now we have the potential for a different kind of wrong answer. The first kind, to repeat, arises because what 3VL thinks is correct is incorrect in real world terms. By contrast, the second kind arises because either the system or the user might be performing invalid transformations, with the result that the query the system executes isn't the query the user wanted.

Of course, it's true that this second kind of wrong answer is (in principle) avoidable, but in practice it's *not* avoided. There are SQL products on the market today that perform invalid transformations.[6] And even if there weren't, it's a virtual certainty that users would perform invalid transformations anyway.

The importance of all this can't be overstressed: Once we know that *some* answers produced by the system might be wrong, all bets are off—*all* answers become suspect. And, to repeat, the problem isn't fixable. So long as the system is using 3VL, "Type 1" wrong answers are guaranteed, and "Type 2" wrong answers are extremely likely as well.

"Unknown" Isn't a Truth Value (I)

The point I want to make here is illustrated nicely by an old riddle: How many legs does a dog have, if we call a tail a leg? The answer, of course, is four. Calling a tail a leg doesn't make it a leg.

So, to repeat an argument I made in Chapter 1 (in Date's Rebuttal IV), how many truth values are there? The answer, of course, is two, viz., *true* and *false*. Now, we might *say* that *unknown* is "a third truth value," but that doesn't make it one. After all, I might *say* that oggle-poggle is another integer, but that doesn't make it one; it has absolutely no effect on the set of all integers. Likewise, the set of all truth values just is the set {*true, false*}, and there's nothing more to be said.

Suppose we have a box containing, let's say, 100 marbles. Now, I might not know how many marbles there are in the box, and I might therefore say that "the number of marbles is unknown" (or even "null"?); but that certainly doesn't mean that "unknown" is another integer, nor that 100 and "unknown" (or "null"?) are the same thing. Does it?

---

[6] This claim was certainly true when I first made it. I don't know if it still is, but I'd be very surprised if it weren't.

"Unknown" Isn't a Truth Value (II)

Something I mentioned in passing in Chapter 1, without getting into details, was the two special relations TABLE_DUM and TABLE_DEE. TABLE_DUM and TABLE_DEE are the only relations (the only tables, if you prefer) *with no columns at all.* Yes, I'm serious! Now, I don't want to get into a lot of detail here either (see reference [9] for more discussion); all I want to do here is make the following points.

- Tables with no columns are important.[7]

- A table with no columns can have either no rows at all or exactly one row. These are the only possibilities, Why? Because such rows must obviously be empty (i.e., contain no column values), and all empty rows are duplicates of one another. Equivalently, there's only one empty row.

- If a table with no columns has no rows at all, it's TABLE_DUM; if it has one row, it's TABLE_DEE.

- TABLE_DUM corresponds to *false* and TABLE_DEE corresponds to *true.*

So what corresponds to *unknown*?

Gallagher's Comments

Reference [7] closed with the following "puzzle corner problem." Recall the database DB1 from Fig. 1 in Chapter 1 (repeated here for convenience):

DEPT

DNO
D2

EMP

ENO	DNO
E1	???

---

[7] Loosely speaking, such tables play a role in the relational algebra that's analogous to the role played by zero in ordinary arithmetic. Can you imagine an arithmetic without zero? Of course not. Can you imagine a relational algebra without TABLE_DUM and TABLE_DEE? Well, I claim you shouldn't be able to. But SQL apparently can.

The problem is as follows: Assuming that EMP.DNO is a foreign key matching DEPT.DNO, show the 3VL and real world answers corresponding to the following pseudoSQL expression:

```
SELECT  ENO
FROM    EMP
WHERE   MAYBE ( DNO = 'D1' )
```

(The expression is only "pseudoSQL" because it involves the logical operator MAYBE. I remind you that MAYBE is defined to return *true* if its operand is *unknown*, *false* if its operand is *true* or *false*.)

Well, soon after reference [7] first appeared, I received a letter from Leonard Gallagher, at that time FIPS SQL Project Leader for the National Institute of Standards and Technology (NIST) in Gaithersburg, Maryland. Here are some edited extracts from Gallagher's letter:

> I strongly disagree with the conclusion that three-valued logic leads to "wrong answers" ...
>
> It is not practical to use default values for missing information in columns where every value of the data type already has a meaning, as is the case in many numeric columns ...
>
> An inexperienced SQL programmer may experience some confusion when first confronted with truth tables for three-valued logic. This confusion flows from the fact that NOT(*true*) is defined to be *false* instead of the **sometimes** more intuitively pleasing (*false* OR *unknown*),[8] and that NOT(*unknown*) is defined to be *unknown* instead of the **sometimes** more intuitively pleasing (*true* OR *false*). Many of the confusing examples in the column derive from intentional obfuscation of these distinct alternatives for negation ... The second example examines a database in which an employee's department number is null.[9] An unstated assumption is that the null really means the department number exists, but is missing because it is not known at the moment. This is an invalid assumption with the given schema and data. Instead, the null could mean that the value is missing because it really does not exist at all. For example, the president

---

[8] There seems to some confusion here. In 3VL, the expression Gallagher cites, (*false* OR *unknown*), evaluates by definition to *unknown*. Probably what Gallagher meant to say was something like this: In 3VL, if something isn't true, then it might be false or it might be unknown. In other words, Gallagher is unwittingly drawing attention to the fact that, in 3VL, just as "NOT is not not" [12], it's also the case that "OR is not or."

[9] That "second example" is the example I discussed in Chapter 1 under Date's Rebuttal II, having to do with the database DB1 of Fig. 1 in that chapter.

of a company often is not assigned to any department ... Date's conclusion that the result is *false* is incorrect because it is based on an invalid existence assumption ...

I close by noting that [the SQL standard] provides an understandable and intuitively pleasing answer to the puzzle corner problem. The pseudoSQL query

```
SELECT  ENO
FROM    EMP
WHERE   MAYBE ( DNO = 'D1' )
```

is easily [represented] in standard SQL by the query

```
SELECT  ENO
FROM    EMP
WHERE   DNO = 'D1' IS NOT FALSE
```

I responded to these comments as follows. First, Gallagher "strongly disagrees" with my conclusion that three-valued logic (3VL) "leads to wrong answers." Well, naturally I "strongly disagree" with Gallagher! He makes a number of specific points that I wish to respond to in more detail, but the overriding and most serious criticism of his letter is that it fails to address *any* of the major objections to 3VL raised in my original article [7]:

■ The fact that 3VL doesn't have a sensible interpretation

■ The fact that 3VL is virtually certain to lead to incorrect expression transformations on the part of either the system or the user (and probably both)

■ The fact that 3VL and nulls are *not* what we use in the real world

Let me now turn to some points of detail.

1. Note first how much more complicated the question of data *interpretation* becomes in 3VL. Consider, e.g., a relation EMP with columns ENO and DNO. If we stay in 2VL (no nulls allowed), the interpretation of this relation is simply

   Employee ENO works in department DNO.

Or to spell it out more precisely:

ENO identifies an employee, and DNO identifies a department, and employee ENO works in department DNO.

But if DNO can be null, the interpretation becomes:

ENO identifies an employee, and *either* DNO identifies a department and employee ENO works in department DNO, *or* DNO is null and the department employee ENO works is unknown.

(Of course, this interpretation does assume that the intended meaning of a null in the DNO position is "value exists but is unknown.") And the more columns that can be null, the more complicated the interpretation becomes. *Exercise:* (a) State the interpretation for a relation EMP with columns ENO, DNO, JOB, and SALARY, if any or all of DNO, JOB, and SALARY can be null; (b) state the interpretation for the projection of this EMP relation over DNO and JOB.

Please note that this matter of interpretation isn't just an academic issue. The interpretation of a given relation is what the relation *means*; it's the *criterion for membership* in that relation. Users have to carry that meaning in their heads whenever they use the relation for any purpose whatsoever—in particular, when they do queries involving that relation and when they insert new rows.

2. While I'm on the subject of projection, let me mention another well known anomaly that arises over nulls. The question is whether or not two nulls are duplicates of one another. Advocates of 3VL approach this question as follows: For purposes of duplicate elimination (e.g., for projection and union), they answer "yes"; for purposes of comparison (e.g., for restriction and join), they answer "no." How can this discrepancy be justified?

3. Gallagher points out that default values can't be used for missing information in columns where every value of the data type already has a meaning. Of course this is correct. I omitted consideration of this case from my original article for space reasons, but it's discussed in my book *Relational Database Writings 1989-1991* (Addison-Wesley, 1992), page 346. Here let me just say that it doesn't invalidate the overall idea of using default values.

4. I reject Gallagher's claim that default values are unpractical, since default values are precisely what we use all the time in the real world.

5. I vigorously deny the accusation that "many of the confusing examples in [my] column derive from intentional obfuscation"! Gallagher doesn't seem to appreciate that his point about "distinct alternatives for negation" is exactly the point I'm trying to make when I say that 3VL doesn't have a sensible interpretation. The point is, the NOT of 3VL is *not* the "not" of ordinary English. The NOT of 3VL supports one of the "distinct alternatives for negation" and not the other.

   I further remark that—as previously pointed out, in part, in footnote 7—in the paragraph where he makes this accusation, Gallagher makes use of the expressions "*false* OR *unknown*" and "*true* OR *false*" ... I can't resist pointing out that the OR in these expressions is presumably not the OR of 3VL, it's the "or" of ordinary English. So there are "distinct alternatives" for disjunction, too.

6. Gallagher will doubtless now point out that the foregoing is precisely the reason why the constructs IS TRUE, IS NOT TRUE (etc.) were introduced into the SQL standard, and of course he'd be right in doing so. But note that IS TRUE (etc.) are really additional truth valued operators, just like NOT, AND, and OR. So the 3VL user now has to deal with six new operators, over and above the usual three operators of 2VL. Furthermore, those new operators suffer from several intuitively undesirable properties. For example, the expressions

   ```
   NOT ( EMP.DNO = 'D1' )
   ```

   and

   ```
   ( EMP.DNO = 'D1' ) IS NOT TRUE
   ```

   aren't interchangeable (because, if EMP.DNO is null, the first evaluates to *unknown* and the second to *true*). In other words, NOT TRUE and NOT (TRUE) are different!

7. Gallagher is quite right in saying that I omitted to state the assumption that the null in my second example meant that the department number exists but

is unknown.[10] I apologize if this omission confused anybody. I feel the omission was justified, however, given the well known fact that the behavior of nulls in SQL, and in 3VL generally, *has been defined all along* in accordance with this particular intended interpretation of "null."

8. Finally, I can't resist pointing out that Gallagher himself has fallen into exactly the kind of trap that I was warning about in my column!—his solution to the puzzle corner problem is incorrect ("IS NOT FALSE" in his solution should be replaced by "IS UNKNOWN"). There's probably a moral here.

Celko's Comments

I received a number of letters after reference [8] was first published. One was from Dr Codd, and that was the one that led to the debate that forms the basis of these two chapters. Several others simply agreed with me that as a general principle nulls and 3VL were best avoided altogether. And then there was one from Joe Celko, who wrote to offer some comments on multivalued logic in general. The following is a lightly edited version of his letter:[11]

> It is worth noting that multivalued logic is just as well defined as two-valued logic.[12] The following scheme was proposed by Łukasiewicz in 1920. Any number of truth values can exist if we agree to represent them by numeric values in the range 0 (*absolutely false*) and 1 (*absolutely true*). We can then define generalized implication and negation operators, as follows:

$$
\begin{aligned}
p \text{ IMPLIES } q &\stackrel{\text{def}}{=} 1 \text{ if } p \le q \\
p \text{ IMPLIES } q &\stackrel{\text{def}}{=} 1 - (p - q) \text{ if } p > q \\
\text{NOT } p &\stackrel{\text{def}}{=} 1 - p
\end{aligned}
$$

> From these operators, we derive:

---

[10] Gallagher says that assumption is "invalid." Actually it's not invalid; however, I agree it might be unwarranted.

[11] The footnotes from this point forward are all new—they didn't appear in reference [8].

[12] Here perhaps is an appropriate point to ask the question: Which particular multivalued logic are we talking about anyway? Even if we limit our attention to three-valued logics only, there are many different such logics. Of course, all of those 3VLs support those 19,710 monadic and dyadic operators I mentioned earlier (because if they don't, they're not 3VLs in the first place). But the question is: Which of those 19,710 operators do they call NOT, and which AND, and which OR (and so on)?

```
p OR q   ≡  ( p IMPLIES q ) IMPLIES q
p AND q  ≡  NOT ( NOT p OR NOT q )
p IFF q  ≡  ( p IMPLIES q ) AND ( q IMPLIES p )
MAYBE p  ≡  ( NOT p ) IMPLIES p
```

Such systems have been shown to be consistent. And surprise! They look just like the SQL operators that Chris Date dislikes so much.

I responded to this letter by first thanking Joe Celko for his comments. Then I continued as follows:

Let me make my position on this subject as clear as I possibly can. I don't "dislike" the three-valued logic (3VL) operators. I don't dispute the claim that 3VL (or *n*VL for arbitrary *n* greater than two) might be well defined. I don't dispute the claim that such logics might be consistent. What I do dispute is the claim that such logics are useful for the purpose at hand—namely, dealing with missing information in databases. In reference [7], I showed that answers that were correct according to 3VL weren't necessarily correct in the real world. Hence, if we use a 3VL-based DBMS, we'll sometimes get answers out of the system that are wrong. Further, there's no reliable way of knowing when the answers are wrong and when not. This state of affairs should be sufficient to persuade any reasonable person that 3VL is a disastrously bad approach to the problem we're trying to solve.

Then I went on to dispute a couple of specific points of detail in Celko's letter.

1. First, the 3VL of SQL is *not* the 3VL of Łukasiewicz.[13] Łukasiewicz's operators do *not* "look just like the SQL operators." In particular, if *p* is *unknown*, then Łukasiewicz defines *p* IMPLIES *p* to be *true*, whereas I believe SQL would define it as (NOT *p*) OR *p*, which is *unknown*.[14] What's more, SQL's 3VL includes quantification.

---

[13] I don't quite know how Celko manages to make the transition from Łukasiewicz's multivalued logics (which is what his text is about, up to but excluding his final sentence) and SQL's 3VL (which is what his final sentence is about)—there seems to be a step, or perhaps several steps, missing. Or perhaps there's some sleight of hand somewhere that I'm missing. In any case, I'd like to stress two points. First, Łukasiewicz's 3VL is only one of many possible 3VLs (see the previous footnote). Second, Łukasiewicz's 3VL is quite definitely not the one that SQL "supports" (as we'll see in a moment), so I'm not even sure of the relevance of Celko's commentary overall.

[14] It's hard to be sure, because SQL's 3VL doesn't include an implication operator anyway—another reason why it doesn't make sense to claim that SQL's 3VL and Łukasiewicz's are the same thing.

2. Second, Celko's formula for MAYBE is wrong (if *p* is *true*, MAYBE *p* should be *false*, but Celko's formula gives *true*). In fact, I'm extremely doubtful as to whether it's even possible to define MAYBE in terms of negation and SQL-style implication.[15] And the same goes for a whole host of other 3VL operators.

---

[15] Such as it is, I suppose I should add, since (as noted in footnote 14) I'm not aware that "SQL-style implication" as such is even defined anywhere.

Chapter 3

TABLE_DUM and TABLE_DEE

"TABLE_DUM" and "TABLE_DEE" are pet names, originally due to Hugh Darwen [2], [1] for two very special relations—namely, the only relations with no attributes, or (in more "user friendly" terms) the only tables that have no columns. This isn't a joke! Perhaps rather surprisingly, these two relations turn out to be of major importance, both theoretical and practical.

Publishing history: This is a combined and revised version of two short papers that first appeared as installments in my regular series for Database Programming & Design, viz., "Tables with No Columns" (DBP&D 6, No. 3, March 1993) and "More on DEE and DUM" (DBP&D 7, No. 3, March 1994) and were later republished in my book Relational Database Writings 1991-1994 (Addison-Wesley, 1995). This version copyright © C. J. Date 2022.

Let me begin by saying a few words about the term *table*. Of course, we use that term all the time in the database world, largely because of SQL; I mean, the SQL language is all about defining and processing information in the form of tables. But as a matter of fact the term has two quite distinct (though overlapping) meanings. The first is the specific SQL meaning:

1. A table in SQL is SQL's counterpart to a relation in the relational model.

The second meaning is rather different, and in some ways more general:

---

[1] And here let me acknowledge the huge debt this chapter owes to Hugh and his original work in this area [2].

2. A table is a picture of a relation (typically on paper or some other "flat" medium, such as a display screen).

In both cases, of coure, the rows and columns of the table correspond to the tuples and attributes, respectively, of the pertinent relation. But in this chapter I want to focus on the second case—and from this point forward, I'll use the term *table* exclusively to mean a table in that second, pictorial, sense (unless the context demands otherwise, of course). Here's a simple example, a picture of a relation—let's call it EMP—representing the employees of a certain company:

EMP

ENO	SAL	DNO
E1	80K	D1
E2	95K	D2
E3	75K	D1
E4	95K	D2

So if a table's just a picture of a relation, then what's a relation? *Answer:* A relation is a certain abstract mathematical construct, with certain formal and precisely defined properties (the appendix to this chapter gives precise definitions).

Now, it's actually a very nice feature of the relational model that its basic abstract construct, the relation, has such a simple pictorial representation. In fact, it's largely because of that simple pictorial representation that relational systems are so intuitively attractive—it makes them easy to understand, and easy to use, and it makes it easy to reason about the way those systems behave. Unfortunately, however, there's a downside too. The downside is: Those pictures suggest rather strongly some things that aren't true. To be specific:

a. They suggest that relations have a top to bottom ordering to their tuples, which they don't.

b. They suggest that relations have a left to right ordering to their attributes, which they don't.

c. They suggest that relations might legitimately contain duplicate tuples, which they don't.

To elaborate briefly:

- Regarding point a.: A relation contains a *set* of tuples (see the appendix), and sets in mathematics have no ordering to their elements.

- Regarding point b.: A relation also has a *set* of attributes (again see the appendix), and again sets in mathematics have no ordering to their elements.

- Regarding point c.: Again, a relation contains a *set* of tuples, and sets in mathematics have no duplicate elements.

As an aside, I note that SQL tables differ from relations on points b. and point c.—with extremely unfortunate consequences in both cases, I might add (see references [3] and [4])—and perhaps it was a confusion over the two meanings of the term *table* that allowed those SQL mistakes to occur in the first place. But I digress. Let me get back to the notion of tables as pictures. The fact is, there's a logical difference between a thing of any kind and a picture of that thing (tables vs. relations is just one example of this general truth). There's a famous painting—see *en.wikipedia. org/wiki/The_Treachery_of_Images*—by Magritte that beautifully illustrates the point: The painting is of an ordinary tobacco pipe, but underneath Magritte has written *Ceci n'est pas une pipe*—the point being, of course, that *obviously* the painting isn't a pipe; instead, it's a picture of a pipe.

So there's a logical difference between tables and relations. In practice, of course, we often use the term *table* when *relation* is what we really mean, and in informal contexts that practice can often be acceptable. But when we're trying to be precise—and in this chapter I do need to try to be fairly precise—then we do need to recognize that the two concepts aren't identical.

EMPTY SETS

As soon as we understand that relations are defined in terms of sets (meaning they have a set of tuples and a set of attributes), we need to consider the possibility that the sets in question might be empty. After all, empty sets are still sets, and theorems and results in mathematics that hold true of sets in general are required to hold true for empty sets in particular (as far as possible, at any rate). As Hugh Darwen once said to me (in a private communication):

> When mathematicians discover rules that seem to hold true for any value of n, they detest it if $n = 0$ turns out to be an exception. So do computer programmers, for whom the undefined division by zero is a famous *bête noire*, and who don't like having to use a language that has forgotten to support, for instance, arrays with zero elements.

So a relation should certainly be allowed to have an empty set of tuples or an empty set of attributes. The "empty set of tuples" case is familiar, of course; it's just like a file with no records, and it's what we mean when we talk, perhaps a trifle sloppily, about an "empty relation." But the "empty set of attributes" case is much less familiar.

RELATIONS AND PREDICATES

Before I can discuss the "empty set of attributes" case in any detail, I first need to say something about relations and *predicates*. Now, a predicate is basically just a truth valued operator.[2] For example, the expression

```
IN ( value , set )
```

might denote an invocation of a predicate called IN, which returns *true* if the specified value is an element of the specified set and *false* otherwise. In this example, the predicate is said to be *dyadic* or *2-place*, because it's defined in terms of two parameters. When we invoke that predicate (or as the logicians say, when we *instantiate* it), we replace those parameters by arguments—say the arguments 3 and {9,3,4}, respectively—and then what we get is what's called a *proposition*. In the example, the proposition is:

```
IN ( 3 , { 9 , 3 , 4 } )
```

---

[2] As so often happens, the true situation is muddied here by SQL. To be specific, SQL does use the term *predicate*—quite a lot, in fact—but only for one rather special case: basically, the case of the boolean expression that appears in a WHERE clause. Thus, it talks about *<comparison predicate>*s, *<between predicate>*s, *<like predicate>*s, and so on. While this specialized usage isn't entirely incorrect, it's certainly unfortunate, because it makes it harder to employ the term in its more general sense, which is what I need to do here.

A proposition in logic is a statement that's categorically either *true* or *false* (the one just shown is *true*, of course).

Here's another example: When it's invoked (or "instantiated"), the dyadic or 2-place predicate

```
> ( x , y )
```

—more conventionally written

```
x > y
```

—returns *true* if the argument corresponding to the parameter *x* is greater than (and *false* if that argument is less than) the argument corresponding to the parameter *y*.

Turning now to relations: The important point here is that *every relation represents some predicate*. For instance, the EMP relation shown earlier, with its attributes ENO, SAL, and DNO, represents the triadic or 3-place predicate

Employee ENO earns salary SAL and works in department DNO.

Loosely speaking, this predicate is what the relation *means*. Each tuple in the relation represents a certain proposition—namely, the proposition that's obtained from the predicate by replacing the parameters ENO, SAL, and DNO by corresponding argument values from the tuple in question—and by convention we assume that the proposition such a tuple represents is *true*. For example, the tuple (E1,80K,D1) appears in the EMP relation shown earlier, and so we're entitled to assume that the following proposition is *true*:

Employee E1 earns salary 80K and works in department D1.

More generally, given a relation *r*, and given also a tuple *t* of the appropriate form,[3] then (a) *t* appears in *r* if the corresponding proposition is *true*, and (b) fails to appear in *r* if the corresponding proposition is *false* [5]. For example, the tuple (E1,92K,D2) *doesn't* appear in the EMP relation value shown earlier, and we're therefore entitled to assume that the following proposition is *false*:

---

[3] By "of the appropriate form" here, I mean the tuple is of the right *type*—meaning in the case at hand that it consists of a possible ENO value, a possible SAL value, and a possible DNO value.

Employee E1 earns salary 92K and works in department D2.

Note in particular, therefore, that if a relation is empty (contains no tuples), it means *there doesn't exist* a tuple of the appropriate form such that the corresponding proposition is *true*. For example, if the employees relation were empty, it would mean there doesn't exist a tuple (*e,s,d*) such the following proposition is *true*:

Employee e earns salary s and works in department d.

PREDICATES AND PROJECTIONS

Now (at last!) I can begin to home in on my main point. Consider the relation ES, with heading {ENO, SAL},[4] that's obtained from the EMP relation by "projecting away" the DNO attribute—equivalently, by projecting it "on" the other two attributes, viz., ENO and SAL.[5] The predicate for that relation ES is:

There exists a department DNO **such that** employee ENO earns salary SAL *and works in department DNO.*

For example, if the EMP relation is as shown earlier, the ES projection looks like this:

ES

ENO	SAL
E1	80K
E2	95K
E3	75K
E4	95K

---

[44] The heading of a relation is basically just the corresponding set of attribute names. See the appendix for further discussion.

[5] It's often more convenient in practice when discussing projection to talk in terms of the attributes that are to be thrown away rather than the ones that are to be kept. A concrete language should ideally support both perceptions, though of course SQL (unfortunately) supports the second one only.

Note that, for example, the tuple (E1,80K) appears in ES, because the following proposition is *true*:

> *There exists a department DNO such that employee E1 earns salary 80K and works in department DNO.*

By contrast, the tuple (E1,92K) doesn't appear, because this proposition is *false*:

> *There exists a department DNO such that employee E1 earns salary 92K and works in department DNO.*

Thus, I hope you can see that:

■ Projecting away an attribute is equivalent to introducing a "There exists <*something*> such that"—in other words, a corresponding *existential quantifier*—into the predicate. (Of course, the <*something*> in question is "some value of the attribute that's projected away.")

■ If the predicate for the relation that's input to the projection operation is *n*-place or *n*-adic, the predicate for the result is (*n*−1)-place or (*n*−1)-adic. In the example, the predicate for the input relation is triadic but that for the result is dyadic—it has just two parameters, ENO and SAL; DNO isn't a parameter any more, it's what's called a *bound variable*, thanks to that quantifier.

> *Please take a moment to make sure you understand these points, because what's to come later is crucially dependent on them.*

PREDICATES AND PROJECTIONS (cont.)

Now let's project away attribute ENO from ES. The result is a relation S, say, with heading {SAL}, that given our running example looks like this:

```
S
┌─────────┐
│ SAL     │
├═════════┤
│ 80K     │
│ 95K     │
│ 75K     │
└─────────┘
```

Since we've projected away an attribute (viz., ENO), we need to introduce a corresponding existential quantifier into the predicate, and so the predicate for relation S is as follows:

> *There exists a department DNO such that **there exists** an employee ENO **such that** employee ENO earns salary SAL and works in department DNO.*

For example, the salary 95K appears in the result, because there does exist an employee *e* and a department *d* such that *e* works in *d* and earns 95K (in fact there are two such (*e,d*) combinations in our running example). By contrast, the salary 99K, say, doesn't appear, because there's no employee in any department who earns such a salary.

Note also that the predicate for relation S is monadic—it has just one parameter, SAL (DNO and ENO are now both bound variables).

And now, for the final step in this progression, let's project away attribute SAL from relation S, to yield a relation Z, say. Do not let your mind be boggled! That result Z is still a relation; it still has a set of attributes; but that set just happens to be empty. In other words, relation Z is of degree zero and has *no attributes at all*: Its heading is the empty set, i.e., the set of zero attributes, { }. What's its predicate? Well, we've projected away an attribute, so we need to introduce a corresponding existential quantifier into the predicate. Thus, the predicate for relation S is:

> *There exists a department DNO such that there exists an employee ENO such that **there exists** a salary SAL **such that** employee ENO earns salary SAL and works in department DNO.*

This predicate looks rather complicated, but I hope you can see on closer inspection that it's actually very simple. It's simple because it's niladic or 0-place; it has no parameters at all, merely three bound variables. As a consequence, it evaluates to *true* or *false*, unequivocally. To be specific, it evaluates to *true* if there does exist at least one employee *e* and at least one department *d* and at least one salary *s* such that "*e* earns *s* and works in *d*" is *true*, and it evaluates to *false* otherwise. Another way of saying the same thing is: It evaluates to *true* if the original EMP relation contained at least one tuple, and to *false* otherwise (i.e., if it contained no tuples at all).

But if the predicate in question evaluates to *true* or *false* unequivocally, then by definition it's a proposition! And indeed so it is. A proposition is just a special kind of predicate—in fact, it's *exactly* a niladic predicate. In other words, all propositions are predicates (they're an important special case), but "most" predicates aren't propositions.

RELATIONS WITH NO ATTRIBUTES

So now we've arrived at the point where we see that the notion of a relation with no attributes, like relation Z above, is at least a respectable one—by which I mean it's respectable from a logical or mathematical point of view.[6] But I can hear my critics now: "I don't care whether it's respectable. The question is, is it *useful*?" Well, of course the answer is *yes*, it certainly is useful; but before I can demonstrate the truth of this claim, I first need to consider the question of whether a relation with no attributes can contain any tuples.

You might want to think about that question for a moment or two before reading any further.

Discussion: Well, if such a relation can contain any tuples, the tuples in question must certainly be *0-tuples* (i.e., tuples of degree zero, which is to say tuples with zero components, also known as *empty tuples*). But that's OK! You see, a tuple is a set too—basically a set of attribute values—and since the empty set is, as always, a perfectly respectable set, the notion of a 0-tuple or empty tuple is a perfectly respectable notion as well. Note further that there's really only one 0-tuple (and we're therefore within our rights to refer to it as *the* 0-tuple), because all 0-tuples are duplicates of one another (!). So it follows that a relation with no attributes can contain *at most one tuple*: namely, the 0-tuple.

Our relation Z, then, can contain either one tuple or no tuples at all; these are the only possibilities. It'll contain one tuple if the original EMP relation was nonempty (and the existence of that one tuple means the 0-place predicate corresponding to Z evaluates to *true*); it'll contain no tuples at all if that original

---

[6] Or both! Apparently some mathematicians regard logic as part of math and some logicians regard math as part of logic. I incline to the latter view myself, but there's no need to worry about such matters here.

EMP relation was empty (and that lack of tuples means the 0-place predicate corresponding to Z evaluates to *false*).

Note carefully that all of the foregoing is perfectly consistent with the rules for projection: Any projection of an empty relation is empty; any projection of a relation with at least one tuple is a relation with at least one tuple, with redundant duplicate tuples eliminated.

So important are these relations with no attributes that we have pet names for them: We call the one with no tuples TABLE_DUM, and we call the one with one tuple TABLE_DEE.[7] And, as we've seen, TABLE_DUM (DUM for short) corresponds to *false*, or *no*, and TABLE_DEE (DEE for short) corresponds to *true*, or *yes*. They have the most fundamental meanings of all!—and that's why they're so important. One of the reasons yes/no questions (e.g., "Does employee E1 work in department D1?") are hard to deal with in SQL—a point I'll come back to in a moment—is precisely because SQL doesn't support DUM and DEE.

By the way, to help you remember which relation is which, note that DEE and YES both have an E, and DUM and NO don't.

Of course, it's a little difficult to draw pictures of TABLE_DUM and TABLE_DEE! In fact, it's ironic that we refer to these special relations by those particular names, since they're the only ones that can't sensibly be drawn as tables; they're the ones where our intuitive mode of thinking—i.e., of relations as tables—tends to break down. In other words, although the idea of a relation with no attributes is utterly respectable as we've seen, the idea of a table with no columns is somewhat counterintuitive to say the least.

YES / NO QUERIES

Consider again that query I mentioned a few moments ago: "Does employee E1 work in department D1?" One way of dealing with this query relationally is as follows:

---

[7] For the benefit of any readers who might not be native English speakers, I should explain that those names are basically just wordplay on Tweedledum and Tweedledee, who were originally characters in a children's nursery rhyme and were subsequently incorporated into Lewis Carroll's *Through the Looking-Glass and What Alice Found There* (1871).

1. Restrict the employees relation to just the set of tuples for employee E1 and department D1. (Actually that set will contain at most one tuple, of course, since employee numbers are unique.)

2. Project that restriction on the set of no attributes.

   Then, if the result of that projection is TABLE_DEE, it means yes, employee E1 does work in department D1; if it's TABLE_DUM, it means no, employee E1 doesn't work in department D1.

   Now recall that, in SQL, restriction is done by means of the WHERE clause (on the result of the pertinent FROM clause), and projection is done by means of the SELECT clause (on the result of the pertinent WHERE clause). So if the SQL analog of the original EMP relation is an EMP table, an SQL analog of the foregoing relational formulation of the query ought to look something like this:

```
SELECT  /* no columns at all */
FROM    EMP
WHERE   ENO = 'E1'
AND     DNO = 'D1'
```

And this formulation then ought to yield either TABLE_DEE or TABLE_DUM. But of course it won't; instead, it'll fail at compile time, because an empty SELECT clause—meaning, more precisely, a SELECT clause with an empty commalist of items to be "selected"—is illegal in SQL. Instead, therefore, the SQL user will have to do something like this:

1. SELECT *something* (it could be ENO, or DNO, or both, or in fact anything at all, perhaps just the literal 0), with FROM and WHERE clauses as shown above, and then

2. Test to see whether the overall result table is empty, and then

3. If it is, return "false"; if it isn't, return "true."

All very cumbersome—and all quite unnecessary, if only SQL supported DUM and DEE.

Aside: Here for interest is an SQL formulation of the query that does at least, in effect, combine the foregoing three steps into a single expression. The expression in question returns a one-column, one-row table containing the character string 'YES' if E1 does work in D1 and the character string 'NO' otherwise:

```
SELECT  'YES'
FROM    EMP
WHERE   EXISTS ( SELECT *
                 FROM    EMP
                 WHERE   ENO = 'E1'
                 AND     DNO = 'D1' )
UNION
SELECT  'NO'
FROM    EMP
WHERE   NOT EXISTS ( SELECT *
                     FROM    EMP
                     WHERE   ENO = 'E1'
                     AND DNO = 'D1' )
```

Note, however, that what this expression evaluates to, even though it'll be understood (or rather interpreted) by the user readily enough, will *not* be understood by SQL as a truth value, nor as a table that corresponds to—or even contains—a truth value. *End of aside.*

INTERPRETATION

I've said, a trifle loosely, that TABLE_DEE and TABLE_DUM "have the most fundamental meanings of all," because they "correspond to" *yes* and *no*, respectively. But I don't want you to think I was saying those relations actually "mean" *yes* and *no*, respectively. After all, *yes* and *no* don't really have any meaning out of context, anyway—they have meaning only when they're understood to be the answer to some specific yes/no question. And the same goes for DEE and DUM, mutatis mutandis. Here's an example to illustrate the point. Consider the familiar suppliers-and-parts database; consider in particular the projections SC, of suppliers on supplier cities, and PC, of parts on part cities. Suppose those projections have values as shown here:

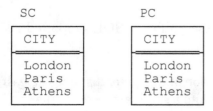

Well, these two relations obviously have the same value, but equally obviously their meanings are quite different. For example, the fact that London appears in SC means "There exists at least one London supplier," while the fact that London appears in table PC means "There exists at least one London part."

In exactly the same way, two relations in the database, or (more realistically) two relations derived from the relations in the database, might both have DEE, say, as their value, but the meaning would be quite different in the two cases. In other words, the meanings of DEE and DUM *depend on context*— just as the meanings of *yes* and *no* depend on context, as I've already said.

TABLE_DEE IS THE IDENTITY FOR JOIN

The concept of *identity*[8] is of fundamental importance in mathematics. In ordinary arithmetic, for example, the number 0 is the identity with respect to addition ("+")—that is, 0 is that special number with the special property that

```
a + 0 = 0 + a = a
```

for all numbers *a*.

By way of another example, the number 1 is the identity with respect to multiplication ("×"). That is, 1 is that special number with the special property that

```
a × 1 = 1 × a = a
```

for all numbers *a*.

Well, in exactly the same kind of way, *TABLE_DEE is the identity with respect to (natural) join.* That is, TABLE_DEE (DEE for short) is that special relation with the special property that

```
r JOIN DEE = DEE JOIN r = r
```

for all relations *r*, as I now explain.

---

[8] Not to confused with the concept of *equivalence* in logic, which is also sometimes known as identity. For example, the logical equivalence (or tautology) NOT (NOT (*p*)) ≡ *p* would sometimes be referred to as an identity, but it's not the kind of identity I'm talking about here.

First of all, please note that in my own preferred version of the relational algebra, (a) "join" means natural join specifically (unless the context demands otherwise, of course); (b) relations *r1* and *r2* can be joined if and only if they're *joinable*; and (c) "joinable" means that attributes with the same name—attributes of the relations in question, that is—are of the same type. Here are precise definitions:

> **Definition (joinable):** Relations *r1* and *r2* are joinable if and only if the set theory union of their headings is a legal heading—equivalently, if and only if attributes with the same name are of the same type.

> **Definition (join):** Let relations *r1* and *r2* be joinable. Then (and only then) the expression *r1* JOIN *r2* denotes the natural join of *r1* and *r2*, and it returns the relation with heading the set theory union of the headings of *r1* and *r2* and body the set of all tuples *t* such that *t* is the set theory union of a tuple from *r1* and a tuple from *r2*.

Points arising:

- Of course, the foregoing definitions depend on certain other definitions in turn—specifically, on precise definitions of *heading* and *attribute* and *body* and *tuple*, all of which are given in the appendix to this chapter. For now, though, I'm just going to assume that the definitions above make sense as they stand.

- Note that both definitions are purely dyadic—the first defines what it means for exactly two relations to be joinable, and the second explains what the join of exactly two joinable relations looks like. But both can be generalized to the *n*-adic case for arbitrary $n \geq 0$, and I'll come back to those generalizations in the next section ("*N*-adic Joins").

- Suppose relations *r1* and *r2* actually have no attribute names at all in common. By the first of the foregoing definitions, then, *r1* and *r2* are certainly joinable—and by the second, their join *r1* JOIN *r2* reduces to their (cartesian) product, which I'll write as *r1* TIMES *r2*. So in "my" version of the relational algebra, TIMES is just a special case of JOIN—it's the special case where the set of common attribute names is empty—and JOIN (meaning, to say it again, natural join specifically) is really the more fundamental operator.

Now let me get back to that business of identities. I'll focus first on the special case of product (TIMES), because I think the argument is a little easier to follow in that special case. Have you ever wondered why that operator is called "product"? One reason is that it does behave in some respects like multiplication in ordinary arithmetic. And just as in ordinary arithmetic the number 1 is the identity with respect to multiplication as we've seen, so TABLE_DEE—DEE for short, remember—is the identity with respect to TIMES, because *r* TIMES DEE = DEE TIMES *r* = *r* for all relations *r*. For example, consider the product *r* TIMES DEE. By definition, the relation resulting from evaluation of that expression clearly has:

- A heading that's the set theory union of the heading of *r* and the heading of DEE—which reduces to just the heading of *r*, since the heading of DEE is empty; and

- A body that consists of all possible set theory unions of a tuple *t* of *r* with a tuple—actually the only tuple, the 0-tuple or empty tuple—of DEE. But the set theory union of any tuple *t* and the 0-tuple reduces to just *t*, and so the body of the product reduces to just the body of *r*.

More fundamentally, if you think about it for a moment, you'll see that TABLE_DEE is in fact the identity with respect to natural join (and product is just a special case). In other words (to repeat), *r* JOIN DEE = DEE JOIN *r* = *r* for all relations *r*. So we see that DEE behaves with respect to join in much the same way as 1 does with respect to multiplication in ordinary arithmetic (or as 0 does with respect to addition in ordinary arithmetic).

Aside: But what about DUM? Well, consider the product *r* TIMES DUM. By definition (again), the relation resulting from evaluation of that expression clearly has:

- A heading that's the set theory union of the heading of *r* and the heading of DEE—which reduces to just the heading of *r*, since the heading of DUM is empty; and

■ A body that consists of all possible set theory unions of a tuple *t* of *r* with a tuple of DUM. But there aren't any "tuples of DUM"!—DUM is empty, by definition—and so there aren't any set theory unions of a tuple *t* of *r* with a tuple of DUM, either, and the body of the product is also empty.

Thus, *r* TIMES DUM, DUM TIMES *r* (and, more generally, *r* JOIN DUM and DUM JOIN *r*) all yield an empty result for all relations *r*. In other words, DUM behaves with respect to TIMES (and, more generally, JOIN) in much the same way as 0 behaves with respect to multiplication in ordinary arithmetic. *End of aside.*

Now, I know from experience that some people find the idea of relations with no attributes a little difficult "to get their head around." If you're one of those people, then I suggest you ask yourself this question:

Do you agree it would be somehow incomplete to support the operations of addition and multiplication in ordinary arithmetic without the special numbers 0 and 1?

I presume your answer is *yes*.[9] So what about this question?—

Do you agree it would be somehow incomplete to support the operations of join and cartesian product in relational agebra without the special relations DUM and DEE?

Well, I hope your answer is *yes* again! Though I suppose SQL apologists would have to answer *no*, because SQL doesn't support TABLE_DUM and TABLE_DEE. But that's just a deficiency—a very major deficiency—in SQL.[10] Let me say it one more time, because it's so important: TABLE_DUM and TABLE_DEE have roles to play with respect to the relational algebra that are analogous to the roles that 0 and 1 play in ordinary arithmetic; in all cases, in fact, the concept is absolutely crucial.

---

[9] Well, I guess the ancient Romans would have had to answer *no*, because they didn't support 0—but we know better now. But have you ever tried to do arithmetic with Roman numerals?

[10] Perhaps I should add that like SQL, Codd's "relational model Version 2" (RM/V2) apparently doesn't support TABLE_DUM or TABLE_DEE either [1]. (I say "apparently" here because reference [1] goes out of its way to justify the notion of a relation with just one attribute—a notion that some people might find counterintuitive, given the usual natural language meaning of the word *relation*—and yet never mentions the arguably much more counterintuitive notion of a relation with no attributes at all.)

Note: I don't want you to misconstrue my message here, though. More particularly, I don't want you to think that DUM and DEE correspond directly to 0 and 1, respectively. Which of DUM and DEE is "like" 0 and which is "like" 1 depends—obviously enough, I hope—on which particular relational operator we're talking about.

N-ADIC JOINS

Now I come as promised to those *n*-adic generalizations of the notions of join and joinability. Here are the definitions (note that they're formulated in terms of the dyadic case, definitions for which I've already given):

> **Definition (joinable, *n*-adic case):** Relations $r1, r2, ..., rn$ $(n \geq 0)$ are joinable—sometimes *n*-way joinable, for emphasis—if and only if for all i and j, relations ri and rj are joinable $(1 \leq i \leq n, \ 1 \leq j \leq n)$.[11]

> **Definition (join, *n*-adic case):** Let relations $r1, r2, ..., rn$ $(n \geq 0)$ be *n*-way joinable. Then (and only then) the expression JOIN $\{r1,r2,...,rn\}$ denotes the natural join of $r1, r2, ..., rn$, and it returns a relation r defined as follows: If $n = 0$, r is TABLE_DEE; if $n = 1$, r is $r1$; otherwise, choose any two relations from the set $r1, r2, ..., rn$ and replace them by their (dyadic) natural join, and repeat this process until the set consists of just one relation r, which is the final result.

Let me get back to ordinary arithmetic for a moment. Suppose we're given a collection of *n* numbers, *CN*. Suppose further that we want to compute the sum of the numbers in *CN*. Then the following code does the trick:

```
SUM := 0 ;
for each X in CN do
    SUM := SUM + X ;
```

---

[11] Let *CR* be a collection of relations (I deliberately don't call it a set, because there's no need here to prohibit the possibility that *CR* might contain duplicates). Then there are two points arising from this definition that are worth calling out explicitly. First, if *CR* contains either just one relation or no relations at all, then the relations in *CR* are certainly joinable, albeit trivially so. Second, note that dyadic joinability isn't transitive; in other words, even if relations *r1* and *r2* are joinable and relations *r2* and *r3* are joinable, it doesn't necessarily follow that relations *r1* and *r3* are joinable. (*Exercise:* Find sample relations *r1*, *r2*, *r3* to illustrate this point.) That's why the definition requires that every relation in *CR* be dyadically joinable with every relation in *CR* (including itself, of course—but every relation *is* dyadically joinable with itself, thanks to the first point).

Note the initialization step, which sets SUM to 0; note further that we choose 0 as that initial value precisely because 0 is the identity with respect to ordinary addition. Now, what happens if *n* is 0, and the collection *CN* is empty? The answer, of course, is that the loop is executed zero times, and the final value of SUM is just the initial value, 0. Thus we can say that *the sum of no numbers is 0* (the identity with respect to "+").[12]

Exactly analogous reasoning shows that the product of no numbers is 1, the identity with respect to multiplication. And exactly analogous reasoning also shows that *the join of no relations is TABLE_DEE*, the identity with respect to join. (And as a special case, the product of no relations is TABLE_DEE as well, of course.)

To close this section, let me say a few words about SQL. We've already seen that SQL ought to (but doesn't) allow the SELECT clause to be "empty," meaning more precisely that it should allow that clause to contain an empty commalist of items to be "selected." Well, now we see that it ought to allow the FROM clause to be empty too, meaning that it should allow that clause to contain an empty commalist of tables for the SELECT items to be selected from. Why? Because the FROM clause really means "form the product of the tables mentioned"; so SQL ought to (but doesn't) allow it to mention no tables at all, in which case the FROM clause in question would be understood as meaning FROM TABLE_DEE. Why might this be useful? Well, suppose we want to ask SQL the time of day. We might try:

```
SELECT  CURRENT_TIME
FROM    EMP
```

Of course, the particular table we choose to mention in the FROM clause here is both arbitrary and irrelevant—but it has to be *some* table, because SQL doesn't allow an empty FROM clause. Though I note that if we did use EMP as just shown, then we'd probably (and very annoyingly) have to revise the expression to say:

```
SELECT  DISTINCT CURRENT_TIME
FROM    EMP
```

(What would happen if we didn't?) But why couldn't we just say this?—

---

[12] Not in SQL, of course—SQL would say the sum is null. But that's just another logical error on SQL's part, and in fact another serious defect.

```
SELECT CURRENT_TIME
FROM    /* no explicit tables */
```

(meaning, of course, "selecting" from TABLE_DEE). And if we were to adopt the obvious convention[13] that such an empty clause can simply be omitted, this would become just—

```
SELECT CURRENT_TIME
```

—which is at last beginning to look almost user friendly.

So the SELECT clause and the FROM clause should both be allowed to be empty. Putting this together, therefore, we see that the following ought to be (but isn't) a legal SQL expression:

```
SELECT /* no explicit columns */
FROM   /* no explicit tables */
```

And the result would be TABLE_DEE. Moreover, if (again) we adopt the obvious convention that empty clauses can be omitted, the foregoing expression would reduce to just—

```
/* no explicit columns */
/* no explicit tables */
```

—and (to repeat) the result would be TABLE_DEE. Come to that, the following should also be (but isn't) a legal SELECT – FROM – WHERE expression—

```
/* no explicit columns */
/* no explicit tables */
WHERE FALSE
```

—and the result would be TABLE_DUM.

OTHER ALGEBRAIC OPERATORS

It's a fact that, once you know about TABLE_DUM and TABLE_DEE, you find them popping up all over the place. For reference purposes, therefore, this

---

[13] A convention, incidentally, that SQL already adheres to in the case of the GROUP BY clause.

section briefly considers the effects of those two special relations on the algebraic operators union, intersection, difference, restrict, project, divide, extend, and summarize. (The effects on join and product have already been considered at length, of course.)

Union, Intersection, Difference

Each of these operators requires its relational operands to be of the same type, or equivalently to have the same heading. The only relations that are of the same type as DUM and DEE are DUM and DEE themselves. We have:

```
union | DEE DUM    intersection | DEE DUM   difference | DEE DUM
──────┼────────    ─────────────┼────────   ───────────┼────────
 DEE  | DEE DEE         DEE      | DEE DUM       DEE    | DUM DEE
 DUM  | DEE DUM         DUM      | DUM DUM       DUM    | DUM DUM
```

In the case of difference, the first operand is shown at the left of the table and the second at the top (the other two operators are commutative, of course, so the order of the operands doesn't matter). Note how reminiscent these tables are of the truth tables for OR, AND, and AND NOT, respectively. Of course, the resemblance isn't a coincidence.

Restrict and Project

■ Any restriction of DEE yields DEE if the restriction condition is *true*, DUM if it's *false*.

■ Any restriction of DUM yields DUM.[14]

■ Projection of any relation on no attributes yields DUM if the original relation is empty, DEE otherwise. In particular, projection of DEE or DUM, necessarily on no attributes at all, returns its input.

Divide

The following notes assume a *generalized form* of the division operator (one that permits any relation to be divided by any relation, loosely speaking)—see "A Brief History of the Relational Divide Operator," in *Database Explorations:*

---

[14] Even the restriction DUM WHERE FALSE! You might want to think about that.

Essays on The Third Manifesto and Related Topics, by Hugh Darwen and myself (Trafford Publishing, 2010).

- Any relation *r* divided by DEE yields *r*.

- Any relation *r* divided by DUM yields an empty relation with the same heading as *r*.

- DEE divided by any relation *r* yields *r*.

- DEE divided by any relation *r* yields an empty relation with the same heading as *r*.

- Any nonempty relation divided by itself yields DEE.

- Any empty relation divided by itself yields DUM.

Extend and Summarize

- Extending DEE or DUM to add a new attribute yields a relation of one attribute and the same number of tuples as its input.

- Summarizing DEE or DUM, necessarily by no attributes at all, to add a new attribute yields a relation of one attribute and the same number of tuples as its input. *Note:* If (a) the input is DUM and (b) the aggregate expression involves AVG or any other operator that's undefined for an empty operand, the effect will be to raise an exception.

CONCLUDING REMARKS

To repeat, it's a fact that, once you know about DUM and DEE, you find them popping up all over the place—which makes it increasingly annoying that SQL doesn't support them. SQL's overriding failure in this connection is that it violates the important closure property of the relational algebra—by which I mean the following:

■ Of course, the relational algebra is properly closed. That is, every expression of the relational algebra evaluates to a relation, and such expressions can therefore always be used (recursively, in fact) as subexpressions of other such expressions.

■ SQL, by contrast, fails to support certain relations, and therefore doesn't support any expression that would evaluate to such a relation—an omission that leads to all kinds of further omissions and failures on SQL's part.

Some of those "further omissions and failures" have already been mentioned, viz.:

■ Difficulties over yes/no queries

■ No empty SELECT clauses

■ No empty FROM clauses

And here are a few more:

■ No empty keys. But this is a big topic in its own right—among other things, it leads to the need to discuss the logical difference between relation values and relation variables. See, e.g., my book *SQL and Relational Theory: How to Write Accurate SQL Code* (3rd edition, O'Reilly, 2015) for further discussion.

■ SQL doesn't let you create a base table without any columns—i.e., it's not possible for CREATE TABLE not to include any column definitions. Note that such a feature might be exactly what you'd like to use at database design time, when you might want to document the fact that you've found some new "entity type" that needs to be dealt with, without having to bother yourself (yet) with any properties the entity type in question might possess.

■ SQL also doesn't let you say (e.g.) ALTER TABLE *T* DROP COLUMN *C* if *C* happens to be the only column of *T*. Of course, this might not be a burning issue, but it's at least worth mentioning as another minor anomaly. Note in particular that it does mean that the reference manuals have to include additional text to tell you there's something you can't do. That's what always happens when a language violates orthogonality in some way [6]—the language gets smaller (in the sense that there's something you can't do), but the manuals get bigger (because they have to have rules to tell you not to try and do the something you can't do).

REFERENCES

1. E. F. Codd: *The Relational Model for Database Management Version 2* (Addison-Wesley, 1990).

2. Hugh Darwen: "The Nullologist in Relationland, *or* Nothing Really Matters," in C. J. Date, *Relational Database Writings 1989-1991* (Addison-Wesley, 1992).

3. C. J. Date: Chapter 9 ("A Sweet Disorder") of *Date on Database: Writings 2000-2006* (Apress, 2006).

4. C. J. Date: Chapter 4 ("No Duplicates, No Nulls") of *SQL and Relational Theory: How to Write Accurate SQL Code* (3rd edition, O'Reilly, 2015).

5. C. J. Date: Chapter 5 ("*The Closed World Assumption*") of *Logic and Relational Theory: Thoughts and Essays on Database Matters* (Technics Publications, 2020).

6. C. J. Date: Chapter 7 ("Some Principles of Good Language Design") of the companion volume to the present book..

7. C. J. Date: *E. F. Codd and Relational Theory, Revised Edition: A Detailed Review and Analysis of Codd's Major Database Writings* (Technics Publications, 2021).

APPENDIX

The following definitions are taken from reference [7]. Together they pin down the notion of a relation precisely, and they form the basis for a sound, thorough, modern, and detailed understanding of what the relational model is all about. Do note, however, that they all fundamentally rely on the definition (not included here) of the notion of *type*.

> **Definition (heading):** A *heading H* is a set, the elements of which are *attributes*. Let *H* have cardinality n ($n \geq 0$); then the value n is the *degree* of *H*. A heading of degree zero is *nullary*, a heading of degree one is *unary*, a heading of degree two is *binary*, ..., and more generally a heading of degree n is *n-ary*. Each attribute in *H* is of the form $<Aj,Tj>$, where Aj is the *attribute name* and Tj is the corresponding *type name* ($0 < j \leq n$), and the attribute names Aj are all distinct.

> **Definition (tuple):** Let heading *H* be of degree n. For each attribute $<Aj,Tj>$ in *H*, define a *component* of the form $<Aj,Tj,vj>$, where the *attribute value vj* is a value of type Tj. The set—call it *t*—of all n components so defined is a *tuple value* (or just a *tuple* for short) over the attributes of *H*. *H* is the *tuple heading* (or just the heading for short) for *t*, and the degree and attributes of *H* are, respectively, the degree and attributes of *t*.

> **Definition (body):** Given a heading *H*, a *body B* conforming to *H* is a set of m tuples ($m \geq 0$), each with heading *H*. The value m is the *cardinality* of *B*.

> **Definition (relation):** Let *H* be a heading, and let *B* be a body conforming to *H*. The pair $<H,B>$—call it *r*—is a *relation value* (or just a *relation* for short) over the attributes of *H*. *H* is the *relation heading* (or just the heading for short) for *r*, and the degree and attributes of *H* and the cardinality of *B* are, respectively, the degree, attributes, and cardinality of *r*.

Chapter 4

All Logical Differences

Are Big Differences

This chapter explains the fundamental principle identified in the title and discusses its usefulness, with good and bad examples.
Publishing history: This is a revised version of a paper that first appeared under the title "On the Notion of Logical Difference" in my book Date on Database: Writings 2000-2006 (Apress, 2006). This version copyright © C. J. Date 2022.

If you're familiar with other writings by myself—especially the book I wrote with Hugh Darwen called *Databases, Types, and the Relational Model: The Third Manifesto* (3rd edition, Addison-Wesley, 2007), referred to in what follows as just *The Third Manifesto*, or the *Manifesto* for short—you'll know I often appeal in those writings to the notion of logical difference. It's a notion I find extraordinarily useful in my own work; it's a great aid to clear and precise thinking (not that my thinking is always as clear and precise as it might be, I'm sorry to say). I also find it helpful when I'm trying to understand, learn, and inwardly digest the contributions of others in the database field. And, last but certainly not least, I find it an extremely useful "mind tool" when I'm trying to pinpoint and analyze some of the confusions that are, unfortunately, all too common in that same field. It's a rock to cling to in what can sometimes seem to be an ocean of muddle.

The intent of what follows, then, is to offer a brief general introduction to the concept of logical difference, and thereby to set the scene for an occasional and open-ended series of writings on specific important examples of that concept—including the next two chapters of the present book in particular.

WHY IS IT IMPORTANT TO THINK PRECISELY?

If it hadn't been for the fact that it doesn't exactly trip off the tongue, the title for this chapter might have been, more specifically, "Some Logical Differences or Fundamental Distinctions that Lie at the Heart of the Database Field." It's my claim, or rather my thesis, that many of the confusions to be found in the database literature—especially in the "object oriented" or OO portions of that literature—stem from confusion over one or other of the fundamental logical differences I have in mind. Examples to follow!

This isn't the first time I've addressed this issue. In addition to the coverage already alluded to above in *The Third Manifesto,* I've at least touched on the concept of logical difference in several other places, and in 1997 I published a four-part piece on the same general subject titled "Why Is It Important to Think Precisely?" (republished in my book *Relational Database Writings 1994-1997*, Addison-Wesley, 1998). So what follows isn't entirely new. But quite a lot of it *is* new, and in any case I believe it's useful to bring the material all together in one place to serve as a central reference.

Here for the record is what that earlier four-part article did. After a little background, it discussed four specific logical differences:

1. Model vs. implementation
2. Value vs. variable
3. Type vs. relation
4. Type vs. representation

In particular, in each case it:

■ Explained exactly what the difference in question was;

■ Gave examples from the literature of where writers had apparently failed to understand that difference; and

■ Discussed some of the consequences of such failure.

Let me also explain why that four-part article had the title it did. As you might know, I've been teaching seminars on database topics for many years, and by now you might expect me to be a little bored with the whole subject. But I'm not. One reason I'm not is the fact that it doesn't matter how many times you teach a given seminar, you can always get questions you've never heard before ... On one occasion, I was claiming that one of the virtues of the relational model was that it helped you to *think precisely*—in particular, it helped you to articulate problems in a precise manner. Whereupon one student asked: "Why is it important to think precisely?" This question was right out of left field so far as I was concerned! Certainly it was one I'd never heard before. So I replied: "Well, I don't know exactly." Which I thought was a pretty good response, off the top of my head.

WITTGENSTEIN'S DICTUM

Throughout our database work in general, Hugh Darwen and I have always tried very hard to follow certain guiding principles (and, of course, this remark is true of our work on the *Manifesto* in particular). Of those principles, the most important—indeed, it underpins all the rest—is the one the present chapter is all about:

```
All Logical Differences Are Big Differences
```

This dictum is due to Ludwig Wittgenstein.[1] What does it mean? Well, the subject matter of the *Manifesto* is, essentially, the relational model. And the relational model is at heart a *formal system*: just as a DBMS is, or an operating system, or indeed any computer program, come to that. Formal systems are what computers are, or can be made to be, good at. And, of course, the basis of any

---

[1] At this point in the paper on which this chapter is based I wrote the following: "At least, I think it is, though, sadly, Hugh and I have never been able to track it down to its source, and we'd be grateful to anyone who could help us in that connection." Little did I know that help was on its way at that very moment. The complete quote is: "As I once heard Wittgenstein say, all logical differences are big differences; in logic we are not making *subtle* distinctions, as it were between flavours that pass over into one another by delicate gradations" (from a lecture titled "History of the Corruptions of Logic," by P. T. Geach, published in his book *Logic Matters,* Basil Blackwell, 1972). Thanks to Stephen A. Wilson for passing on this discovery. Though I can't resist pointing out that it really isn't clear how much of the quote is due to Wittgenstein and how much is due to Geach! Logicians themselves—who really ought to know better—aren't always as precise as they might be.

formal system is logic. It follows that—with respect to formal systems in general, and hence with respect to programming in general, and with respect to database management and the relational model in particular—differences that are logical in nature are very important ones, and we need to pay very careful attention to them. To put it another way:

- Computers do what they're formally instructed to do, no more and no less.

- In computing above all, therefore, clarity, accuracy, and precision are paramount.

- These remarks are true of database management in particular.

- As a consequence, any endeavor having to do with database management, if it's confused over issues as basic as (for example) the difference between a value and a variable, or the difference between a type and a relation, is *doomed to eventual failure*.

We (i.e., Hugh and I) also pointed out in the *Manifesto*, slightly—but only slightly!—tongue in cheek, that Wittgenstein's dictum had an interesting corollary: namely, that *all logical mistakes are big mistakes*. Because, of course, a mistake is a difference: It's a difference between right and wrong. And it's certainly possible to observe a number of logical mistakes that have been made, and still are being made, in the database industry as a whole ... We also went on to conjecture that the inverse of Wittgenstein's maxim was true as well: namely, that *all nonlogical differences are small differences*—by which we meant, not that differences that are (e.g.) merely psychological in nature are unimportant in absolute terms, but that they *are* unimportant from the point of view of formal systems in particular. We therefore paid little attention in our *Manifesto* to nonlogical considerations, such as matters of syntax.

Note: Syntax is important from a human factors point of view, of course, and we naturally tried to choose good syntax over bad when we came to design our own language **Tutorial D**.[2] But we don't regard differences that are mere differences in syntax as logical differences, nor for present purposes as very important ones.

---

[2] See *www.thethirdmanifesto.com*.

SOME THINGS ARE MUCH THE SAME

In practice, we unfortunately but not infrequently encounter a situation that truly does involve some particular logical difference, and yet either

a. The logically different concepts are referred to by the same name, or

b. The concepts do have distinct names, but those names tend to be used very sloppily—sometimes almost interchangeably.

Both of these situations can certainly give rise to confusion, of course. As an illustration of Case a., consider the term *data model*, which is used to refer to two very different concepts.[3] As an illustration of Case b., consider the terms *argument* and *parameter*, which certainly refer to different concepts but are often used as if they were interchangeable.

As another illustration of Case a., I note that the SQL language often considers two things to be the same even when they're clearly different.[4] For example, in SQL the character strings 'XYZ' and 'XYZ ' (note the trailing space in the second of these) are considered to be equal if PAD SPACE applies to the pertinent "collation"; similarly, the character strings 'XYZ' and 'xyz' are considered to be equal if the pertinent collation is case insensitive. In other words, SQL actually *enshrines* certain confusions over the notion of logical difference in its very definition! A case of "If you can't fix it, feature it"?

So perhaps the concern isn't so much about logical differences per se as it is about the confusions that can occur when we fail to recognize and act on such differences. But the opposite phenomenon can occur, too; that is, we can find ourselves in a situation in which we're told, in effect, that there's a logical difference between two concepts, and it turns out later that the concepts are in fact one and the same (or at least overlap considerably, and usually unpleasantly). In other words:

---

[3] Case a. is reminiscent of the phenomenon found in many programming languages called *overloading*. Overloading occurs when the language provides several distinct operators with the same name; for example, the name "+" might refer to two distinct "add" operators, one to add two fixed point numbers and one to add two floating point numbers. Then again, some writers use the term *overloading* to refer to something completely different—in which case the term *overloading* is itself overloaded, and we have a genuine example of Case a. on our hands (a state of affairs that Lewis Carroll might have enjoyed).

[4] See Chapter 1 ("Equality") of my book *Stating the Obvious, and Other Database Writings* (Technics Publications, 2020).

■ Problems occur over *logical difference* when somebody fails to recognize that two concepts are in fact distinct.

■ Problems occur over *logical sameness* when somebody fails to recognize that two allegedly distinct concepts are in fact the same, or at least have a great deal in common.

In fairness, I observe that the logical sameness issue is sometimes unavoidable, especially when we're trying to build a bridge between disciplines that have been constructed on different foundations. For example, the relational model has its roots in the mathematics of relations; when Codd first introduced it, therefore, he used the mathematical term *domain* to refer to the sets over which relations were defined. At the same time, the relational model quite explicitly did *not* have its roots in language theory. As a consequence, it was several years before it was generally recognized and understood that what the database community called *domains* and what the language community called *types* were really one and the same concept.

(As an aside, I observe that some people don't understand even today that domains and types are the same thing. SQL muddies the issue, too, because it uses the term *domain* to mean something else—not to mention that (a) SQL's notion of *type* is much more complicated than it ought to be and (b) SQL is also confused over types vs. representations.)

As another example of logical sameness, consider the terms *intension* and *extension*, which come from logic and mathematics, and their synonyms (perhaps more commonly encountered in the relational world) *heading* and *body*, respectively. The latter terms were introduced by someone who wasn't as familiar with logic as he might have been: namely, yours truly.[5] That said, however, I don't know how the term "relation schema"—sometimes "relation *scheme*," possibly because of a mistaken belief that "schema" was plural and "scheme" was the corresponding singular (!)—came into occasional use, even by logicians, as another synonym for *intension*.

To repeat, then, the logical sameness problem is sometimes unavoidable; nevertheless, we should strive to avoid it as much as we can. The next three

---

[5] Let me quickly add in my own defense here that I think the terms *heading* and *body* are preferable, at least from the point of view of immediate and intuitive comprehensibility. Not to mention the problems that can be caused by confusipn over the word *intension* and its homophone *intention*.

subsections briefly illustrate some cases where I think we should have been able to avoid it, but we didn't.

Object Orientation

It sometimes seems to me that *every* term used in the world of object orientation is just a new label for something that's been known for years in other contexts under some more familiar name. Of course, the problem is exacerbated by the fact that there doesn't seem to be consensus on the meanings of terms even *within* the object world; however, I think it's fair to say that the key concepts, regardless of what names they go by, are *class*, *method*, *message*, *encapsulation*, and of course *object* itself. I'll defer discussion of the last of these to a chapter of its own, Chapter 7 (there's a lot to say about it!). As for the rest:

- *Class* seems to be indistinguishable from *type*, as this latter term is classically understood.

- *Method* seems to be indistinguishable from *operator*, as this latter term is classically understood—except that in some object systems methods are "selfish," meaning they're effectively *a special kind* of operator: namely, one that treats one particular parameter as special (a state of affairs that makes life easier for the system but harder for the user).[6]

- *Message* seems to be indistinguishable from *operator invocation*, as this latter term is classically understood—unless the method concerned is "selfish," in which case the minor exception noted under the previous point applies essentially unchanged.

- Finally, to say something is *encapsulated* seems to be indistinguishable from saying it's *scalar*, as this latter term is classically understood.[7]

Another term that's frequently encountered in the object world is *class hierarchy*. Here are some synonyms for *that* term:

---

[6] But even that "special kind of operator" is special only in the sense that it's given special syntactic treatment. Fundamentally, it's still just an operator.

[7] See Chapter 7 ("Thinking Clearly about Encapsulation") of my book *Stating the Obvious, and Other Database Writings* (Technics Publications, 2020).

type hierarchy
inheritance hierarchy
generalization hierarchy
specialization hierarchy
"is a" hierarchy

Note: I make the foregoing claims—i.e., regarding logical sameness in the object world—in full knowledge of the fact that many people will object to them (pun intended). For example, take the case of *class* and *type.* Here's a quote from a textbook on object database systems—*Object-Oriented Database Systems: Concepts and Architectures,* by Elisa Bertino and Lorenzo Martino (Addison-Wesley, 1993)—that discusses that very issue (the annotation in brackets is mine):

> Object-oriented systems can be classified into two main categories—systems supporting the notion of *class* and those supporting the notion of *type* ... [Although] there are no clear lines of demarcation between them, the two concepts are fundamentally different [*sic!*] ... Often the concepts type and class are used interchangeably. [*But I thought they were "fundamentally different"?*]. However, when both are present in the same language, the type is used to indicate the specification of the interface of a set of objects, while class is an implementational notion. [*In that case, why is the class concept "in the language" at all?*]. Therefore ... a type is a set of objects which share the same behavior ... [and] a class is a set of objects which have exactly the same internal structure and therefore the same attributes and the same methods. [*But if all objects in a class have the same attributes and the same methods, isn't that class a type, by the book's own definition?*] The class defines the implementation of a set of objects, while a type describes how such objects can be used. [*Contrast ODMG,*[8] *which— at least in some contexts if not in all—uses the terms "type" and "class" in a very different way.*]

A little later in the same book, we also find this:

> With inheritance, a class called a *subclass* can be defined on the basis of the definition of another class called a *superclass.* [*Surely—in accordance with its own earlier definitions—the book should be talking in terms of types here, not*

---

[8] See R. G. G. Cattell and Douglas K. Barry (eds.): *The Object Data Standard: ODMG 3.0.* San Francisco, Calif.: Morgan Kaufmann (2000), also Chapter 9 ("An Overview and Analysis of ODMG") of my book *Stating the Obvious, and Other Database Writings* (Technics Publications, 2020).

classes?] ... The **specification hierarchy** (often called *subtype hierarchy*) expresses ... subtyping relationships which mean that an instance of the subtype can be used in every context in which an instance of the supertype can correctly appear (*substitutability*). [*Observe that now it does speak of types, not classes. Observe too that we now have two more terms (specification hierarchy, subtype hierarchy—and why not subclass hierarchy?—for the class, or type, hierarchy.*]

As an aside, I'd like to quote here a passage from the preface to *A Dictionary of Modern American Usage,* by Bryan A. Garner (Oxford University Press, 1998):

> I should address a question that many readers will wonder about. Should I really name names? Should I give full citations in the way that I do? Won't it mortify a [writer] to find some badly written sentence [quoted] for all the world to see? ... Well, I hope it isn't mortifying, and for me it's nothing new ... The citations appear for three reasons. First, they show that the examples are real, not fabricated. Second, they show the great variety of evidence on which [my] judgments are based ... And third, ... they reflect how the language is being used in our culture in our time.

I concur!

The Unified Modeling Language

A particularly rich source of examples of the logical sameness phenomenon is provided by the book *The Unified Modeling Language User Guide*, by Grady Booch, James Rumbaugh, and Ivar Jacobson (Addison-Wesley, 1999). For example, here are some definitions from that reference that all have something to do with the general—and, I would have thought, fairly familiar—notion of *data type*:

■ *Datatype* [*sic one word*]: A type whose values have no identity. Datatypes include primitive builtin types (such as numbers and strings), as well as enumeration types (such as boolean).

■ *Type*: A stereotype of class used to specify a domain of objects, together with the operations (but not methods) applicable to the objects.

■ *Stereotype*: An extension of the vocabulary of the [Unified Modeling Language] UML, which allows you to create new kinds of building blocks that are derived from existing ones but that are specific to your problem.

■ *Class*: A description of a set of objects that share the same attributes, operations, relationships, and semantics.

■ *Domain*: An area of knowledge or activity characterized by a set of concepts and terminology understood by practitioners in that area.

■ *Interface*: A collection of operations that are used to specify a service of a class or a component.

■ *Component*: A physical and replaceable part of a system that conforms to and provides the realization of a set of interfaces.

■ *Primitive type*: A basic type, such as integer or a string.

■ *Value*: An element of a type domain.

Well, I don't want to comment further on the lack of precision in these definitions, though it's ubiquitous; I think the overall message—that there are far more terms than concepts—is clear enough without my needing to add anything. Nor do I want to discuss in detail the truly astounding nature and implications of some of those definitions: for example, the idea that values have no identity (?). Nor do I want to get into the many questions those definitions raise. For example, if "a type whose values have no identity" is called a "datatype," then what's a type whose values do have identity called?

My second exhibit involves a similar set of definitions surrounding the general concept of *operator* (a term that doesn't actually seem to be used in UML, though the term *operation* is):

■ *Precondition*: A constraint that must be true when an operation is invoked.

■ *Postcondition*: A constraint that must be true at the completion of an operation.

■ *Operation*: The implementation of a service that can be requested from any object of the class in order to affect [*effect?*] behavior.

■ *Request*: The specification of a stimulus sent to an object.

■ *Stimulus*: An operation or signal.

■ *Activation*: The execution of an operation.

- *Execution*: The running of a dynamic model.

- *Action*: An executable atomic computation that results in a change of state of the system or the return of a value.

- *Method*: The implementation of an operation.

- *Message*: A specification of a communication between objects that conveys information with the expectation that activity will ensue; the receipt of a message instance is normally considered an instance of an event.

- *Send:* The passing of a message instance from a sender object to a receiver object.

And one more exhibit:

- *Parameter*: The specification of a variable that can be changed, passed, or returned.

- *Argument*: A specific value corresponding to a parameter.

- *Formal parameter*: A parameter.

- *Actual parameter*: A function or procedure argument.

Miscellaneous Examples

Sometimes it seems as if people are *actively exploiting* the logical sameness problem. For example, in his original paper on the entity/relationship model,[9] Chen reinvented the concept of domains (among other things), but called them *value sets*; and then he went on to analyze the relational model in terms of the constructs of his E/R model and concluded that domains were just value sets (!).

Talking of entities and relationships: Of course, we all know that in many approaches—including but not limited to UML, the E/R model, prerelational systems such as IMS and IDMS, and most object systems—a distinction is made between entities and relationships. Well, there certainly is a distinction to be made, but it's not an either/or kind of distinction; to be more specific, all

---

[9] Peter Pin-Shan Chen: "The Entity-Relationship Model—Toward a Unified View of Data," *ACM TODS 1*, No. 1 (March 1976).

relationships are entities, but some entities aren't relationships. (In that respect the distinction is analogous to that between, e.g., predicates and propositions—all propositions are predicates, but some predicates aren't propositions.) So in this case we have two terms and two concepts, but the concepts aren't totally separate (since one subsumes the other).

My last example of the logical sameness problem concerns what has come to be called, especially in XML contexts, *the semistructured data model*. Although this term is comparatively new, I have great difficulty in detecting any difference of substance between the thing it's supposed to refer to and the old-fashioned *hierarchic* data model—or, at least, the structural aspects of that model. But this is clearly a subject that deserves extended discussion, so I won't pursue it any further here.

CONCLUDING REMARKS

I've been wanting to write about these matters for some time. An airing is certainly needed! One of Codd's objectives when he introduced the relational model was to bring some clarity of thought and expression into a field, database management, that was in sore need of it at the time—and evidently still is. Confusion is rife; confusion leads to mistakes; and we can't even *discuss* those mistakes sensibly if we're confused over basic concepts!

I'll finish up with another quote that I think is highly relevant to the topic at hand. It's from Bertrand Russell's own preface to *The Bertrand Russell Dictionary of Mind, Matter and Morals* (ed., Lester E. Denonn), Citadel Press, 1993:[10]

> **Clarity, above all, has been my aim**. I prefer a clear statement subsequently disproved to a misty dictum capable of some profound interpretation which can be welcomed as a "great thought." It is not by "great thoughts," but by careful and detailed analysis, that the kind of technical philosophy which I value can be advanced [*boldface added*].

These wonderful remarks need no further elaboration by me.

---

[10] I've used this quote in other places, too—in particular in the preface to my own book *An Introduction to Database Systems*, 8th edition (Addison-Wesley, 2004).

ACKNOWLEDGMENTS

I'd like to thank Hugh Darwen and Fabian Pascal for their comments on earlier drafts of this chapter.

APPENDIX

I'm well aware that the body of this chapter is a little light on technical substance. In fact the same is true of this appendix—but I thought it might help bolster my argument a little to display a few pertinent quotes from the literature (not just the technical literature), with occasional commentary. My aim is partly to edify, partly just to amuse.

With regard to the technical quotes, by the way, I should say that some of them are quite old. One reason for this state of affairs is that I've more or less stopped reading the trade press over the past few years (I don't think I need say why). Another is that it's impossible to keep up!—the nonsense comes so thick and fast. Indeed, what I do see from time to time (especially in material taken off the Internet) tends to confirm my suspicion that little has changed, except perhaps for the worse. Thus, even when the quotes are old, the attitudes and confusions expressed therein still exist and in fact seem to be widespread, and there's still a need to fight the good fight.

And another remark on those technical quotes: Most of them are *extremely* sloppily phrased. As I've written elsewhere, it's very distressing to find such sloppiness in writings dealing with relational technology of all things, given that (to say it again) it was exactly one of the objectives of the relational model to inject some precision and clarity of thinking into the database field.

Without further ado, let's turn to the quotes. My first is *not* from the trade press; it's from Bertrand Russell again. In comparing mathematics and logic, Russell asserted:

> It has become wholly impossible to draw a line between the two; in fact, the two are one. (Quoted in William Dunham, *The Mathematical Universe*, John Wiley and Sons Inc., 1994.)

No logical difference here, then! Though I'm not sure Russell subscribed to the stated position all his life—I have a feeling he might have changed his mind at some later time (?).

Anyway, talking of logic, here's another beautiful quote from Wittgenstein:

Logic takes care of itself; all we have to do is look and see how it does it. (From *Notebooks 1914-1916, entry for October 13th, 1914,* ed. Anscombe, 1961; also in *Tractatus Logico-Philosophicus, sct. 5:473,* 1921; tr. 1922.)

Thanks to Declan Brady for drawing my attention to this one.

Here's another of Wittgenstein's famous dictums (this one is from the preface to *Tractatus Logico-Philosophicus*):

Was sich überhaupt sagen lässt, lässt sich klar sagen; und wovon man nicht reden kann, darüber muss man schweigen. (What can be said at all can be said clearly; and whereof one cannot speak, thereof one must be silent.)

There's a logical difference, then, between that which can be spoken of and that which can't. Which might well be taken, incidentally, as a directive to avoid nulls!—since to say "*x* is null" is to say, in effect, that there's nothing we can say about *x*.

I have a few more nice quotes to do with this business of speaking clearly. The first is due to Descartes:

When transcendental questions are under discussion, be transcendentally clear. (Quoted in Simon Singh, *Fermat's Enigma*, Walker and Co., 1997.)

The second is from Ben Jonson (he's discussing "the shame of speaking [and writing] unskilfully"):

Neither can his Mind be thought to be in Tune, whose words do jarre; nor his reason in frame, whose sentence is preposterous; nor his Elocution clear and perfect, whose utterance breaks itself into fragments and uncertainties. Negligent speech doth not onely discredit the person of the Speaker, but it discrediteth the opinion of his reason and judgement; it discrediteth the force and uniformity of the matter and substance. If it be so then in words, which fly and 'scape censure, and where one good Phrase asks pardon for many incongruities and faults, how then shall he be thought wise whose penning is thin and shallow? How shall you look for wit from him whose leasure and head, assisted with the examination of his eyes, yeeld you no life or sharpnesse in his writing?

These remarks are quoted by Richard Mitchell in an essay entitled "Hopefully, We Could Care Less" in his book *The Leaning Tower of Babel* (The Akadine Press, 2000).

My third and last quote on this issue of speaking clearly is from Dijkstra, and is perhaps more directly relevant to my thesis. He's talking about the process by which he believes software products should be designed and built:

> I have described this [process] at some length because I remember it so well and because I believe it to be quite typical. Eventually you come up with a very formal and well-defined product, but this eventual birth is preceded by a period of gestation during which new ideas are tried and discarded or developed. That is the *only* way I know of in which the mind can cope with such conceptual problems. From experience I have learned that in that gestation period, when a new jargon has to be created, an excellent mastery of their native tongue is an absolute requirement for all participants. A programmer that talks sloppily is just a disaster. Excellent mastery of his [*sic*] native tongue is my first selection criterion for a prospective programmer; good taste in mathematics is the second important criterion. (As luck will have it, they often go hand in hand.)

This quote is from E. W. Dijkstra, EWD 648, "Why Is Software So Expensive? An Explanation to the Hardware Designer," in *Selected Writings on Computing: A Personal Perspective* (Springer-Verlag, 1982). I particularly appreciate Dijkstra's final, parenthesized sentence.

Following all of these beautifully clear remarks on the importance of clarity, what are we to make of extracts like this one (from an article in a trade magazine)?

> Database vendors are displacing SQL with Java because SQL isn't portable and because object developers cringe at using legacy procedural code in interchangeable component frameworks.

Or this one (from another magazine article)?

> JDO also complements EJB (Enterprise JavaBeans). For example, programmers can use JDO and EJBs together to access data, either using persistent classes in Session Beans, delegate classes in BMP (Bean-Managed Persistence) Entity Beans, or a container implementation alternative to JDBC in CMP (Container-Managed Persistence) Entity Beans. Developers need not modify existing applications that use EJBs, but they may wish to implement JDO with EJBs to simplify data access methods.

I've suppressed attributions on these two quotes in order to protect the guilty; but remember what I said about sloppy writing? Examples like these are so badly expressed that it's not even clear what the writers are trying to say, and I'm sometimes forced to invoke what I've referred to elsewhere as *The Principle of Incoherence* (sometimes known, a trifle unkindly, as *The Incoherent Principle*):

> *It's hard to criticize something coherently if what you're trying to criticize is itself not very coherent in the first place.*

Well, never mind that. Let's take a look at some more quotes from the world of objects. The first is from a textbook titled *C++ Object Databases: Programming with the ODMG Standard*, by David Jordan (Addison-Wesley, 1998; italics as in the original):

> An *entity* is any *thing* that needs to be modeled. The definitions of entities and objects are intertwined. Texts on ER modeling describe an entity as an object, and texts on object modeling describe an object as an entity in the problem domain. *Webster's* describes both *entity* and *object* as "*things*" and *Roget's* treats *entity*, *object*, and *thing* as synonyms. Novices in object technology often ask, "What is an object?" The answer is to explore the "*things*" that need to be managed by the application, which often turn out to be the objects that the application must model: people, places, inanimate objects, concepts, events, and so on. Entities are the most common form of object modeled in applications.

The next is from an interview with Peter Chen in the *FOCUS Systems Journal*, May 1988—Chen speaking:

> What's the difference between an entity and an object? In the database world, people tend to be more type-oriented and to need more semantics. That's why we call them entities. [*What, the people?*] In the programming environment, people want more freedom, so they call them objects ... [Entities] are objects with more semantic value, classified into types, which give more information. We often define entities as "identifiable objects of interest." Everything is an object. Some are identifiable ones [*meaning some aren't?*] that we have an interest in, and these are entities.

Next, here's Hugh Darwen (part of a review of an early draft of a text on object databases):

> [A] brief but awful treatise on OODB ... [It] exhibits all of the usual muddles we find in OO literature, arising from the excess of terminology, conflation of

important distinct concepts, and distinction of concepts that aren't really distinct. For example, an object, we're told, is something that has instance variables and methods. An example of an object of class INTEGER is the *self-identifying* (?) object, 3. I don't know what 3's instance variables are. For another example, we're told that every object is an instance of some class. We aren't told about any instances (of classes) that aren't objects. So it isn't clear why we need both terms, nor is it clear what considerations lead one to choose between these terms, nor is it clear why sometimes both are used simultaneously, in *object instance*. And then there are *messages*. Apparently a message is a method invocation that is sent from one object (the sender) to another (the receiver). Not only does the sender not appear to have any effect on anything, but also there are frequent subsequent references to messages being sent, not by objects, but by *methods*. I could go on.

Perhaps we have to content ourselves with this thought: "Objects in the real world have only one thing in common—they're all different" (anon.). A logical difference with a vengeance!

Let's get back to the philosophers for a moment. The following is taken from *Beyond the Wall* by Edward Abbey (Henry Holt, 1991):

> What did the wall-eyed Jean-Paul Sartre say to Albert Camus when they ran into each other in the doorway of the Café Flore? Sartre said, *Pourquoi ne regards-tu pas où tu vas, Albert?* And what did Albert Camus say? *Pourquoi ne vas-tu pas vers ce que tu regards, J.-P?*

(So what's the logical difference here?)

Another nice quote on logic, to remind us that it isn't a closed subject:

> [In] Boole's time, it was common for writers on logic to equate the entire subject with what Aristotle had done so many centuries earlier. As Boole put it, this was to maintain that "the science of Logic enjoys an immunity from those conditions of imperfection and of progress to which all other sciences are subject." (From Martin Davis, *Engines of Logic: Mathematics and the Origins of the Computer*, W. W. Norton and Company, 2000.)

Next, I have a quote—or paraphrase, at any rate—from Ted Codd. This piece first appeared in 1974 in Installment No. 4 of an occasional series by Codd entitled "Understanding Relations" in the ACM SIGMOD bulletin *FDT* (subsequently renamed *SIGMOD Record*), *Vol. 6*, No. 4. It has to do with logical difference (or logical sameness, rather). I've published versions of it in a variety of different writings of my own since that time, so it's far from new, but I still think it's worth repeating here:

> Regarding the general question of whether any two concepts *A* and *B* are "the same" and can thus be equated, there's a simple general principle that can usefully be applied: Simply ask yourself "Is every example of *A* an example of *B*?" and, conversely, "Is every example of *B* an example of *A*?" Only if the answer is *yes* to both of these questions is it true that *A* and *B* are identical.

Back to the matter of clarity. I think we all know some speakers and writers who *deliberately* try not to be clear (they usually succeed, too), because they know the paucity of their thinking would be revealed if they made themselves too easily understood. Here's Plato on this subject:

> [They] are always in motion; but as for dwelling upon an argument or a question, and quietly asking and answering in turn, they can no more do so than they can fly ... If you ask any of them a question, he will produce, as from a quiver, sayings brief and dark, and shoot them at you; and if you enquire the reason of what he has said, you will be hit with some other new-fangled word, and you will make no way with any of them. Their great care is, not to allow of any settled principle either in their arguments or in their minds ... for they are at war with the stationary, and do what they can to drive it out everywhere. (Quoted by Richard Mitchell in his essay "Sayings Brief and Dark" in the book *The Leaning Tower of Babel* already referred to earlier.)

Now a few miscellaneous quotes. I'll leave it to you (mostly) to figure out what the relevance, if any, of the concepts of logical difference and logical sameness might be in each case.

■ In language there are only differences (Ferdinand de Saussure).

■ Information is any difference that makes a difference (Gregory Bateson).

■ He is no better, he is much the same (Alfred Austin).

■ *N-ary association*: An association among three or more classes (another definition from *The Unified Modeling Language User Guide*, by Grady Booch, James Rumbaugh, and Ivar Jacobson, Addison-Wesley, 1999).

■ In no engineering discipline does the successful pursuit of academic ideals pay more material dividends than in software engineering (C. A. R. Hoare; I'm not sure I have the wording here exactly right, but the sense is right).

■ All large companies know today that speed and being early to market are often more important than being right (Lou Gerstner, IBM chairman, quoted in *Informationweek*, February 9th, 1998). Well, I certainly agree there's a logical difference between being early to market and being right. Some might say there are a few other logical differences involved here, too.

I'll close with a few quotes taken off the Internet. To my mind, these quotes demonstrate both an extreme lack of clarity of expression and a desperate confusion over concepts (the latter, of course, equating—in most cases if not all—to a lack of appreciation of certain logical differences). Note the frightening implications of some of the things said! ("I am supposed to teach a class in this starting next week" ... ?!?). I give the quotes absolutely verbatim.

■ I need to make a search option into my website. It needs to display products and the user can use any words. Right now I am using access database with all my products in one table. I need help in connecting my database to the internet. I know nothing about database, just creating queries and tables that's it. I would appreciate if you would e-mail me back.

■ I have been trying to find the correct way of normalizing tables in Access. From what I understand, it goes from the 1st normal form to 2nd, then 3rd. Usually, that's as far as it goes, but sometimes to the 5th and 6th. Then, there's also the Cobb 3rd. This all makes sense to me. I am supposed to teach a class in this starting next week, and I just got the textbook. It says something entirely different. It says 2nd normal form is only for tables with a multiple-field primary key, 3rd normal form is only for tables with a single-field key. 4th normal form can go from 1st to 4th, where there are no independent one-to-many relationships between primary key and non-key fields. Can someone clear this up for me please?

The third example consists of an exchange involving four individuals:

A: How is data independence implemented?

B: What do you mean by data independence?

A: Data independence is the independence between levels in a DBMS, when you can modify a level without interference in another or in your programs.

C: Can you be more specific? I have not heard of this concept in relation to how you have described it. It sounds more like an application design concept rather than an SQL principle.

D: C's right it is a design approach. There is both physical and logical data independence, but there is no way to add data independence to a SQL statement.

Finally—talking about confusion—how about this one for an example of being "unclear on the concept"?

Ultimately, respect for a free press comes with democratic development and economic growth, in part because only a robust private sector can provide enough advertising to give the media independence (*New York Times editorial*, September 5th, 2000).

Chapter 5

Types, Values, and Variables

Part 1

To be is to be a value of a variable
(or to be some values of some variables)

—George Boolos

This chapter examines and describes the fundamental concepts
identified in the title, along with a variety of related concepts, and
clarifies the logical differences between and among them.
    Publishing history: This is a revised version of a paper that
first appeared under the title "On the Logical Differences Between
Types, Values, and Variables" in my book Date on Database:
Writings 2000-2006 (Apress, 2006). I've divided this revised version
into two parts in order, I hope, to make it a little more digestible.
This version (both parts) copyright © 2022 C. J. Date.

I'll begin with a few remarks on *The Third Manifesto* (the *Manifesto* for short). The *Manifesto* is described in detail in the book *Databases, Types, and the Relational Model: The Third Manifesto* (3rd edition, Addison-Wesley, 2007), by Hugh Darwen and myself—the *Manifesto* book for short. [1] In essence, the *Manifesto* is a detailed, formal, and rigorous proposal for the future direction of databases and DBMSs; it can be seen as an abstract blueprint for the design of a

---

[1] The most up to date information regarding the *Manifesto* in general can always be found on the website *www.thethirdmanifesto.com*.

DBMS and the language interface to such a DBMS. It's based on the four classical core concepts *type*, *value*, *variable*, and *operator*. In these two chapters, I propose to examine the various logical differences that exist between and among these concepts. *Note:* The main emphasis of the discussion is on the first three concepts in particular (i.e., types, values, and variables); there's a great deal of confusion in the database community over these matters, as I'll show. I don't think there's quite so much confusion over operators, but even there there's some—again, as I'll show.

Incidentally, I said the *Manifesto* could be seen as "an abstract blueprint for the design of a DBMS and the language interface to such a DBMS." Let me now point out that exactly the same could be said of the relational model as originally defined by Codd. Indeed, the *Manifesto* is 100 percent in the spirit of Codd's work; it continues along the path he originally laid down and is thus (of course deliberately) very definitely evolutionary, not revolutionary, in nature.

With regard to those "four classical core concepts," here's a simple motivating example:

- We might have a *type* called INTEGER.

- The integer 3 will then be a *value* of that type.

- N might be a *variable* of that type, whose value at any given time is some integer value (i.e., some value of type INTEGER).

- PLUS ("+") might be an *operator* that takes two integer values (i.e., two values of type INTEGER) and returns another.

If you ever find yourself getting confused over any of the matters being discussed in what follows, I suggest you refer back to this simple example for guidance. Note in particular that, as the example clearly shows, types are in a sense the most fundamental concept of all—values are typed; variables are typed; and operators apply to typed arguments and, if they return a value, are themselves typed as well (the type in question being the type of that returned value). In other words, the value, variable, and operator concepts all rely in turn on the more fundamental notion of *type*.

Let me now draw your attention to the *Manifesto* book's subtitle: *a detailed study of the impact of type theory on the relational model of data, including a comprehensive model of type inheritance*. Indeed, the *Manifesto* is very heavily concerned with type theory. Part of the reason for this state of affairs is that type theory and the relational model are more or less independent of one another. To be more specific, the relational model does not prescribe support for any particular types (with one exception, type BOOLEAN); it merely says that attributes of relations must be typed, thus implying that *some* (unspecified) types need to be supported—but that's *all* it says.[2]

A couple of points of clarification:

- First, please note that I use the term "operator" to include *all* operators, not just ones like PLUS that happen to be expressed in a certain special syntactic style. In particular, I use it to include operators that are invoked using some functional notation, as in the case of, e.g., SQRT (N). What's more, the operator PLUS is a little special in other ways as well: It takes exactly two operands, those operands are of the same type, and the result is of the same type as well. In general, of course, (a) an operator can take any number of operands; (b) those operands don't all have to be of the same type; and (c) the result if any can be of a different type again.

- Second, the term "type" is short for "data type," of course. Moreover, types—as you're probably aware—are also known (especially in relational contexts) as *domains*; personally, however, I greatly prefer the term *types*, and I'll use that term in what follows (except once in the next chapter, when I quote from another writer). Just as an aside, though, I note that the very fact that the term *domain* was used instead of *type* in the first place—i.e., in the original relational model—has itself been the source of a considerable amount of confusion over the years, in SQL contexts (but not only SQL contexts) especially. But I don't want to go into detail on that particular issue just now.

TYPES ARE FUNDAMENTAL

I've already said that types are fundamental. So what *is* a type? Basically, it's just *a set of values*. Examples might include type INTEGER (the set of all

---

[2] Well, maybe not quite all. Given that there do have to be some underlying types (BOOLEAN, at least, and probably several others such as INTEGER and CHAR), it follows that certain tuple and relation types are implicitly defined as well. I'll have a little more to say about such matters later in this chapter.

integers); type CHAR (the set of all character strings);[3] type PNO (the set of all part numbers); and so on. Thus, when we say that some relation has an attribute of type INTEGER, for example, what we mean is that the values the attribute in question is permitted to take are integers, and nothing but integers.

Paragraphs 1-6 below—which are meant to be fairly precise and might not be fully understandable on a first reading—spell out the crucial importance of the type concept in more detail:

1. *Values:* Every value v is of exactly one type T.[4]

2. *Variables:* Every variable V is explicitly declared to be of some type T, meaning that every possible value v that can legitimately be assigned to V must be a value of type T.

3. *Operators:* Every operator is either a read-only operator or an update operator. To simplify slightly, update operators update at least one of their arguments when they're invoked, but read-only operators don't; conversely, read-only operators return a result when they're invoked, but update operators don't. If operator Op is read-only, then it's explicitly declared to be of some type T, meaning that every possible result that can be returned by an invocation of Op is a value of type T.

4. *Parameters:* Every parameter P of every operator Op is explicitly declared to be of some type T. If Op is read-only, or if it's an update operator but it doesn't update the argument that's substituted for P, then every possible argument that can legitimately be substituted for P is a value of type T; otherwise, every possible argument that can legitimately be substituted for P is a variable of type T.

5. *Expressions:* Every expression X is at least implicitly declared to be of type T, where T is the type of the outermost operator in X.

---

[3] Not to be confused with type CHAR in SQL, which is the set of all character strings of length one.

[4] Unless type inheritance is supported—but even if it is, every value still has exactly one *most specific* type, which for the purposes of these two chapters can be taken as "the" type of the value in question. For simplicity, I'll ignore type inheritance from this point forward, except to note that several of the concepts I'll be discussing do need some slight extension to their definitions if inheritance is supported.

6. *Attributes:* Every attribute *A* of every tuple type *TT* and every attribute *A* of every relation type *RT* is explicitly declared to be of some type *T*, meaning that every value of *A* in a tuple of type *TT* or a relation of type *RT* is a value of type *T*.

Note: The remarks in paragraphs 3-5 above concerning operators and parameters need some slight refinement if the operator in question is *polymorphic*. For example, if the operator "+" can be invoked either on integers (returning another integer) or on rational numbers (returning another rational number), then we say that operator "+" is polymorphic. However, such talk is misleading. What's really going on in this example is this: There are actually two distinct addition operators, one for integers and one for rationals, but they both have the same name (viz., "+"); in fact, that name is *overloaded*. For simplicity I'll ignore the possibility of such overloading for the remainder of this discussion.

Now let me illustrate the definitions just given in paragraphs 1-6 in terms of the simple INTEGER example from the introduction to this chapter:

1. First of all, integer *values* (or just integers for short) are self-explanatory. Note carefully, however, that if some given value is of type INTEGER, then *it isn't of any other type*. For example, the value denoted by the numeral 3 is of type INTEGER, and type INTEGER *only*.[5] To say it again, every value is of exactly one type; equivalently, (a) no value is of two or more types, (b) no value is typeless, and (c) types are *disjoint*.

2. Here's a possible definition for an integer variable called N:

   ```
   VAR N INTEGER ;
   ```

   N here is explicitly declared to be of type INTEGER; thus its value at any given time is some integer value.
   Note: Barring explicit statements to the contrary, all coding examples in this chapter and the next are based on a language called **Tutorial D** (note the boldface!), which is the language we use for examples in the *Manifesto* book.

---

[5] In particular, it mustn't be confused with the value 3.0, which is a value of type RATIONAL. Of course, it's possible to convert that RATIONAL value to a value of INTEGER (and vice versa), but such "conversions" are really just *mappings* between values of the one type and values of the other, and the existence of such a mapping doesn't alter the fact that there are two distinct values involved.

3. Here's a possible definition for an operator called DOUBLE_R that takes an integer and doubles it:

```
OPERATOR DOUBLE_R ( I INTEGER ) RETURNS INTEGER ;
    RETURN ( 2 × I ) ;
END OPERATOR ;
```

DOUBLE_R is a *read-only* operator (it doesn't update anything), and it's explicitly declared to be of type INTEGER (see the RETURNS clause), meaning the value it returns when it's invoked is an integer. The sole parameter I is also explicitly declared to be of type INTEGER, meaning the argument that corresponds to that parameter when the operator is invoked must be an integer value.

4. Alternatively, we could make the "doubling" operator an *update* operator instead ("DOUBLE_U"):

```
OPERATOR DOUBLE_U ( I INTEGER ) UPDATES { I } ;
    I := 2 × I ;
END OPERATOR ;
```

Operator DOUBLE_U has no declared type and returns no value when it's invoked (there's no RETURN statement, and the RETURNS clause has been replaced by an UPDATES clause, showing that arguments corresponding to the parameter I are *subject to update*). As a consequence, the argument that corresponds to the parameter I when the operator is invoked must be an integer variable specifically. The assignment statement causes that variable to be updated appropriately.

Note: It follows that "DOUBLE_U (*V*)"—where *V* is an integer variable—(a) doesn't return or "have" a value, and therefore (b) doesn't have a type, and more generally (c) isn't regarded as an expression. Hence the operator must be invoked by means of some kind of explicit CALL statement, as in this example:

```
CALL DOUBLE_U ( V ) ;
```

5. In contrast to the foregoing, "DOUBLE_R (*v*)," where *v* is an integer value, (a) does have a value (an integer), (b) therefore does have a type

(INTEGER), and (c) is regarded as an expression—in fact, it can appear wherever an integer literal is allowed. Here's an example:

```
( 5 * DOUBLE_R ( J ) ) + DOUBLE_R ( K - 4 )
```

This expression has a type, too: namely, the type of the outermost operator involved, which happens to be integer addition ("+") in this example.

Note: To avoid possible confusion, I should explain that simple literals and simple variable names are both legal expressions. The "outermost operator" involved in, e.g., the expression 3 is a *literal* (or *literal reference*), and it's of the obvious type. Likewise, the "outermost operator" involved in, e.g., the expression N is a *variable reference*, and it too is of the obvious type.

6. Finally, consider the following *relation* type:

```
RELATION { PNO PNO , PNAME NAME , COLOR COLOR ,
                  WEIGHT WEIGHT , CITY CHAR }
```

This relation type involves five attributes PNO, PNAME, COLOR, WEIGHT, and CITY, of types PNO, NAME, COLOR, WEIGHT, and CHAR, respectively. (Don't worry if this example doesn't make too much sense to you yet. I'll have more to say about relation types in the next chapter, in the section "Relation Values and Variables.")

MORE ON TYPES

There's still quite a lot more groundwork I need to lay regarding types as such before I can get to the real substance of the chapter, and that's the purpose of the present section.

First of all, types can be *system defined* (in other words built in) or *user defined*. In this connection, by the way, I'd like to stress the fact that the relational model *never* said all types had to be system defined!—it simply said there had to *be* some types, so we could define relations over them. It's true that, in principle, a DBMS could provide a totally faithful implementation of the relational model while supporting system defined types only; however, such a DBMS would be of limited usefulness, since implementers could never foresee all of the types that users might ever want to use. Thus, the idea that a means should be available for users to define their own types was always present in the relational model, at least implicitly, right at the very outset. That's why I categorically reject claims to the effect that user defined types represent an "extension" to the relational model. In fact, type theory and the relational model are essentially *orthogonal*, or independent of one another.

Next, *any type whatsoever*, regardless of whether it's system or user defined, can be used as the basis for defining variables, parameters, attributes, and so on. *Note:* You might think the foregoing is pretty obvious, and indeed so it is—but SQL in particular manages to violate it in numerous ways. Indeed, SQL's type support suffers from a serious lack of orthogonality, but I don't want to get into a detailed discussion of that issue here.[6]

Third, any given type *T* has an associated set of *operators* that can legitimately be applied to values and variables of type *T*; in other words, values and variables of type *T* can be operated upon solely by means of the operators defined for type *T* (where by "defined for type *T*" I mean, very precisely, that the operator in question has a parameter of type *T*—no more and no less). For example, assume for definiteness that type INTEGER is system defined. Then:

- The system will provide operators "=", "<", and so on, for comparing integers.

- It will also provide operators "+", "×", and so on, for performing arithmetic on integers.

- It will *not* provide operators "| |" (concatenate), SUBSTR (substring), and so on, for performing string operations on integers; in other words, string operations on integers won't be supported.

- However, users can provide further operators of their own for operating on integers in whatever ways they want.

By contrast, if type PNO (part numbers) is user defined, then there obviously won't be any system defined operators for operating on part numbers.

---

[6] A detailed discussion of types in SQL can be found in Chapter 22 of my book *Type Inheritance and Relational Theory: Subtypes, Supertypes, and Substitutability* (O'Reilly, 2016). *Note:* Despite the title, that book does contain an extended discussion (over 30 pages) of types in SQL without, as well as with, inheritance as such.

But there *will* be user defined operators; in particular, the user in question—probably the type definer—will certainly define operators for comparing part numbers (for equality at the very least). But he or she probably won't define operators for performing arithmetic on them (why would we ever want to add or multiply two part numbers?), and arithmetic on part numbers will thus not be supported.

Next, types can be *scalar* or *nonscalar*:

■ A *nonscalar* type has user visible components. In particular, relation types are nonscalar, because such types do have user visible components: namely, their attributes.[7]

■ A *scalar* type has no user visible components. INTEGER and BOOLEAN are examples of scalar types.

Note carefully, however, that even though scalar types have no user visible components, they can and often do have user visible *possible representations* ("possreps" for short), and those possreps *can* have user visible components, as we'll see in a moment. Don't be confused, however: The components in question are *not* components of the type, they're components of the possrep. For example, suppose we have a user defined scalar type called QTY ("quantity"). Suppose too that a possrep is declared for this type that says, in effect, that quantities can "possibly be represented" by nonnegative integers. Then that possrep certainly does have user visible components—in fact, it has exactly one such, of type INTEGER—but quantities per se don't.

Here's a slightly more complicated example to illustrate the same point:

```
TYPE POINT /* geometric points in two-dimensional space */
     POSSREP CARTESIAN { X RATIONAL , Y RATIONAL }
     POSSREP POLAR { RHO RATIONAL , THETA RATIONAL } ;
```

This definition for type POINT includes declarations of two distinct possreps, CARTESIAN and POLAR, reflecting the fact that points in two-dimensional space can indeed "possibly be represented" by either cartesian or polar coordinates. Each of those possreps in turn has two components, both of type RATIONAL. But type POINT as such is still scalar—it still has no user visible components.

_____

[7] Can you think of any exceptions here? If so, what are the implications?

Note: Please understand that the *physical* representation of values of type POINT might be cartesian coordinates, or polar coordinates, or something else entirely. In other words, possreps (which are, to repeat, user visible) are indeed only *possible* representations. Physical representations, by contrast, are an implementation matter merely—they're not part of the model, and (as far as *The Third Manifesto* is concerned, at any rate) they're not user visible.

Each possrep declaration causes automatic definition of the following more or less self-explanatory operators:

■ A *selector* operator, which allows the user to specify or "select" a value of the type in question by supplying a value for each possrep component

■ A set of *THE_* operators (one such for each possrep component), which allow the user to access the corresponding possrep components of values of the type in question

Note: Most of the literature talks in terms not of THE_ operators as such but of "GET_ and SET_" operators instead: GET_ for retrieval and SET_ for update. Hugh Darwen and I prefer our THE_ operators, for reasons explained in the *Manifesto* book.

Here by way of example are some selector and THE_ operator invocations for type POINT:

```
CARTESIAN ( 5.0 , 2.5 )
/* selects the point with x = 5.0, y = 2.5 */

CARTESIAN ( X1 , Y1 )
/* selects the point with x = X1, y = Y1, where */
/* X1 and Y1 are variables of type RATIONAL      */

POLAR ( 2.7 , 1.0 )
/* selects the point with rho = 2.7, theta = 1.0 */

THE_X ( VP )
/* denotes the x coordinate of the point value in VP, */
/* where VP is a variable of type POINT                */

THE_THETA ( VP )
/* denotes the theta coordinate of the point value in VP */

THE_Y ( pz )
/* denotes the y coordinate of the point denoted */
/* by the expression pz (which is of type POINT) */
```

As these examples suggest, selectors—more precisely, selector *invocations*—are a generalization of the more familiar concept of a literal. Briefly, all literals are selector invocations, but not all selector invocations are literals; in fact, a selector invocation is a literal if and only if all of its arguments are denoted by literals in turn. *Note:* I'll have more to say about literals in the section immediately following this one.

By convention, selectors have the same name as the corresponding possrep. Also, if type *T* has a possrep with no explicitly declared name, then that possrep is named *T* by default. Taken together, these two conventions mean that, e.g., we might legitimately define type PNO (part numbers) thus:

```
TYPE PNO POSSREP { C CHAR } ;
```

And the expression PNO ('P1') would then be a valid selector invocation for this type—in fact, it would be a valid part number literal.

Every type, then, has at least one associated selector and at least one associated set of THE_ operators.[8] In addition, there are certain other operators that *must* be defined for every type, including the following in particular:

- *Equality* ("="): Given values *v1* and *v2* of the same type, the comparison *v1* = *v2* evaluates to TRUE if *v1* and *v2* are in fact the very same value and to FALSE otherwise.

- *Assignment* (":="): Given a variable *V* and a value *v* of the same type, the assignment *V* := *v* has the effect of establishing *v* as the current value of *V*.

Points arising:

- Observe that the variable reference *V* denotes (a) the variable *V* itself in a target position (in particular, on the left side of an assignment) and (b) the current value of that variable in a source position (in particular, on the right side of an assignment).

- After the assignment *V* := *v*, the comparison *V* = *v* is required to evaluate to TRUE. *Note:* This fact—viz., that successful assignment of some value *v*

---

[8] Every scalar type, that is. Nonscalar types have selectors too, but no THE_ operators; they don't need THE_ operators as such, because they have other operators that allow the user to access the components (which are user visible, by definition) of values of the nonscalar type in question.

to some variable *V* causes the comparison *V* = *v* to evaluate to TRUE—is known as *The Assignment Principle*. While this principle might sound obvious, even trivial, in fact it's not quite as obvious as it sounds, and it has several far-reaching consequences. Unfortunately those consequences are beyond the scope of this discussion; you can find more detail in Chapter 2 ("Assignment") of my book *Stating the Obvious, and Other Database Writings* (Technics Publications, 2020).

■ Note that the operators "=" and ":=" are both polymorphic—in fact, they apply to values and variables of *every* type.

VALUES AND VARIABLES

I've now discussed types at some length (and said quite a bit about operators, too); it's time to turn to the other two core concepts, viz., values and variables. Here are some definitions:

Definition (value): A value is an "individual constant" (for example, the individual constant 3). Values have no location in time or space. However, they can be represented by certain encodings, and of course such encodings do have location in time and space (see the definition of *variable* below). Indeed, the very same value can have many distinct encodings (in general), and each of those encodings can appear at many distinct locations in time or space (again in general)—meaning, loosely, that any number of distinct variables can have the same value, at the same time or different times. Note that, by definition, values can't be updated (because if they could, then after such an update they wouldn't be the same value any longer, in general).

Definition (variable): A variable is a holder, or container, for an appearance of an encoded representation of a value ("an appearance of a value," or just "an appearance," or even—informally—just "a value," for short). Variables do have location in time and space. If variable *V* currently holds an appearance of value *v*, *v* is said to be the current value of *V* (any given variable always has exactly one value at any given time); equivalently, *V* is said to "have" *v* as its current value. Unlike values, variables can be updated—that is, their current value can be replaced by another value, probably different from the previous one. (Of course, the variable in question is still the same variable after the update.)

These definitions are based on ones given in *An Introduction to Data Types*, by J. Craig Cleaveland (Addison-Wesley, 1986). I hope you agree they're straightforward enough, even if they might seem a little wordy. Yet they have a wealth of implications, not all of which are immediately obvious (at least, not if the existing literature is anything to go by). Here are a few implications that I think are worth mentioning right away:

■ It follows from the definition that a value might equally well be called a *constant*, and I do indeed usually take the terms to be equivalent. However, it's sometimes useful to have a term for a declared "variable" whose value by design never changes, and the term *constant* is sometimes used for this purpose. ("Named constant" might be a better term.)

■ The terms *constant* and *value* are thus (usually) interchangeable. By contrast, the terms *constant* and *literal* aren't! A literal isn't a value, it's a *symbol* that *denotes* a value (another logical difference here, incidentally— namely, that between *notation* and *denotation*). The value in question is determined by the symbol in question (and since every value is of exactly one type, the type of that value is also determined by the symbol in question, a fortiori). Loosely, we can say that a literal is *self-defining*. Here are some **Tutorial D** examples:

```
FALSE                       /* a literal of type BOOLEAN  */
4                           /* a literal of type INTEGER  */
2.7                         /* a literal of type RATIONAL */
'ABC'                       /* a literal of type CHAR     */
PNO ('P1')                  /* a literal of type PNO      */
CARTESIAN ( 5.0 , 2.5 )     /* a literal of type POINT    */
```

■ Following on from the previous point, it's worth noting that distinct literals can denote the same value. For example, the following are three SQL literals of type TIME WITH TIME ZONE that all denote the same absolute value (viz., 6:00 pm London time, which is, let's agree for the sake of the example, the same as 10:00 am San Francisco time and 8:00 pm Helsinki time):

```
TIME '18:00:00-00:00'              /* London         */
TIME '10:00:00-08:00'              /* San Francisco  */
TIME '20:00:00+02:00'              /* Helsinki       */
```

This example thus serves to emphasize the point that (as already noted) there's a logical difference between a literal and a value.

I now proceed to explore a variety of important aspects and implications of the value vs. variable distinction.

VALUES AND VARIABLES CAN BE ARBITRARILY COMPLEX

Note carefully that there's nothing in the definitions of the previous section to say that values have to be limited to simple things like the integer 3. On the contrary, values can be as complex as we like. But what does "complex" mean here? There are two possibilities, both of which are valid:

- A value can be scalar—meaning it's a value of some scalar type and therefore has no user visible components—and yet have a "possrep" of arbitrary complexity, whose components *are* (by definition) visible to the user. For example, values of type POINT (in other words, individual point values, or just points for short) are scalar values, and yet we can talk, loosely, of such points as having cartesian and/or polar coordinates. Strictly speaking, however, those coordinates aren't components of the pertinent point value as such; rather, they're components of the corresponding possible representation, or representations plural, of that point value.

- A value can be nonscalar, meaning it's a value of some nonscalar type and has a set of user visible components. For our purposes, the obvious example here is a *relation* value, where the user visible components are the pertinent attributes. Another is a *tuple* value, where again the user visible components are the pertinent attributes.

To say it again, then, values can be arbitrarily complex, and so, e.g., arrays, stacks, lists, tuples, relations, part numbers, points, polygons, X rays, fingerprints, XML documents (and on and on) are all legitimate examples of values.

Remarks analogous to the foregoing apply to variables too, of course; thus, variables too can be arbitrarily complex (meaning, more precisely, that they can hold or contain values that are arbitrarily complex). In particular, variables, like values, are considered to be scalar or nonscalar according as their type is scalar or nonscalar. Similarly for read-only operators—such an operator is considered to be scalar or nonscalar depending on whether its result is scalar or nonscalar.

VARIABLES ARE UPDATABLE, VALUES AREN'T

Of course, there's one obvious logical difference between values and variables: *Variables are updatable, values aren't.* To elaborate:

- Values are nonupdatable by definition, as we've already seen.

- As for variables, to say that something's a variable is *precisely* to say it's updatable—no more and no less. That's what "variable" *means:* The current value varies over time. Furthermore, the way to effect those changes in value (the *only* way) is by updating the variable in question. *Note:* For simplicity, I'm ignoring here the case of a variable that happens never to be actually updated. This simplification doesn't materially affect the discussion, of course.

By the way, I've always thought the term *variable* as used in mathematics, at least in some contexts, is a little bit of a misnomer. Certainly variables in the (mathematical) sense I have in mind don't have values that vary over time, unlike variables in the computer science sense. For example, consider the equation

```
x + 3 = 5
```

Mathematicians would call x a variable here, but it obviously has the constant value 2. Perhaps *unknown* would be a better term; solving a set of equations is the activity of determining the values the unknowns in those equations stand for. Of course, it's true that the set of equations might not have a unique solution, as in the case of, e.g., the set consisting of the single equation $x + y = 0$. In such a case, referring to the unknowns as variables is perhaps a little more reasonable. But it's still the case that those variables don't vary over time; rather, they vary over some prescribed range.

Back to values vs. variables in the computing sense. The fact that there's a logical difference between these concepts accounts in turn for another logical difference: namely, that between read-only and update operators. Read-only operators operate on *values*; in particular, they operate, harmlessly, on those values that happen to be the current values of variables. Update operators, by contrast, operate on *variables*—I'm speaking just a trifle loosely here—and they have the effect of replacing the current values of such variables by other values, probably different ones.

And talking of update operators, let me now point out that, logically speaking, there's only one such operator that's really needed: namely, the *assignment* operator. All other update operators are really just shorthand for some assignment. (I'll explore this issue in detail in connection with the relational update operators in particular in the section "Relation Values and Variables" in the next chapter.) Since we already know that to say something's a variable is to say it's updatable, no more and no less, it follows that to say something's a variable is to say it's assignable to, no more and no less. In other words, to say that *V* is a variable is to say, precisely, that the following assignment is legal—

```
V := v
```

—where *v* is a value of the same type as *V*. Of course, *v* can be denoted by an arbitrary expression of the appropriate type; thus, the assignment operation takes the general syntactic form—

```
target := source
```

—where *target* is a variable reference (syntactically, just a variable name), denoting some variable *V* of some type *T*, and *source* is an arbitrary expression of that same type *T* denoting a value *v* also of that same type *T*.

Note: Actually the syntactic form just shown for the assignment operator is *not* the most general. In *The Third Manifesto*, Darwen and I require support for a more general form that we call "multiple" assignment, which allows several variables to be updated at the same time (I'm speaking pretty loosely here). In these two chapters, however, I'll limit my attention to assignments of the simple (or "single") form already discussed. Multiple assignment is discussed in Chapters 10 and 11.

PSEUDOVARIABLES

Consider the following example:

```
VAR VC CHAR ;

VC := 'Middle' ;
SUBSTR ( VC , 2 , 1 ) := 'u' ;
```

After the first assignment here, the variable VC has the value 'Middle'. After the second, it has the value 'Muddle'—the effect of that second assignment is to "zap" the second character position within that variable, replacing the *i* by a *u*. Note in particular that the left side of that second assignment doesn't consist of a simple variable reference; so is it really true that assignments always take the specific syntactic form shown in the previous section?

Well, yes, fundamentally it *is* true. The second assignment in the example is really just shorthand for the following longer one:

```
VC := SUBSTR ( VC , 1 , 1 ) || 'u' || SUBSTR ( VC , 3 , 4 );
```

Now the left side is a simple variable reference, as required. As for the right side, the expression on that side denotes the character string obtained by concatenating, in left to right order, the first character of the current value of VC, the character 'u', and the last four characters of the current value of VC. It follows that the overall assignment has exactly the effect previously explained.

Here's another example:

```
VAR VV VECTOR INTEGER ;

VV := VECTOR ( 1 , 2 , 3 , 4 , 5 ) ;
VV[4] := 0 ;
```

After the first assignment, the variable VV has as its value a vector (in other words, a one-dimensional array) of five integers, with the *i*th element equal to *i* ($i = 1, 2, 3, 4, 5$). After the second assignment, the fourth element is 0 instead of 4, while the others remain unchanged. Again, the left side of the second assignment isn't just a simple variable reference; again, however, the assignment is really just shorthand for another one in which the left side *is* such a variable reference. Here's the expanded version:

```
VV := VECTOR ( VV[1] , VV[2] , VV[3] , 0 , VV[5] ) ;
```

Note: The expression on the right side here is a *vector selector invocation*. (The same remark applies to the original assignment to VV in this example also, of course.)

Another example:

```
VAR VE TUPLE { ENO ENO , DNO DNO , SALARY MONEY } ;

VE := TUPLE { ENO ENO ('E1') , DNO DNO ('D1') ,
                               SALARY MONEY(50000) } ;
VE.DNO := DNO ('D2') ;
```

VE here is a tuple variable (i.e., a variable whose permitted values are tuples); I've used dot qualification to express the operator that gives access to tuple components. The second assignment here is shorthand for:

```
VE := TUPLE { ENO VE.ENO , DNO DNO ('D2'),
                           SALARY VE.SALARY } ;
```

And one last example:

```
VAR VP POINT ;

VP := CARTESIAN ( 5.0 , 2.5 ) ;
THE_X ( VP ) := 6.0 ;
```

Note the appearance in the second assignment here of a THE_ operator invocation on the left side. That assignment is shorthand for:

```
VP := CARTESIAN ( 6.0 , THE_Y ( VP ) ) ;
```

It's time to introduce some more terminology. Here again are the expressions appearing on the left sides of the four "shorthand" assignments in the foregoing examples:

```
SUBSTR ( VC , 2 , 1 )
VV[4]
VE.DNO
THE_X ( VP )
```

Each of these expressions is being used as a *pseudovariable reference* and (in the context at hand, in which the expression in question appears in a target position) denotes a *pseudovariable*. A pseudovariable isn't a variable, but you can think of it, loosely, as something rather like a variable, inasmuch as it's assignable to (i.e., updatable). And a pseudovariable reference isn't an expression—at least, not as the term *expression* is usually understood—precisely because it appears on the left side of an assignment, [9] where expressions in general aren't allowed. So pseudovariables are a kind of fiction, in a way. But they're a very convenient fiction: They provide a mechanism for simplifying the formulation of certain assignments, and they make it easier to talk about the effects of such assignments, because they allow us to think in terms of "zapping" certain components of the target variable (even in situations where, as in the case of variable VP of type POINT, the target variable doesn't really *have* any user visible components as such).

Note: The term *pseudovariable* is taken from PL/I, but the PL/I concept differs from what I've been describing in at least three respects:

■ First, the PL/I term is used only in connection with built-in functions like SUBSTR, not in connection with references of the form VV[4] or VE.DNO (though PL/I certainly does allow references such as these latter two to appear in a target position).

■ Second, PL/I doesn't allow pseudovariable references to be nested, but the scheme I've been describing does. For example, suppose we have a type LINESEG (line segments), defined as follows:

```
TYPE LINESEG
     POSSREP { BEGIN POINT , END POINT }
     /* begin and end points -- corresp selector */
     /* is called LINESEG by default          */ ;
```

Also, let LS be a variable of this type:

```
VAR LS LINESEG ;
```

Now consider the following assignments:

```
Z := THE_X ( THE_BEGIN ( LS ) ) ;
THE_X ( THE_BEGIN ( LS ) ) := Z ;
```

---

[9] More generally, it's used to denote an argument to some update operator, where the argument in question is subject to update and is thus supposed to be a variable.

The first of these assignments assigns the X coordinate of the begin point of the current value of LS to the RATIONAL variable Z, while the second uses the current value of that variable Z to update the X coordinate of the begin point of the variable LS—and of course it's that second statement specifically that illustrates the idea of pseudovariable nesting. Note that the ability to nest THE_ pseudovariables in this fashion means, loosely speaking, that arbitrarily complex updates are possible (just as the ability to nest regular THE_ operator invocations means that arbitrarily complex retrievals are also possible).

- Third, assignment to a pseudovariable in PL/I is sometimes not just shorthand. For example, the "completion status" of a PL/I variable E of type EVENT can be set *only* by assigning to COMPLETION(E), and COMPLETION here is considered by PL/I to be a pseudovariable.

There's one more (important!) issue I want to address in this section. Here again is the vector example:

```
VAR VV VECTOR INTEGER ;

VV := VECTOR ( 1 , 2 , 3 , 4 , 5 ) ;
VV[4] := 0 ;
```

Just to remind you, the second assignment here is shorthand for this one:

```
VV := VECTOR ( VV[1] , VV[2] , VV[3] , 0 , VV[5] ) ;
```

Recall now that the two expressions of the form VECTOR (...) in this example are vector selector invocations; they "select" or specify certain vector values, which are then assigned to the vector variable VV. Now, you might possibly have had some difficulty with the idea that the variable VV is indeed a single variable; many people would say rather that it's a kind of "collection" of several separate variables, called VV[1], VV[2], and so on. Here's a quote in this connection (it's from Chapter 11, "Array Variables," of *A Discipline of Programming*, by Edsger W. Dijkstra, Prentice Hall, 1976):[10]

---

[10] As previously noted, vectors are arrays, of course—they're just a special case—and so the term "array variables" does include vector variables in particular.

I [was] trained to regard an array [*he means an array variable specifically*] ... as a finite set of elementary, consecutively numbered variables, whose "identifiers" could be "computed."

However, Dijkstra then goes on to give two good and sound reasons (details of which I omit here for space reasons) for his subsequent rejection of this point of view. And he concludes:

The moral of the story is that we must regard the array in its entirety as a single variable, a so called "array variable," in contrast to the "scalar variables" discussed so far.

It follows that the assignment

```
VV[4]  :=  0  ;
```

really does have to be considered, not as an assignment to a hypothetical "elementary variable" called VV[4], but as an assignment—one that just happens to be expressed in a certain shorthand syntactic style—to the entire vector variable VV.

As an aside, I remark that pseudovariables aren't just convenient for the user—they make life easier for the system too, because they're easier to implement efficiently. Now, I'm no implementer, but it seems to me that the implementation would have to do quite a lot of work to recognize that the assignment

```
VV  :=  VECTOR ( VV[1] , VV[2] , VV[3] , 0 , VV[5] ) ;
```

"really" involves assigning just to VV[4]. Historically, however, I think we let ourselves be beguiled by such considerations into thinking that the individual elements of an array variable—VV[4], for example—are variables in their own right. But they're not.

Remarks analogous to the foregoing apply to variables of all types (all nonscalar types in particular). A variable of type *T* is a variable of type *T*—it's never a "collection" of variables (not of any type). In a way, in fact, the frequently used term "collection" for things like vector variables is really quite misleading. In my examples, therefore, the variables VC, VV, VE, and VP must indeed all be regarded as single variables, and the idea that we might be able to "zap" some "component" of them is only (as previously claimed) a convenient fiction, and one that isn't wholly accurate.

VARIABLES HAVE ADDRESSES, VALUES DON'T

This next logical difference is an immediate consequence of the fact that variables have locations in time and space and values don't. Fundamentally, in fact, a variable is *an abstraction of a piece of storage*, while values (or appearances of values, rather) are the things we can put in those "pieces of storage." It follows that variables have addresses, and values don't.

Let me immediately emphasize that I'm not talking about physical addresses here, of course. I'm not interested in physical addresses. What I mean is that, at least conceptually, any given variable does have a location in space, and that location in space can be identified by some kind of address. We can *point to* variables.

It follows that certain operators—certain additional operators, that is, over and above the update operators already discussed—can and must be defined, operators that (like those update operators) have to do with variables specifically. The operators in question are called *referencing* and *dereferencing*. Here are rough definitions:

> **Definition (referencing):** Given a variable V, the referencing operator applied to V returns the value that's the address of V.

> **Definition (dereferencing):** Given a value v of type address (or type pointer), the dereferencing operator applied to v returns the variable whose address is v.

As you can see, these operators assume support for a type whose values are addresses or pointers. Such types are often called *REF types*. *Note:* In practice we'd probably have not just one REF type but many (one for each individual type), so that pointers themselves would be typed in turn: pointers to variables of type INTEGER, pointers to variables of type CHAR, and so on. In other words, REF here isn't really a type as such at all, but rather a type *generator*. However, I'm afraid type generators are another topic I don't want to get into detail on here; if you're interested, you can find further details in my book *SQL and*

Relational Theory: How to Write Accurate SQL Code, 3rd edition (O'Reilly, 2015).

The specific syntax used for referencing and dereferencing will naturally depend on the specific language involved.[11] For present purposes, I'll use syntax as indicated below.

- *Referencing:* The expression REF (*V*), where *V* is a variable, returns a pointer to *V*. For example:

```
VAR VP POINT ;
VAR PADDR REF_( POINT ) ;  /* REF(POINT) = pointers to */
                           /* variables of type POINT  */

PADDR := REF ( VP ) ;              /* PADDR now contains */
                                   /* a pointer to VP    */
```

Note: REF is a rather unusual operator, in that it requires its argument *V* to be a variable specifically, even though it's read-only. Moreover, that argument must indeed be a variable as such, not a pseudovariable. (But why? Do you think this restriction is reasonable? Justify your answer!)

- *Dereferencing:* The expression DEREF (*v*), where *v* is an address or pointer, returns the variable *v* points to. For example (following on from the REF example above):

```
VAR VQ POINT ;

VQ := DEREF ( PADDR ) ;            /* assigns VP to VQ */
DEREF ( PADDR ) := VQ ;            /* assigns VQ to VP */
```

Note: DEREF is a rather unusual operator too, in at least two ways. First, although its argument can in principle be denoted by an arbitrary pointer valued expression, in practice it's almost always a variable reference specifically, as in both of the DEREF invocations in the example. Second, it returns—or denotes—a *variable*, not a value; this fact allows a DEREF invocation to appear in a target position, as in the second

---

[11] And, I might add, is often a trifle cryptic. For example, the language C uses expressions of the form "&V" and "*P" for referencing and dereferencing, respectively (where V is any variable and P is a variable of some reference type). The language Pascal uses "^V" and "P^".

assignment in the example.[12] (Of course, such an invocation can also be regarded, harmlessly, as returning the *value* of that variable, if the invocation appears in a source position—e.g., on the right side of an assignment, as in the first assignment in the example—where a value is all that's required.)

Before going any further, I'd like to offer a brief comment on terminology here. I've "gone with the flow" and used the kind of terminology that's used in most of the literature on this topic, but I'm bound to say I don't think much of it for at least three reasons:

1. The "referencing" terminology is very reminiscent of foreign keys in the relational model, but foreign keys and "references" in the present sense aren't the same thing at all (another logical difference here, in fact).

2. Languages already have a concept (a very different concept!) of *variable reference*; in fact, I've used the term myself several times in this very chapter. To be specific, the use of the variable name *V* to denote either that variable per se or its current value—using it on the left and right sides of an assignment, respectively, in particular—is a variable reference in the more conventional (and more usual) sense.

3. As we've seen, the expression DEREF (*v*) must generally be understood as returning a *variable*. As a consequence, that *de*referencing expression might very reasonably be interpreted as serving as a *reference* to the variable in question ... After all, in the DEREF examples above, the expression DEREF (PADDR) does effectively denote—and thereby serve, in effect, as a reference to—the variable VP both times it appears. At the very least, therefore, I'd have to say the terminology is confusing, and likely to be misconstrued.

---

[12] Two points: First, this fact allows a DEREF invocation, more generally, to be used to denote an argument to some update operator, where the argument in question is supposed to be a variable specifically. Second, such an invocation (either on the left side of an explicit assignment, or more generally denoting an argument to be updated by an update operator) does *not* constitute a pseudovariable reference in our sense of that term, even though it does look rather like one, because the assignment in question, either explicit or implicit, isn't shorthand for anything. So we need to extend our definition of the assignment operator accordingly. The details are left as an exercise. (If you try that exercise, however, you might begin to understand, if you didn't already, why the relational model refuses to have anything to do with pointers at all.)

To return to the main thread of the discussion: We've seen that variables typically imply the existence of at least one REF type, or in other words support for *values of type pointer*. In principle, therefore, we're faced with the possibility that such values—like values of any other kind—might be stored in the database. In practice, however, such a possibility is very strongly contraindicated (in fact, of course, the relational model expressly prohibits it).

Note: Since relation variables in particular (see the next section) are indeed variables, they have addresses, at least in principle. However, *the relational model provides no corresponding REF and DEREF operators*. Thus, there's no way in the relational model of obtaining a pointer to a relation variable, and hence no way in the relational model of storing such a pointer in the database a fortiori. As far as the relational model is concerned, in fact, relation variables are sufficiently identified by their *name*, and the concept of a relation variable having an address is never appealed to (and is effectively rendered harmless in consequence).

To be continued.

Chapter 6

Types, Values, and Variables

Part 2

For a description of the background to this chapter, please see the preamble to Chapter 5. This version copyright © 2022 C. J. Date.

RELATION VALUES AND VARIABLES

In the relational world, relations themselves provide the most immediately obvious example of the importance of the value vs. variable distinction. *Note:* I've included a discussion similar to the one that follows in several other writings. Nonetheless, I believe it bears repeating here. The concepts are important.

Let's consider the usual suppliers-and-parts database; to fix our ideas, let's focus on parts specifically. Fig. 1 shows the usual sample value:

P

PNO	PNAME	COLOR	WEIGHT	CITY
P1	Nut	Red	12.0	London
P2	Bolt	Green	17.0	Paris
P3	Screw	Blue	17.0	Oslo
P4	Screw	Red	14.0	London
P5	Cam	Blue	12.0	Paris
P6	Cog	Red	19.0	London

Fig. 1: Relation variable P, initial value

Suppose we now execute the following DELETE statement:

```
DELETE P WHERE CITY = 'London' ;
```

The result, given the sample value shown in Fig. 1, is as shown in Fig. 2:

P

PNO	PNAME	COLOR	WEIGHT	CITY
P2	Bolt	Green	17.0	Paris
P3	Screw	Blue	17.0	Oslo
P5	Cam	Blue	12.0	Paris

Fig. 2: Relation variable P after deleting parts in London

Now, I hope it's obvious from this example that the symbol P as used here really denotes a *variable*: a relation variable, to be precise, or in other words a variable whose values are relation values (different values at different times). And what that DELETE operation does is this: It updates that relation variable, replacing the current value of that variable—which is a relation value, by definition—by another such value. In fact, of course, the DELETE in question is basically just shorthand for a certain assignment operation that might look like this:

```
P  :=  P WHERE NOT ( CITY = 'London' ) ;
```

As in all assignments, what's happening here, conceptually, is that (a) the source expression on the right side is evaluated, and then (b) the result of that evaluation is assigned to the target variable on the left side.

In analogous fashion, relational INSERT and UPDATE operations are also basically just shorthand for certain relational assignments. For example, the INSERT statement

```
INSERT P RELATION { TUPLE { PNO     PNO ('P7') ,
                            PNAME   NAME ('Bolt') ,
                            COLOR   COLOR ('Red') ,
                            WEIGHT  WEIGHT ( 15.0 ) ,
                            CITY    'London' } } ;
```

(which "inserts a tuple" into the relation variable called P) is really shorthand for an assignment that might look like this:[1]

```
P  :=  P UNION RELATION { TUPLE { PNO    PNO ('P7') ,
                                  PNAME  NAME ('Bolt') ,
                                  COLOR  COLOR ('Red') ,
                                  WEIGHT WEIGHT ( 15.0 ) ,
                                  CITY   'London' } } ;
```

By the way, the expression RELATION {...} appearing in both the original INSERT statement and the assignment statement equivalent is an example of a *relation selector invocation* (actually a relation literal). Likewise, the expression TUPLE {...} in both cases is an example of a *tuple* selector invocation (actually a tuple literal).

In similar fashion, the UPDATE statement

```
UPDATE P WHERE CITY = 'Paris' : { CITY := 'Rome' } ;
```

(which "updates the city" for Paris parts) is shorthand for:

```
P := ( P WHERE CITY ≠ 'Paris' )
       UNION
     ( EXTEND ( P WHERE CITY = 'Paris' ) :
                     { CITY := 'Rome' } ) ;
```

Now, historically we've tended to use the term *relation* when what we really meant was *relation variable* (as well as when we meant a relation per se— that is, a relation *value*). But the practice is unfortunate, and has certainly led to some confusion (I'll give some examples later). In *The Third Manifesto*, therefore, Darwen and I introduced the term **relvar**—short for relation variable— and we took care to phrase our remarks in terms of relvars, not relations, when it really was relvars that we meant. We also took the unqualified term *relation* to mean a relation value specifically (just as we take, e.g., the unqualified term *integer* to mean an integer value specifically), and we took care to phrase our remarks in terms of relations, not relvars, when it really was relations that we meant. And I'll do the same in the present chapter from this point forward.

---

[1] Note that the "longhand" version (i.e., the explicit assignment) will succeed if the specified tuple for part P7 already exists. In practice, we'd surely want to refine the semantics of INSERT (and we can) in such a way as to raise an exception in such a situation. For simplicity, however, I'll ignore this issue here. Of course, analogous remarks apply to DELETE and UPDATE also.

A remark on SQL: Of course, SQL doesn't make the foregoing distinctions at all (not explicitly, at any rate); instead, it uses the same term *table* to refer to both relation values and relation variables.[2] In particular, the keyword TABLE in CREATE TABLE refers to a variable specifically (more precisely, it refers to what we might call a *base tablevar*). In **Tutorial D**, by contrast, we deliberately use the same keyword VAR—short for variable, of course—in the definition of variables of all kinds. For example, the **Tutorial D** counterpart to the SQL statement

```
CREATE TABLE P ... ;        /* P is a "base table variable" */
```

is

```
VAR P RELATION ... ;        /* P is a relation variable      */
```

I'd like to elaborate for a moment on the foregoing example. Here again is the **Tutorial D** definition of relvar P, now shown complete:

```
VAR P RELATION { PNO PNO , PNAME NAME , COLOR COLOR ,
                              WEIGHT WEIGHT , CITY CHAR }
     KEY { PNO } ;
```

The expression RELATION {...} here denotes a certain relation *type*: namely, the type of the relation variable P, and also (of course) the type of every possible relation that might ever be assigned to that variable. The braces enclose a set of attribute-name / type-name pairs that go to make up that relation type; braces are used to emphasize the fact that what they contain is indeed a set, with no ordering to its elements and no duplicate elements.

Another point: Don't make the mistake of thinking a relation variable is a collection of tuple variables! A relation variable is a single variable, just as an array or vector variable is a single variable (see the section "Pseudovariables" in the previous chapter). A relation variable is a variable whose value is a relation value. A relation value in turn contains a set of tuple values (or just tuples for short; we abbreviate *tuple value* to *tuple*, just as we abbreviate *relation value* to *relation*). What a relation value *doesn't* do, and couldn't possibly do, is contain a

---

[2] Of course, it's a bit of a stretch to say the term *table* in SQL stands for either a relation or a relvar at all!—we have to overlook all kinds of SQL quirks (nulls, duplicate rows, left to right column ordering, and so on) if we're even to begin to contemplate the notion that SQL's tables have anything to do with relations as such. See Chapter 1 ("What's a Relational DBMS?") of my book *E. F. Codd and Relational Theory, Revised Edition* (Technics Publications, 2021) for further discussion.

set of tuple variables (or indeed variables of any kind—in fact, the very notion of a value of any kind containing a variable of any kind is a logical absurdity).

Of course, the foregoing paragraph mustn't be taken to mean there's no such thing as a tuple variable (*tuplevar* for short). A tuplevar is simply a variable whose values are tuples. Here's an example:

```
VAR PTV TUPLE { PNO PNO , PNAME NAME , COLOR COLOR ,
                WEIGHT WEIGHT , CITY CHAR } ;
```

Values of the tuplevar called PTV are part tuples. So (to repeat) tuplevars are certainly legal. *But such variables aren't allowed in a relational database*; the only kind of variable recognized in the relational model is the relvar, and the only kind of variable allowed in a relational database is the relvar.

In closing this section, let me point out what I'm sure you've already realized for yourself: namely, that the term *relvar* is not in common usage. But it should be! It really is important to be clear about the distinction between relation values and relation variables in particular, just as it's important to be clear about the distinction between values and variables in general.

EXAMPLES OF CONFUSION: VALUES vs. VARIABLES

Confusion over types vs. values vs. variables is rife in the object world in particular, and so I'll use the object world as the source for most (not all) of the examples I'll be discussing in this section.

First of all, I want to forget about types (for the moment) and focus on just values vs. variables. Now, you might find it hard to believe that people could get confused over the difference between notions as fundamental and as straightforward as these two. In fact, however, it seems to be all too easy to fall into traps in this area. Consider, for example, the following somewhat compressed extract from a tutorial on object databases (Stanley B. Zdonik and David Maier, "Fundamentals of Object-Oriented Databases," in Zdonik and Maier (eds.), *Readings in Object-Oriented Database Systems,* Morgan Kaufmann, 1990):

> We distinguish the declared type of a variable from ... the type of the object that is the current value of the variable ... We distinguish objects from values ... A *mutator* [is an operator such that it's] possible to observe its effect on some object.

I want to examine (or deconstruct) this quote in detail.

■ First, the phrase "the object that is the current value of the variable" clearly implies that an object is a value. (At least, it implies that some, or perhaps all, values are objects, and hence that some or perhaps all objects are values.)

■ Second, the assertion that "[we] distinguish objects from values" clearly implies that an object isn't a value. (More precisely, it implies that no objects are values and no values are objects.)

■ Third, the existence of mutators—that is, operators that have an "effect on some object," or in other words update some object[3]—clearly implies that the particular object in question is a variable; so some objects, at least, are variables.

What *are* we to make of such a muddle?

Before I go any further, there's another confusion I need to head off at the pass. Throughout this chapter so far, I've used the term *variable* in its conventional programming language sense (and of course I'll continue to do so in what follows). Be aware, however, that some object languages and systems use that term to mean, very specifically, *a variable whose value is an object ID*—that is, a variable whose value is a pointer to some object (*object ID* being the usual object term for what I called a *reference* in the section "Variables Have Addresses, Values Don't" in the previous chapter). You can get into some very frustrating conversations if you're not aware of this fact.

Back to values vs. variables. Actually, some object systems and texts do draw a distinction between *mutable* and *immutable* objects, and it seems to me that "mutable objects" are basically just variables and "immutable objects" are basically just values. Indeed, in *Database Systems: The Complete Book*, by Hector Garcia-Molina, Jeffrey D. Ullman, and Jennifer Widom (Prentice Hall, 2002), we find a statement to that exact effect:

---

[3] The object term *mutator* thus corresponds to our *update operator*. The object term for *read-only operator* is *observer*. I remark in passing that SQL uses the terms mutator and observer too, but SQL's mutators aren't really mutators in the usual object sense of the term (i.e., they aren't update operators). However, they can be used in such a way as to achieve mutator functionality. For example, the SQL statement SET P.X = Z—which, believe it or not, doesn't explicitly contain a mutator invocation—is defined to be shorthand for the statement SET P = P.X(Z), which does. See Chapter 11 for further exlanation.

A *class* consists of a type and possibly one or more functions or procedures ... that can be executed on objects of that class. The objects of a class are either values of that type (called *immutable objects*) or variables whose value is of that type (called *mutable objects*).

But if they're truly just variables and values as claimed, then why in the name of *<please fill in the gap here as you think fit>* does the object community see a need to drag in the new terminology? What on earth does it buy us, other than additional complexity and confusion?

In any case, writers on object matters often talk as if objects are always mutable, and forget about the immutable ones.

Note: I said earlier that to say that *V* is a variable is to say that *V* is assignable to, no more and no less. It might therefore be claimed that a mutable object isn't really a variable because the available "methods"[4] typically don't include one for assigning a value—sorry, an immutable object—to it (i.e., replacing the previous value in its entirety, lock, stock, and barrel). However, as we saw in the section "Pseudovariables" in the previous chapter, any method that allows us to "zap" some "component" of an object is really shorthand for one that allows us to assign a new value to the object in its entirety (and if there aren't any such methods, then the object isn't mutable in the first place!). So I stand by my position that mutable and immutable objects are really just variables and values, respectively.

Other object systems use different terminology in an attempt to get at the same value vs. variable distinction. ODMG, for example, regards all objects as mutable and uses the term *literal* for an immutable object.[5] But this latter term illustrates a confusion of a different kind; as we saw in the previous chapter, a literal (at least as that term is conventionally understood) simply isn't a value (or "immutable object")—rather, it's a *symbol* that *denotes* such a value.

---

[4] And why that term *method*, anyway? Considered purely as a regular noun, it doesn't even mean what the object advocates seem to want it to mean (at least, not according to any regular dictionary that I'm aware of). Not to mention the fact that there are already several perfectly good terms that do mean what they seem to want it to mean, including the term *operator* in particular.

[5] In this connection, you might care to meditate on the following quotes from the first edition of the ODMG book, viz., R. G. G. Cattell, ed., *The Object Database Standard: ODMG-93* (Morgan Kaufmann, 1994). Page 16: "[The] type *Denotable_Object* [has disjoint subtypes] *Object* and *Literal* [*so a denotable object isn't necessarily an object, and no object is a literal, and no literal is an object*] ... Objects are mutable; literals are immutable." Page 20: "Literals are objects."

While I'm on the topic of ODMG, incidentally, I note that ODMG regards objects and literals as being fundamentally different things,[6] in the sense that no object is of the same type as any literal! The (weird) implications of this state of affairs are well beyond the scope of the present discussion, however.

Back to objects per se. Here's another extract from that same object database tutorial (the one by Zdonik and Maier) that manages to confuse values and variables and several other things as well:

> A *class* (sometimes called a *type*) is a template for its *instances*. Often the terms *type* and *class* are used interchangeably, but when the two terms are used in the same system, *type* usually refers to specifications, whereas *class* refers to the extension (i.e., all current instances) of the corresponding type. Every object is an instance of some class ... [*Later:*] Some types might also support operations that will alter the state of [their] instances.

Points arising:

■ First, notice that we now have another term for *object* ("instance"),[7] and another term for *value* ("state"), and a certain amount of confusion over the terms *type* and *class*. I see no need for either *instance* or *state* at all. As for type vs. class, let me remind you of the brief discussion of that topic in Chapter 4 ("All Logical Differences Are Big Differences"). Let me also draw your attention to the slightly different (?) meanings those terms seem to have in the extract from Garcia-Molina, Ullman, and Widom quoted earlier.

■ Second, the term *extension* is usually understood to refer to a set of values: to be specific, the set of values that satisfy some given predicate. For example, the extension of the predicate "i is an integer such that $0 < i < 6$" is precisely the set of values $\{1, 2, 3, 4, 5\}$. Thus, the phrase "extension (i.e., all current instances)" strongly suggests that an "instance" is a value. But the final sentence in the extract clearly implies that an "instance" is a variable.

By the way, a type that *didn't* "support operations that will alter the state of [its] instances" would seem to be not very useful, since apparently

---

[6] Except when it doesn't (see previous footnote).

[7] The same tutorial elsewhere uses yet a third term: *object instance* (!).

we wouldn't be able to define variables of that type. (Well, perhaps we could *define* them, but we could certainly never assign anything to them!)

Here's yet another quote from the same source:

> An intensional specification is a template specifying all possible objects with a given structure ... [Objects have] an *object identity* ... that remains invariant across all possible modifications of the object's value.

To talk of "all possible objects" (regardless of whether or not the objects in question are ones "with a given structure") surely implies that an object is a value (think of all possible relations with a certain heading, for example—or all possible rectangles, or even all possible integers, come to that). To talk of "all possible modifications of the object's value" surely implies that an object is a variable.

The next two quotes are taken from an interview with Mary Loomis in *Data Base Newsletter 22*, No. 6 (November/December 1994):

> One of the simplest ways to think about state is as the current values of the properties of an object—much like the values of a record's variables at a particular point in time.

By the term "record," Loomis must mean either a record value or a record variable. If it's the former, it obviously can't contain any variables. If it's the latter it can't either!—a record variable, like an array variable or a tuple variable or a relvar, is *a single variable*, not a "collection" of other variables. So what does Loomis mean by that phrase "a record's variables"?

Note: I think I know what's going on here, though. Objects in the object world are supposed to contain a set of components, known variously as *properties* or *attributes* or *members* or *instance variables*, and those components are indeed thought of as variables in their own right. (At least, they are if the objects in question are mutable. I don't know what the "instance variables" in an immutable object might be.) It seems to me, therefore, that the concept of a "mutable object" is flawed at the very outset, since we saw earlier that it's logically wrong to think of a variable of any kind as containing others (other variables, I mean).

By the way: If "one of the simplest ways to think about state" is in terms of values, then why not *use* the term "values" (or "value," singular, rather)? And what other ways are there that might be simpler?

My second quote is:

An object can be viewed as a dynamic instance that changes over time as it is operated upon.

So now we have yet another term for object ("dynamic instance")? Presumably this term means a *mutable* object, however; do we therefore have to refer to immutable objects as "static instances"? (At least I'm pleased to see the use of the phrase "operated upon" instead of some strange circumlocution involving "methods," however.)

Logical Sameness

This subsection is a small digression from my main topic, but I think it's worth including. As you'll surely have realized by now, what we're looking at in this area is a minor epidemic of the "logical sameness" problem (again see Chapter 4, "All Logical Differences Are Big Differences"). We have:

- Type vs. class—not to mention the term *interface*, which is used in ODMG, at least, to mean another kind of type (or class?)

- Value vs. immutable object vs. state vs. static object

- Variable vs. mutable object vs. dynamic object

- Operator vs. method vs. function vs. procedure[8]

- Read-only operator vs. observer, update operator vs. mutator[9]

---

[8] I haven't discussed this one in detail in this chapter so far, so let me elaborate on it briefly here. First, *procedures* resemble our update operators in that they have to be explicitly called; however, they don't necessarily have to update anything. *Functions* resemble our read-only operators in that they can be invoked inline, but they aren't necessarily read-only (also, the term "functions" seems to be used even for operators that aren't true functions, in that they return more than one result). *Methods* seem to be just operators, except that the operators in question are often assumed to be "selfish" ones. (But the term *method* is also sometimes used to mean not an operator as such but rather the implementation of an operator.) Overall, I prefer the generic term *operator*, with *read-only* and *update* as qualifiers when appropriate. In other words, I believe the distinction between read-only and update operators is an important logical difference, whereas that between procedures and functions and methods is mainly just a syntactic one.

[9] See footnote 3.

■   Object vs. instance vs. object instance vs. value (and/or variable?)

Regarding this last one, by the way, you might care to ponder over the following definitions, which are taken from *The Unified Modeling Language User Guide*, by Grady Booch, James Rumbaugh, and Ivar Jacobson (Addison-Wesley, 1999):

■   *Object:* A concrete manifestation of an abstraction; an entity with a well-defined boundary that encapsulates state and behavior; an instance of a class.

■   *Instance:* A concrete manifestation of an abstraction; an entity to which a set of operations can be applied and that has a state that stores the effects of the operations.

The same book includes a rather strange definition for *value* and no definition at all for *variable*.

By the way, the SQL standard uses the fuzzy term *instance* as well, and "defines" it thus:

■   *Instance:* A physical representation of a value.

I have no idea what the standard means by "physical representation" here; however, I do know it actually uses the term *instance* to refer to variables as well as values—possibly even to variables exclusively, other than in the foregoing "definition."

A Conjecture

I have a possible explanation for the widespread failure in the object world to distinguish properly between values and variables. As I've indicated elsewhere (see in particular Chapter 7, "Why the Object Model Isn't a Data Model"), it seems to me that "the object model" is much closer to being a model of *storage* than it is to being a model of *data*. Certainly this conjecture, if true, would explain a lot about the "the object model"!—its provision of so many different ways of structuring data, for example, also its heavy reliance on pointers. In fact, it seems to me undeniable that object advocates try to achieve good performance—always one of their key objectives—by "moving users closer to the metal," so to speak (the relational model, by contrast, being "further from the metal" and at a higher level of abstraction).

Now, the distinction between values and variables doesn't make much sense at the storage level; in fact, the concepts don't really even exist, as such, at that level. Instead, what we have is *storage locations*, and those storage locations can be used to hold bit patterns, or in other words encoded representations of values. But there's nothing in general to stop us overwriting any storage location at any time; thus, *all* storage locations effectively correspond to variables in this sense. And I could be wrong, but I strongly suspect that the concept of "objects" grew (maybe only tacitly) out of this notion of storage locations. Whence, it seems to me, the lack of emphasis—if not the total lack of appreciation—in the object world regarding the logical difference between values and variables.

EXAMPLES OF CONFUSION: TYPES vs. VALUES AND VARIABLES

Now I'd like to turn to examples of other confusions: specifically, confusions between types, on the one hand, and values or variables or both, on the other. My first example is taken from an article by John Taschek entitled "ODBMSs Take on Relational Models" [*sic!*] in *PCWeek* (October 9th, 1995):

> The term "classes" describes the behavior of groups of objects ... object classes correspond to relational tables, object attributes map to columns, and instances of objects correspond to rows and columns ... ODBMS vendors ... offer products that bridge object databases and current relational databases. These databases, called hybrids, extend relational databases and add support for objects, which appear as another data type.

Points arising:

- First and foremost, object classes absolutely do *not* "correspond to relational tables"! An object class is (as near as I can tell) a type. What Taschek calls a "relational table" is either a value or—more likely, in this context—a variable. A type isn't a value, nor is it a variable. In fact, the idea of equating classes and tables was referred to in early editions of the *Manifesto* book as a **Great Blunder**: the *first* great blunder, to be precise, because there's a second one too, which I'll get to in the next section. It's true that some products have embraced that equation ("class = table"), but sooner or later those products will fail; in fact, some already have. Here's an edited extract from those early editions of the *Manifesto* book:

> Obviously, systems can be built that are based on this equation. Equally obviously, those systems (like a car with no oil in its engine, or a house that's built on sand) might even provide useful service, for a while—but they're doomed to eventual failure.

■ Next, consider the assertion that "instances of objects [*sic!*] correspond to rows and columns." On the face of it, this claim makes no sense at all. Taken in conjunction with the assertion that "object attributes map to columns," however, I think what the writer meant to say was that "instances of objects" map to *rows*, not to "rows and columns." But if that's indeed what he meant to say, then what he meant to say is simply wrong, for many, many reasons. Those reasons are discussed in detail in the *Manifesto* book; here I'll mention just one of them, which is that in the context at hand "instances of objects" are almost certainly variables, but rows are values.

■ Given the errors mentioned in the previous two bullets, the claim that "object attributes map to columns" has to be wrong too, and it is.

■ "These databases ... extend relational databases and add support for objects, which appear as another data type." So now objects are a data type? (Incidentally, by "databases" here, I believe the writer means "DBMSs," but I'll let that one pass for now.)

In sum, this quote manages to confuse in a few brief lines (a) types vs. variables (or possibly types vs. values), (b) variables vs. values, and (c) values and/or variables vs. types again (not to mention databases vs. DBMSs), as well as making other logical mistakes that I choose not to discuss here.

I turn now to a slide presentation by Jim Melton entitled "ANSI SQL3: New Directions for the SQL Standard." Melton was for many years the editor of the SQL standard, and he gave the presentation in question, describing what subsequently became SQL:1999, at the second annual Object / Relational Summit conference (Boston, Mass., August 3rd-6th, 1997). His presentation explained among other things SQL's support for abstract data types (ADTs), which were apparently introduced with the intention of making SQL more "object like." Here are two short bullet items from the slides (edited just slightly here):

■ ADTs are passed by reference

■ But are ADTs objects?

The first bullet item is meant to explain the rule by which an argument is passed to an invocation of some operator (or method?) if that argument is of some abstract data type. But it talks about the "ADT" as if it actually were that argument! Two problems: First, arguments must be either values or variables, so there's a confusion here over types vs. values and/or variables. Second, "pass by reference" means passing the *address* of the argument, so that argument had better be a variable specifically! (So what happens if it's a value I don't know, but I suspect there's simply another failure here to distinguish between values and variables.)

As for the second bullet item: Well, ADTs are types and objects are either values or variables, so once again we have a confusion over types vs. values and/or variables. (Of course, I presume what Melton really meant by his rhetorical question was "Does SQL's support for ADTs constitute full object support?" But it's not what he *said*.)

Now, to be fair to Melton here, I need to add that it isn't just him; the literature in general tends to use the term ADT—also the term UDT, meaning a user defined type—extremely sloppily, treating them both as if they meant sometimes a value, sometimes a variable, of the type in question, rather than the type per se. The following examples, which are quite typical, are all taken from the same conference as the Melton quotes; they mostly come from presentation slides, a fact that explains the rather choppy style (though I've edited them slightly here). The first two are from "DB2 Extenders and the Universal Database," by Nelson Mattos of IBM (note the deprecated use of "database" in that title to mean "DBMS," by the way):

■ How should we replicate UDTs?

■ UDTs are cached close to the application

These examples both use "UDTs" to refer to values and/or variables *of* some user defined type, rather than to UDTs per se.

The next few are from "Object / Relational: Separating the Wheat from the Chaff," by Bruce Lindsay, also of IBM:

- ADTs are mutable

- ADTs / objects live in repository

- Applications manipulate ADTs in queries

- Object / relational databases permit:
  - a.   User defined types in columns
  - b.   User defined types in queries
  - c.   User defined types in applications

The first three of these use "ADTs" to mean variables (probably) or values (possibly)—though the reference to "manipulating" ADTs in queries is slightly puzzling, since queries are read-only and "manipulating" is usually understood to mean updating. The fourth uses "user defined types" in the same way; here I'd just like to add that it shouldn't be necessary to say what Lindsay is trying to say, anyway, if ADT or UDT support is (as of course it should be) properly orthogonal.

My next exhibit consists of a series of quotes from a paper by Andrew E. Wade titled "Object Query Standards" (*ACM SIGMOD Record 25*, No. 1 (March 1996):

A basic difference between an object and traditional data is that the object also includes operations.

Sorry, but I disagree. Strongly! What operations does the object 3 "include"? Or the object N, where N is a variable of type INTEGER?

If *v* is a "velocity object" and *t* is a "time object," and if we can multiply *v* by *t* to obtain a "distance object" *d*, does *v* "include" that multiplication operation, or does *t*? What about *d*?

Really, I think that all Wade's trying to say here is that "objects" of type *T* can be operated upon only by means of the operators defined for type *T* (where, as in the previous chapter, by "defined for type *T*" I mean, precisely, that the operator in question has a parameter of type *T*). In other words, I think he's using the term "object" to mean a type instead of a value or a variable. If I'm right, then where's the claimed "basic difference"? There's absolutely no need to invoke the idea of "objects" "including" "operations" *at all*. Traditional data too can be operated upon by operators defined for the relevant type, no more and no less. It all looks like another example of logical sameness to me.

By the way: If Wade's trying to say rather that "objects" actually *include the code* for the operators, then I disagree still further, on at least two counts. First, it's not the "object" per se that includes the code, it's the "object" *descriptor* (sometimes called the *class-defining object* or CDO).[10] Second, where the code resides is purely an implementation matter—it has nothing to do with the model, and it shouldn't even be mentioned in the context at hand.

> Collections can be thought of as multivalued attributes, [with] individual values, or members, of the collections comprising various, possibly complex, data types, as well as objects.

A "collection" is, e.g., an array or a set; in other words, it's a value (unless the term "collection" is meant to stand for a collection *variable*, in which case it's a variable). Attributes, multivalued or otherwise, are components of a type.[11] Components of a type are neither values nor variables. So it makes no sense to say that collections are—or "can be thought of" as—attributes, multivalued or otherwise. I suppose I can agree that some attribute A of some nonscalar type T might be "collection valued" (e.g., certain attributes of certain relation types are relation valued), meaning that for all values v of type T, the A component of v is some collection c. But then I don't understand at all the notion that "members" of that collection c might be "data types as well as objects"—especially since c is definitely a value here, and in any case Wade himself says those "members" are in fact values! (I think he's using "objects" in this context to mean variables, though it's hard to be sure.)

> The type of the result of the query may be a scalar (including tuples), an object, or a collection of objects, with ... rules specifying which operations on which types produce which other types.

---

[10] More likely, the CDO includes a pointer into some library somewhere and the code physically resides in that library. Be that as it may, the claim that "unlike traditional data, objects include code" is frequently heard but seems to me to be simply wrong, on several levels at once.

[11] Of course, we often talk in the relational world of relation values and variables "having attributes"—but what we mean when we say such things is that (a) relation values and variables are of some relation type, and (b) that relation type has attributes. Now, maybe Wade's text is meant to be understood in a similar fashion; however, later parts of the text in question make it hard to justify such a charitable interpretation.

Comments:

- First, the sentence overall needs to be revised in order to avoid "type vs. value or variable" errors, perhaps as follows: "The result of the query may be a scalar (including tuples), an object, or a collection of objects, with ... rules specifying which operations on *operands of* which types produce *results of* which other types" (italics just to show the additions).

    By the way, operations were called methods earlier in the same paragraph as the sentence quoted.

- Second, I thought it was a basic tenet in the object world that "everything's an object"; so what does "a scalar (including tuples), an object, or a collection of objects" mean? Aren't scalars, tuples, and collections objects?

- Third, what does "a scalar (including tuples)" mean? Scalars aren't tuples and tuples aren't scalars.

- Fourth, the result of a query is always a value; so "scalar," "tuple," "object," and "collection" here all refer to values—which would be fine, except that such terms are widely used elsewhere in Wade's own article to mean variables.

Continuing with extracts from Wade's article:

ODMG attempted to make OQL completely compatible with SQL, in the sense that any SQL query would be a legal OQL query, with the same syntax, semantics, and result [*given the same input, presumably!*]. Although this was achieved to a large extent (perhaps 90%, some suggest), full compatibility was not reached ... For example, if X is of type *T*, then the type of the result of the query SELECT X FROM ... is MULTISET (ROW (*T*)) in SQL but MULTISET (*T*) in OQL. [*I've edited this extract somewhat, but not so as to alter the intended meaning.*]

If the "For example ..." sentence here is correct, then I'd say the degree of compatibility between SQL and OQL is not 90% but 0%.[12] All logical differences are big differences.

---

[12] You might observe that the extract quoted doesn't illustrate any "type vs. value or variable" errors as such and thus doesn't really belong in this section—but I found it so staggering that I couldn't resist quoting it here anyway.

The addition of object capabilities [to SQL] includes the ability to define and access Abstract Data Types (ADTs), which have much the same functionality as ... objects ... The intent is to add "OO-ness" to rows in tables ... These rows may contain ADTs. A mechanism to reference ADTs in other rows exists ...

"The ability to ... access ADTs" suggests confusion over types vs. values and/or variables; so does "ADTs ... have much the same functionality as objects." "These rows may contain ADTs" suggests confusion over types vs. values, unless "rows" is being used (confusingly) to mean row *variables*, in which case it suggests confusion over (a) types vs. variables, (b) the fact that row variables are *not* collections of component variables, and (c) the fact that there's no such thing as a row variable in the relational model. Analogous remarks apply to the final sentence in the quote (which incidentally makes no sense unless "rows" is being used to mean row variables).

For my final examples in this section, I return to that interview with Mary Loomis in *Data Base Newsletter 22*, No. 6 (November/December 1994):

True object-oriented support means extending the database schema to include specifications of operators that act upon data types defined to the DBMS.

First, operators "act upon" values and/or variables, not data types. Second (and perhaps more important), I'm not at all sure I agree that "specifications of operators" should appear in "the database schema," because this latter term—at least as usually understood—applies to *one particular database*, and I don't think that either data types or operators should be specific to one particular database, in general. (What database does type INTEGER belong to? What database does the operator "+" belong to?) I think, rather, that definitions of types and associated operators should be completely separate from, and sharable by, definitions of ("schemas for," if you prefer) specific databases.

Interviewer: C. J. Date [has] argued that object type equates to the relational notion of domains—and not to relations or tables. Do you agree?

Answer: That is absolutely true ...

Interviewer: What corresponds to a relational table in the object model?

Answer: A table is an extent, which is the set of instances of a given type.

I agree completely with that first answer! I agree *partly* with the second answer as well, provided that (a) in the question, "a relational table" means a relation variable, not a relation value, and (b) in the answer, "the set of instances of a given type" means the set of all tuples that correspond to currently true instantiations of some given predicate. But in the object world "instances" usually means "objects," and "objects" usually means variables ... So once again there might be some confusion over type vs. either value or variable, and I'm not sure I'm right to agree, after all.

Furthermore (and perhaps more important), even if I'm right to agree, I must now qualify that agreement by adding that I certainly reject the subsidiary implication that "rows in relational tables" correspond to objects.

 Let me close this section by admitting that I'm well aware that many people will simply dismiss the criticisms I've been articulating as mere quibbles: "Yes, the phrasing might be a little sloppy, but what does it matter? We all know what the writer really means, don't we?" And so on. Well, I think it does matter, and I don't think we can just assume we always know what the writer really means. I agree with Bob Boiko when he says (in an article entitled "Understanding XML," *metatorial.com/papers/xml.asp,* 2000) that "Even in the smallest organization, most conflicts stem from a lack of clearly defined and shared meaning for the words we use." I also agree, strongly, with the following remarks by Richard Mitchell in his book *Less than Words Can Say* (Little, Brown and Company, 1979):

> It is no coincidence that the Greeks who first devised discursive prose also constructed formal logic ... Thinking *is* coherent discourse, and the logic and the prose require one another ... [We] have to suspect that coherent, continuous thought is impossible for those who cannot construct coherent, continuous prose ... The logic of writing is simply logic; it is not some system of arbitrary conventions interesting only to those who write a lot. All logical thought goes on in the form of statements and statements about statements ... If we cannot make those statements and statements about statements logically, clearly, and coherently, then we cannot think and make knowledge. People who cannot put strings of sentences together in good order cannot think.

CONSEQUENCES OF SUCH CONFUSIONS

What are the consequences of confusing values and variables? Well, here's one. Consider the following quote from the article "On Marrying Relations and

Objects: Relation-Centric and Object-Centric Perspectives," by Won Kim, in *Data Base Newsletter 22*, No. 6 (November/December 1994):

> [Some] relational database systems ... assign tuple identifiers to tuples in relations ...

Well, "relational" should probably be SQL and "relations" should certainly be relvars, but I don't want to pursue those issues further here. Rather, the point is that the systems in question are clearly thinking of the "relations" (really relvars) in question as consisting of collections of tuple variables or "tuplevars." After all, there wouldn't be any point in "assigning identifiers to"—or, better, associating identifiers with—tuple *values*. So the systems in question are based on a logically flawed concept; as we know, relvars don't contain tuplevars, they contain relation values, which contain tuple values.

Even this flaw might not matter, however (I mean, it might not be a concern at the model level), were it not for the following:

■ First, the systems in question typically expose those "tuple IDs" to the user (indeed, if they don't, then from the user's point of view those tuple IDs don't exist—they aren't part of the model, and we don't need to talk about them). Exposing them to the user means the user can access and exploit them in a variety of ways. Unless they're represented to the user as just another relational attribute (which they might or might not be), we thus have a violation of *The Information Principle* on our hands.
    Note: In case you're not familiar with it, *The Information Principle* states, loosely, that the user deals with (a) relation values and variables and (b) nothing else.

■ Second, all of the systems in question—so far as I'm aware—associate such IDs only with tuples in base relvars specifically, not with tuples in other kinds of relvars (e.g., views), and certainly not with tuples in relations produced as the result of evaluating some general relational expression (e.g., as the result of some query). One consequence of this state of affairs is that users thus see a logical difference between base relvars and other kinds, and so we have a violation of *The Principle of Interchangeability* on our hands.
    Note: In case you're not familiar with it, *The Principle of Interchangeability* (of base and derived relvars) states, loosely, that the user

shouldn't be able to tell the difference between base relvars and other kinds.

Following on from the foregoing, I now claim that it was at least partly a confusion over the value vs. variable distinction that led to the introduction of object IDs into the object world. *The Third Manifesto* rejects the concept of object IDs, finding them to be both unnecessary and undesirable. The argument to show they're *unnecessary* goes like this:

- By definition, every value is distinct from every other value (i.e., is in fact self-identifying).

- Values thus have no need to carry around with themselves some hidden, secret identifier that's somehow separate from the value itself, and indeed they don't.

- Variables, by contrast, do need some identity that's separate from their current value, and that identification is provided, precisely and sufficiently, by the variable's name.

As for showing the *undesirability* of object IDs, it's sufficient to say just that they're logically indistinguishable from pointers—and we already know we don't want pointers in the database, and I don't think I need give any further justification of this latter position here.

Of course, the relational world too has been guilty in the past of some confusion over values and variables: to be specific, over *relation* values and variables. And that fact has led to some confusion over normalization in particular. For example, in the second edition of my book *An Introduction to Database Systems* (Addison-Wesley, 1977), I wrote:

> Given a relation *R*, we say that attribute *Y* of *R* is functionally dependent on attribute *X* of *R* if and only if each *X* value in *R* has associated with it precisely one *Y* value in *R* (at any one time).

I should have said *relvar*, not *relation*—then I could (and should, and would) have deleted "(at any one time)." To put the point another way: If we call a relvar a relation, what do we call a relation?

Confusions have also arisen over update. In the 6th edition of that same book (Addison-Wesley, 1995)—though only in the first printing!—I wrote:

Tuple assignments are performed (implicitly) during ... [relational] UPDATE operations.

No, they're not. As explained near the beginning of this chapter, relational UPDATE operations—relational INSERT and DELETE operations too, of course—are really shorthand for certain relational assignments, which replace the current value (a relation) of the target variable (a relvar) by another value (another relation). Note clearly that the target of such assignments is always a relvar; what it's categorically not is a tuplevar, as it would have to be in a genuine tuple assignment (not even in the special case where the relvar we're trying to update happens to contain just one tuple). [13]

Further examples of confusion over updating are provided by SQL (were you surprised?). Consider first the SQL INSERT statement. In its simplest and probably commonest form, that statement looks like this:

```
INSERT INTO <table name> ( <column name commalist> )
       VALUES ( <expression commalist>  ) ;
```

For example:

```
INSERT INTO EMP ( ENO ,        DNO ,       SALARY )
       VALUES ( ENO ('E1') , DNO ('D1') , MONEY (50000) ) ;
```

This example would widely be regarded as "inserting a row" into table EMP, but it really shouldn't be—at best, such a characterization is very loose; at worst, it's misleading.

A more serious issue is raised by the "positioned" forms of the DELETE and UPDATE statements (i.e., DELETE and UPDATE via a cursor). For example:

```
UPDATE EMP
SET    SALARY = SALARY × 1.1
WHERE  CURRENT OF EXC ;
```

This statement is *defined* to be a single-row operation—it updates the particular row that cursor EXC happens to be positioned on (I'm assuming here that EXC is a cursor running over the EMP table, of course). But "updating a

---

[13] Nor is it any kind of "collection" of tuplevars, of course.

row" means by definition that the row in question must be a row *variable*—and there's no such thing, in the relational model. In other words, I'm suggesting that SQL's positioned DELETE and UPDATE statements are and always were a logical mistake. Indeed, they would probably never have been included in the language at all if only the original SQL designers had understood the logical difference between relation (or table) values and variables in the first place.

By the way, it's relevant to mention in passing that certain cursor-based updates can never work, anyway. As a trivial example, suppose table EMP is subject to the constraint that employees E1 and E2 must always be in the same department. Then any cursor-based (and hence single-row) update that attempts to change the department number for either E1 or E2 will necessarily fail.

Let me turn now to the issue of confusion over types, on the one hand, and either values or variables or both on the other. I've already alluded to the fact that a failure to distinguish between types and variables constitutes **The First Great Blunder**. I don't want to discuss that blunder any further here, except to say that it really is a blunder (defined by *Chambers Twentieth Century Dictionary* as "a gross mistake"); if you want to learn more about it, a detailed discussion can be found in my book *An Introduction to Database Systems* (8th edition, Addison-Wesley, 2004) and elsewhere. But I do want to say something about **The Second Great Blunder**, which can be characterized, informally, as *mixing pointers and relations*—that is, "allowing an attribute in one relation to contain pointers to tuples in another."

Now, I hope you realized immediately that this notion makes no sense, because "pointers to tuples" has to mean pointers to tuple *variables*, and there's no such thing as a tuple variable in a relational database (hence the quotation marks in the previous paragraph). So we really are talking about another huge blunder ... Again, I don't want to discuss the issue in detail here. because I'll be doing that in Chapter 9 ("Don't Mix Pointers and Relations!"). Instead, I just want to make the following points:

■ A system that commits the first great blunder is inevitably led into committing the second as well. That is, the second is a logical consequence of the first, and so it's also, logically, a consequence of confusing types and variables.

■ However, a system that avoids the first great blunder can still commit the second anyway. To that extent, therefore, the second is independent of the first. Since we've already seen that the second involves "pointers to tuples," however, we can say that the second is also a consequence of confusing values and variables, as well as a consequence of confusing types and variables.

- Third, as I've written elsewhere, if SQL doesn't quite commit the two great blunders, it certainly sails very close to the wind ... To be specific, SQL does include support for "REF types"; it does include support for dereferencing (though, oddly, not for referencing); and it does allow rows in one table to contain "references" to rows in another. Now, advocates of these SQL features claim that those features are all really just shorthand for various combinations of features that already exist in the language. But even if we accept this claim as valid (which it patently isn't, by the way), the fact remains that the new features have the effect of making SQL more complicated than it was before—as if it wasn't complicated enough already!—and (to say it again) they're all consequences, in the last analysis, of confusing types, values, and variables.

CONCLUDING REMARKS

I began these two chapters by identifying types, values, variables, and operators as "four core concepts." They're core concepts because they do indeed form the core of the vast majority of traditional programming languages (among other things), and database and programming language professionals really ought to be thoroughly familiar with them—though I believe these chapters have demonstrated rather convincingly that there's room for improvement in this regard. Let me therefore say a little more about them here by way of additional justification:

- We must have types, because without them we can't catch stupid errors.[14] *Note:* Types don't just allow such errors to be caught; importantly, they allow them to be caught at compile time.

---

[14] The SQL example SELECT ... WHERE SHOE_SIZE = AGE is frequently cited in this connection, SHOE_SIZE and AGE being examples of properties that intuitively should be of different types but might not be. In fact, it's not just often cited, it's often used by object proponents as an example of a stupid query that relational systems allegedly permit (see, e.g., *Object Databases: The Essentials*, by Mary E. S. Loomis, Addison-Wesley, 1995), and hence as a criticism of such systems. Well, the query might be stupid, but so are those criticisms ... Whether such a comparison (SHOE_SIZE = AGE) is allowed has to do with whether the system in question includes proper type support, that's all. It has nothing to do with whether that system is relational.

- We must have values, because values are what we assign to variables. Without them, we couldn't do anything at all.

- We must have variables, because without them everything would be totally static. In particular, we couldn't update the database to reflect changes in the real world.

- We must have operators, because, again, without them we couldn't do anything at all. In particular, we must have update operators (at least an assignment operator), because without them we couldn't update the database.

Once we realize the need for types, in fact, we realize further that types are, in a sense, the most fundamental of the four core concepts. To repeat from the something I said in the previous chapter: Values are typed; variables are typed; and operators apply to typed arguments and, if they return a value, are themselves typed as well. In other words, values, variables, and operators all in turn rely on the notion of type.

I'd like to close by saying a word about integrity constraints (or just constraints for short). Recall the example I mentioned in the previous section, to the effect that employees E1 and E2 were constrained always to be in the same department (not a very realistic example, I have to admit, but a possible one). My actual words were: "Suppose table EMP is subject to" the foregoing constraint. Well, I hope you realized right away that the phrase "table EMP" here must be understood as referring to a table *variable*, not a table *value* (or, as I would greatly prefer to say, a relvar, not a relation). Why?

Well, to say that something, V say, is subject to some constraint is to say that updates on V will be checked against the constraint in question, and hence that V must be updatable. And to say that V is updatable is to say, precisely, that V is a variable. (To be updatable is to be a variable, to be a variable is to be a updatable.) Here's the terminology we use:

- If constraint C applies to variable V, we say C *holds* for V, or equivalently that *V is subject to C*.

■ If constraint *C* applies to variable *V*, and if value *v* is of the same type as *V*, then (a) if *v* causes *C* to evaluate to TRUE, then *v satisfies C*; (b) if *v* causes *C* to evaluate to FALSE, then *v violates C*.

■ Value *v* can be successfully assigned to variable *V* if and only if *v* satisfies all of the constraints that apply to *V*.

So the very notion of constraints implies immediately that we need to be careful over the logical difference between values and variables.

Note: One particular kind of constraint that applies to relation variables (relvars) in particular is *key* constraints. Note carefully, therefore, that it's relvars that "have" keys; relations don't "have" keys, though for relation *r* to be successfully assignable to relvar *R*, *r* must certainly satisfy all of the key constraints (and all other constraints, of course) to which *R* is subject.

Chapter 7

Why the Object Model

Isn't a Data Model

Arguments over the relative merits of objects and relations are often of the "more heat than light" variety. Why is this? The present chapter suggests an answer to this question. Specifically, it suggests that the underlying models are more different than is usually realized—one, the relational model, being a true data model and the other not. One consequence of this state of affairs is that, perhaps without fully realizing the fact, object proponents and relational proponents are likely to be arguing from different premises.

Publishing history: This is a revised version of a paper that first appeared under a very slightly different title in InfoDB 10, No. 4 (August 1996) and was later republished in my book Relational Database Writings 1994-1997 (Addison-Wesley, 1998). This version copyright © C. J. Date 2022.

This chapter discusses an idea that I believe can help shed some light on the debate over the relative merits of objects and relations. The idea is this:

The "object model" is a storage model, not a data model.

Let me immediately explain why I place the term "object model" in quotation marks here. I do so because, as is well known, there's no such thing as a universally agreed, abstract, formally defined "object model" (despite the fact that several attempts have been made to define such a thing—see, e.g., references

[1], [4], and maybe [12]). Nor is there even consensus on an *in*formal model; indeed, there's very little agreement in the object world even on so simple a matter as terminology. However, it's at least safe to say that every candidate "object model" does include, under one name or another, all of the features I need to examine in this chapter (see the next section but one); so I don't think we need to be too concerned about this lack of consensus, at least for present purposes.

As an aside, I note that at this point in the paper that was the original version of this chapter I wrote the following:

> As indicated by my opening sentence, I hope [what follows] will serve to clarify certain aspects of the [debate over] objects vs. relations ... To this end, I invite anyone who disagrees with the thesis adopted ... to take up a dissenting position in public, so that we can at least get the arguments out in the open and thereby stand a better chance of assessing their relative worth—and, perhaps more importantly, a better chance of deciding how best to move forward in our field.

Well, I note for what it's worth that no one responded to my invitation (perhaps I should say rather, no one accepted my challenge). Of course, that lack of response might just mean no one read the original paper ... but I choose to take it as meaning that no one was able to come up with a solid rebuttal of the position it advocated. Be that as it may, I now observe that no one seems very interested in object databases any more, and for my money that's a good thing. But ideas do have a habit of resurfacing from time to time, even—or perhaps especially— bad ones, so I think the present chapter does still have a useful purpose to serve.

One final preliminary remark: Please note that, at least so far as this chapter is concerned, I'm interested in object orientation *solely* as it pertains to database management. Thus, I don't want to discuss object oriented interfaces, or applications, or programming languages, or analysis, or design (etc., etc.). Indeed, I suspect that another reason why the objects vs. relations debate sometimes seems so confusing is that the arguments themselves sometimes conflate these very different contexts. Throughout this paper, therefore, all references to objects, or object orientation, or just "OO"—which I use from this point foward as an abbreviation for either "object oriented" or "object orientation," as the context demands—are to be understood from a database perspective specifically, barring explicit statements to the contrary.

DATA MODELS AND STORAGE MODELS

Perhaps I should begin by explaining what I mean by the terms *data model* and *storage model*—especially as the first of these terms, at least, is used in the literature to denote two quite different things. So here goes:

- First of all, I take a model of anything to be simply a construction, as concrete or as abstract as we please, that captures certain aspects of the thing being modeled—where by "capturing certain aspects" I mean that features or properties of the model mimic, in certain specific ways, features or properties of whatever it is that's being modeled. Study of the model can thereby lead to improved understanding of the thing being modeled.

- In particular, therefore, a model of data[1] is a construction—necessarily somewhat abstract, since data itself is already a fairly abstract concept— that captures certain aspects of data. What aspects? Well, the aspects we're interested in are clearly those that are intrinsic, as opposed to those that are mere artifacts of some particular representation or implementation. We want to study data in its pure form and not be distracted by irrelevancies. To use the usual jargon, we're interested in the logical aspects of data, not the physical aspects.

- It follows that a *good* model of data will be one that's "logical, not physical"—i.e., one that captures only logical aspects, not physical aspects. (Ideally it would capture *all* of those logical aspects, of course, but this goal I take to be unachievable.) Moreover, it shouldn't include anything else!— i.e., there should be no properties or features that don't correspond to anything intrinsic. In IMS, for example, the very same data item can be interpreted either as a character string or as a packed decimal number; but this oddity is merely an artifact of "the IMS model" (if I might use such a term)—it certainly isn't something that's intrinsic to data per se.[2]

- To be more specific, a good data model will include a set of *objects* (using the word here in its generic sense, not its OO sense), together with a set of

---

[1] By *data* here, I mean data in general, not the specific data that some specific database is supposed to contain.

[2] More particularly, it's a consequence of a failure to pay adequate attention to the logical difference between types and representations (see Chapers 5 and 6).

operators for operating on those objects. The objects allow us to model the *structure* of data. The operators allow us to model its *behavior*. Taken together, therefore, the objects and operators effectively constitute an *abstract machine*[3]—and we can thus usefully distinguish the model from its *implementation*, which is the physical realization of that abstract machine on some underlying real machine. In a nutshell: The model is what users have to know about; the implementation is what users don't have to know about.

■   Next, the objects and operators of the model serve as a basis for further investigations into the nature of data. For example, what does it mean for data to be secure? consistent? redundant? (and so on). And those investigations in turn can lead to (compatible!) extensions to the original model; that is, the model can grow over time to become an ever more faithful abstraction of data "as it really is." In other words, a model of data is really a *theory* of data (or at least the beginnings of one), and it's not a static thing.

Note: I remark in passing that it might have been better if, right back in the early days of database research, we'd talked about a theory, not a model, of data. Then there'd have been less likelihood of confusion with the other common interpretation of the term *data model*: namely, as a model of the data of some specific enterprise or business. Also, it might help to point out that the relationship between the two interpretations of the term *data model* is analogous to that between (a) some programming language *L* and (b) some program *P* written in that language *L*. It's also worth stating explicitly that the familiar activity of *data modeling* refers to the second meaning of the term, not to the meaning that's the principal focus of the present chapter.

■   Finally, a model of *storage* is, of course, a model that captures certain aspects of storage, not data.

---

[3] An attendee on one of my seminars suggested rather strongly that I should go further here and demand that the objects and operators form an *algebra* specifically (as they do in the case of the relational model, of course)—and I have to say I'm very sympathetic to this suggestion. So what's an algebra? Generally speaking, it's a formal system, consisting of a set of elements and a set of read-only operators that apply to those elements, such that those elements and operators together satisfy certain laws and properties (almost certainly closure, probably commutativity and associativity, and so on).

In the remainder of this chapter I'll elaborate on this distinction (between data models and storage models, I mean) and explain it in more detail.

AN OVERVIEW OF "THE OBJECT MODEL"

This section summarizes those components of the object model that are relevant to my thesis (it ignores aspects that might be important in themselves but aren't relevant to that thesis, such as inheritance). *Note:* In the interests of readability, I'll drop the quotation marks surrounding "the object model" from this point forward. Too much repetition quickly becomes tiresome.

First of all, we need to understand exactly what objects themselves are. Well, most OO writings will at least agree that:

- Every object is an *instance* of some *object class* (*class* for short).

- Objects are either *mutable* or *immutable*.

In more conventional terms:

- A *class* is essentially just a *data type* (*type* for short). The type in question can be either system defined (i.e., built in) or user defined; either way, however, the only way objects of the type in question can be operated upon is by means of the *operators* (also known as *methods*) defined for that type. In other words, the *representation* of those objects—which can be arbitrarily complex—is always hidden from the user.

    Note: In the case of a user defined type, of course, the representation will presumably be visible to the user who actually defines the type. But it'll be hidden from other users.

- A *mutable* object (or instance) of type (or class) T is essentially just a *variable* of type T.[4]

- An *immutable* object (or instance) of type (or class) T is essentially just a *value* of type T.

---

[4] Be warned, however, that object systems typically usurp the general term *variable* and give it a very specific and limited meaning—namely, a variable whose legal values are object IDs (see later). This chapter uses the term in its more traditional and general sense.

Thus, for example, the system might provide a built-in type called RATIONAL ("rational numbers"), with operators "=", "<", "+", "×", and so on. Users would then be able to declare RATIONAL variables and specify RATIONAL literals, perform comparison and arithmetic operations on RATIONAL values, and so on; however, they wouldn't know, nor would they need to know, how RATIONAL values were represented internally.

As another example, some suitably authorized user might provide a user defined type called CIRCLE, with operators GET_CENTER, GET_RADIUS, SET_CENTER, SET_RADIUS, and so on. Users would then be able to declare CIRCLE variables and specify CIRCLE literals, operate on CIRCLE centers and radii, and so on, but again they wouldn't know, nor would they need to know, how CIRCLE values were represented internally.

Next, the operators associated with any particular class (i.e., type) are required to include at least one *constructor*, the purpose of which is to "construct" a new object (instance) of the class (type) in question.[5] In Smalltalk, for example, the constructor for a given class is invoked by sending a message to that class asking it to create a "new" object of the class in question, as in this example:

```
CIRCLE NEW
```

Constructing an object causes the system to return an *object identifier* (*object ID*, or just *OID* for short) for the new object. That OID can be thought of as a pointer to, or address for, the new object. Thus, the Smalltalk message just shown can be regarded as an expression that evaluates to a pointer to a newly constructed circle. (Of course, when I say "pointer" here, I mean some kind of *logical* pointer—I'm not talking about physical disk addresses. At least, I hope not.)

Next, it's important to understand that in the OO world constructing an object doesn't necessarily initialize that object to any particular value. If it doesn't, such initialization will have to be performed as a separate, follow-on step. For example (Smalltalk again):

```
C_PTR    :=   CIRCLE NEW .
C_PTR SET_CENTER : CENTER_PTR .
C_PTR SET_RADIUS : RADIUS_PTR .
```

---

[5] I assume here, and you can assume too, that the new object is a mutable one specifically. I'll have more to say about this issue in the next section.

The first step here, the assignment statement, constructs a new circle and assigns its OID to the variable C_PTR. The second and third steps then send messages to the object whose OID is contained in that variable C_PTR—in other words, to the circle just constructed. Those messages cause two further operations to be performed, the effect of which is to set the center and radius of that new circle to certain initial values. More precisely, the effect is:

- To set the center of the new circle to the value that's the current value of the object whose OID is contained in the variable CENTER_PTR, and

- To set the radius of that circle to the value that's the current value of the object whose OID is contained in the variable RADIUS_PTR.

The variables C_PTR, CENTER_PTR, and RADIUS_PT here are, of course, all variables "of type OID"—that is, they all contain addresses, or pointers.

Note that, as the example suggests, all references to objects are by means of the corresponding OIDs;[6] in other words, OIDs provide *addressability*—logical addressability, that is—to the objects they identify. Thus, for instance, a request to get the center (GET_CENTER) of a given circle will actually return, not the relevant point per se, but rather the OID of that point (I assume for the sake of the example that POINT is another user defined type).

Finally, the object model requires support for a full complement of *type generators* (also known as type constructors; I use the term "generator" in order to avoid confusion with the constructor operators already discussed). Examples of such generators include STRUCT (or TUPLE), LIST, ARRAY, SET, BAG, and so on. These generators can be combined in arbitrary ways; thus, for example, an array of lists of bags of arrays of real numbers might constitute a single ("complex") object in suitable circumstances. Along with the OID mechanism already discussed, the availability of these type generators essentially means that *any data structure that can be created in an application program can be created as an object in an OO database*—and further that the structure of such objects is *visible to the user*. For example, consider the object, EX say, that is (or rather denotes) the collection of employees in a given department. Then EX

---

[6] Which explains why, as is well known, object systems typically provide (a) two different equality comparison operators (equal OID vs. equal value) and (b) two different assignment operators (assign OID vs. assign value). The two forms in each case are sometimes referred to as "deep vs. shallow," though authorities don't always agree as to which is which.

might be implemented either as a linked list or as an array, and users will have to know which it is (because the access operators will differ accordingly).

Note: This "anything goes" approach to what can be stored in the database is a major point of difference between the object and relational models, of course, and it deserves a little further discussion here. In essence:

- The object model says we can store anything we like (i.e., any data structure we can create with the usual programming language mechanisms).

- The relational model effectively says the same thing—but then goes on to insist that whatever we do store be presented to the user in *pure relational form*.

More precisely, the relational model quite rightly says *nothing* about what can be physically stored (it's a logical model only). It therefore imposes no limits on what data structures are allowed at the physical level; the only requirement is that whatever structures are in fact physically stored must be mapped to relations at the logical level and thus hidden from the user. In other words, relational systems make a clear distinction between the logical and physical levels (data model vs. implementation), and OO systems don't. One consequence is that—contrary to conventional wisdom!—OO systems might very well provide less data independence than relational systems. For example, suppose the implementation in some object database of the object EX mentioned above (denoting the collection of employees in a given department) is changed from an array to a linked list. What are the implications for existing code that accesses that object EX? *Answer:* It breaks.

OBJECT CONSTRUCTION

Now I return to the question of what it means to construct an object.[7] Let me begin by reminding you that there are basically two kinds of objects, *values* ("immutable objects") and *variables* ("mutable objects"). So what exactly do I

---

[7] The discussion that follows appears more or less verbatim in various other writings of mine, but it bears repeating here. In fact I plan to go on repeating it until the message finally gets through and becomes conventional wisdom in our field—which I can say, from experience in teaching this material for many years now, still doesn't seem to have happened.

mean by the terms *value* and *variable*? The following definitions are based on ones given by Cleaveland in reference [5]:

Definition (value): A value is an individual constant (e.g., the individual constant 3). Values have no location in time or space; in effect, they simply exist. What's more, a value can't be updated—for if it could, then after the update it wouldn't be that value any more. However, values can be represented by some encoding, and such representations can be used to denote "current values" of variables, which do have locations in time and space and can be updated (see the next definition).

    Note: I don't mean to suggest that only simple things like integers are legitimate values. On the contrary, values can be arbitrarily complex; for example, a point is a value, a circle is a value, an array is a value, a relation is a value, and so on.

Definition (variable): A variable is a holder for a representation of a value. A variable does have location in time and space, and of course it can be updated; that is, the current value of a variable can be replaced by another, probably different from the previous one.

From the foregoing definitions, it should be clear that:

- The idea of constructing a *value* makes no sense. Consider integers, for example. Nobody ever "constructs" the integer 3; that value simply exists, logically speaking. It's true that a given user at a given time might happen to become interested in that value (for example, in order to be able to specify the number of employees in a given department), but that user doesn't suddenly "construct" that value out of thin air; rather, he or she simply makes use of a value that already exists. And exactly the same argument applies to all conceivable values, no matter how complex they might be—integers, strings, points, circles, relations, lists or arrays of any of the foregoing (etc., etc.).

- By contrast, the idea of constructing a *variable* does make sense—it means, precisely, constructing a holder into which we can put values (or, rather, representations of values). In other words, it means *declaring*, or *creating*, or *defining*, the variable in question.

Let's agree, then, that from this point forward "constructing an object" means constructing a *mutable* object (i.e., a variable) specifically. Thus, for example, execution of the PL/I statement

```
DECLARE N INTEGER ;
```

might be thought of as "constructing" a "mutable object" called N, of "class" INTEGER. And, once that mutable object has been constructed, we know we can go on to place (representations of) various "immutable objects" into that mutable object (different immutable objects at different times, in general). For example, the PL/I assignment statement

```
N = 3 ;
```

causes (a representation of) the immutable object 3 to be placed in the mutable object N.

Now, all I've done so far is introduce certain terms (terms that might be novel to some readers) for concepts that aren't really novel at all. And if matters stopped there—if that were all there were to it—everything would be just fine (well, reasonably fine, anyway; we don't really want too many different terms for the same thing if we can help it). The trouble is, in the object world matters don't stop there, as I now explain.

First of all, no matter what language we're talking about, a variable—a holder for values—has to be implemented under the covers as an area of storage. That is, one of the things the system has to do in order to implement an operation like the PL/I DECLARE statement shown earlier is *allocate storage* for the variable being "constructed." But, of course, the whole point of traditional programming languages is precisely that users shouldn't have to worry about implementation level details like storage allocation; to put it another way, the goal of such languages is *to raise the level of abstraction*. Thus, users of such a language should be able to ignore the physical details of the underlying real machine and focus instead on the logical details of the abstract machine defined by the language at hand. In particular, they should be able to ignore the idiosyncrasies of physical computer storage and operate in terms of the "variable" abstraction instead.

Now, the goal of data models also is to raise the level of abstraction, in an exactly analogous fashion; indeed, in many respects a data model really is a kind of high level programming language, except that it doesn't prescribe any specific concrete syntax. Thus, all of the remarks in the previous paragraph apply equally well, mutatis mutandis, to data models as well as to programming languages.

Given the foregoing definitions and explanations, then, it's my claim that:

> *The OO notion of "constructing an object" is much closer to the implementation notion of allocating storage than it is to the more abstract data model notion of declaring a variable—and hence the object model is really a storage model, not a data model, as a consequence.*

In the next two sections, I present arguments and evidence in support of these claims.

OBJECT IDENTIFICATION

My first argument goes like this:

- In a traditional programming language (or in a data model), when a variable is declared, a name is typically specified for that variable, and that variable can then be referenced by that name from that point forward.

- At the implementation level, by contrast, when an area of storage is allocated, it isn't given a name; instead, the system returns the address of that storage, and that storage can then be referenced by that address from that point forward.

Well, what happens in an object system? When an object is constructed, it isn't given a name; instead, the constructor operation returns an OID—which is to say, an address—for the new object.[8] I conclude that, as already suggested, an OO "object" is more like an area of storage than it is like a conventional variable.

Note: I said earlier that a mutable object was "essentially just a variable." Frankly, I would have preferred to say it was *nothing more nor less* than a variable. However, we now see that it lacks one very important feature of a typical variable (to wit, a *name*); in that respect, at least, it's something less than

---

[8] Remember that *object* here means a variable (mutable object) specifically. Values (immutable objects), which are never "constructed" but simply exist, can be thought of as serving as their own OIDs; in other words, they're *self-identifying*. (Though I ought to mention in passing that the object literature often talks, confusingly, as if address-style OIDs refer not to variables per se but rather to the values those variables happen to contain. See the section "Values vs. Variables," later.)

a true variable. (On the other hand, it's also more than just plain storage, inasmuch as it does usually have a *type*.)

My second point is related to my first. Given a type (class), OO systems permit the construction of *any number* of individual objects of that type (class). For example, given the type CIRCLE introduced in the overview section earlier, the user is at liberty to construct as many CIRCLE "variables" (mutable objects) as he or she desires: one, two, a hundred, a million, or even none at all. As a direct consequence of this fact, individual CIRCLE "variables" don't—in fact, can't—have names in the usual sense but are instead distinguished by address (OID), as we've already seen.

Now, it's interesting, and relevant, to note that an exact parallel to the foregoing state of affairs can be found in PL/I once again, in the form of what are called *based* variables. Consider the following PL/I code fragment (I've numbered the lines for purposes of subsequent reference):

```
1   DECLARE 1 CIRCLE BASED ,
2             2 CENTER ... ,
3             2 RADIUS ... ;
4   DECLARE C_PTR POINTER ;

5   ALLOCATE CIRCLE SET ( C_PTR ) ;
6   C_PTR -> CENTER = some center value ;
7   C_PTR -> RADIUS = some radius value ;
```

Explanation:

- Lines 1-3 declare a based variable—actually a based *structure* variable, in this example—called CIRCLE, with components CENTER and RADIUS. The specification BASED means that the declaration is really just a template; no storage will be allocated at compile time, it'll be allocated at run time instead (see line 5).

- Line 4 declares a regular (nonbased) variable, a pointer variable called C_PTR. Storage *is* allocated for this variable at compile time.

- Line 5 (executed at run time) allocates storage for an unnamed CIRCLE variable—that is, an unnamed variable whose structure conforms to the template defined in lines 1-3. It also returns a pointer to that storage— equivalently, to that unnamed variable—and places it in the pointer variable C_PTR.

■ Lines 6-7 (also executed at run time) then assign values to the CENTER and RADIUS components of the particular CIRCLE variable that the pointer variable C_PTR currently happens to point to.

The parallels with OO are obvious: The based variable declaration for CIRCLE corresponds to an object class definition; ALLOCATE CIRCLE is the corresponding constructor; access to a given CIRCLE variable by means of its address corresponds to access to a given object by means of its OID; construction (storage allocation) and initialization are logically distinct operations. And, of course, storage allocation can be done for any number of individual unnamed CIRCLE variables, each with its own address, just as in OO any number of individual unnamed objects can be constructed, each with its own OID.

Why bother with these OO-PL/I parallels? Well, in his book *Concepts of Programming Languages* [11], Robert Sebesta refers to variables like the allocated CIRCLE variable in the foregoing example as "explicit dynamic variables," and explains what he means by this term as follows:

> Explicit dynamic variables are *nameless objects* whose *storage is allocated* ... by *explicit run-time directives* ... These variables *can only be referenced through pointer variables* (my italics).

And he goes on to say:

> Explicit dynamic variables [and the corresponding pointers] are often used for dynamic structures, such as linked lists and trees, which need to grow and shrink during execution. Such structures can be conveniently built using pointers and explicit dynamic variables.

In other words, just as pointers and explicit dynamic variables can be used to build and maintain "dynamic structures" in programming languages like PL/I, so OIDs and objects can be used to build and maintain such structures in OO. And OO databases n particular do frequently include such structures.

Is this, then, a serious logical distinction between OO and relational systems? No, it isn't. Relational systems can and do involve dynamic structures also. The difference is that in the relational case those structures are built and maintained using, not pointers, but rather the mechanisms—keys and matching foreign keys—prescribed by the relational model. There's no *logical* need to use pointers instead of keys for such a purpose. And there are good reasons not to! To quote Sebesta again [11]:

> The disadvantages of explicit dynamic variables [and pointers ... include] *the difficulty of using them correctly* (my italics again).

To be specific, pointers lead to pointer chasing, and pointer chasing is notoriously error prone. Indeed, it's precisely this aspect of object systems that gives rise to the criticisms, sometimes heard, to the effect that such systems "look like CODASYL warmed over."

By the way, it's worth noting in passing that Codd would certainly agree with the foregoing assessment. When he first defined the relational model, he very deliberately excluded pointers. And in his book *The Relational Model for Database Management Version 2* [6], he explains why:

> It is safe to assume that all kinds of users [including end users in particular] understand the act of comparing values, but that relatively few understand the complexities of pointers. The relational model is based on this fundamental principle ... [The] manipulation of pointers is more bug-prone than is the act of comparing values, even if the user happens to understand the complexities of pointers.

In view of the foregoing, it's curious that so many people seem to regard OIDs as the sine qua non of the object model.[9] For example, *The Object-Oriented Database System Manifesto* [1] says "Thou shalt support object identity"—but it doesn't give any *logical* justification for such an edict. Likewise, Jim Melton [10] says "References in the form of object identifiers are the key [*sic!*] to the object oriented paradigm," but he provides no evidence in support of this strong claim.[10] And in a useful annotated and comprehensive anthology of writings on the subject [2] compiled by Declan Brady (containing "the substance of everything I've managed to unearth on the [subject] of OIDs"), numerous similar assertions can be found. So far as I can see, however, none of those assertions is accompanied by any logical supporting arguments.

---

[9] Personally, I'd have said rather that user defined types were the sine qua non. For the record, therefore, let me state explicitly here that in *The Third Manifesto* [7] Hugh Darwen and I take the position that user defined types can be supported perfectly well without OIDs. Moreover, we concur with Sebesta and Codd that OIDs can be positively harmful and therefore expressly proscribe them. We see no need to burden users with obsolete technology.

[10] The implicit claim, that is, that whatever useful functionality OO might be thought to provide can't be obtained in some way that doesn't require OIDs.

Of course, OO advocates will probably counter with the argument that OIDs are needed for performance reasons. As I've written elsewhere, however, everything to do with performance is, first and foremost, an implementation matter!—it shouldn't be part of a (or the) data model. Anyone who thinks otherwise is seriously confused over the distinction between a data model and its implementation. Let me elaborate:

- The argument that pointers or OIDs are needed is usually based on a claim that following a pointer is more efficient than performing a join based on a key and matching foreign key (or any other join, come to that).

- Well, let's agree for the sake of the argument that following pointers is efficient (though I think there are situations in which this claim is almost certainly invalid). But the point is—again as I've said elsewhere—*there's absolutely no reason why key-to-matching-foreign-key relationships shouldn't be implemented by pointers at the physical level.* (I know they typically aren't implemented that way in today's SQL products, but that's a criticism of those products, not a criticism of the relational model. At least one system, the IBM Starburst prototype, does provide such a pointer based implementation [3].)

In other words, (1) implementing such relationships by pointers is very different from (2) exposing such pointers in the data model. Even if (1) is a good idea, it doesn't follow that (2) is a good idea, and of course it categorically isn't. We *must* keep logical and physical concepts distinct, and not get confused over the two levels in our debates; we've learned the hard way—or at least some of us have—what happens when this principle is violated.

VALUES *vs.* VARIABLES

The fact that, at least in some object models, object construction and object initialization are separate operations lends further weight to my thesis that objects more closely resemble storage areas than they do variables. In fact, an argument could be made that—just like assembler language!—the object model is rather unclear on the distinction between a value and a variable. The following quote, which is taken from a tutorial by Zdonik and Maier on object databases [13], is not atypical:[11]

> We distinguish the declared type of a variable from ... the type of the object that is the current value of the variable ... We distinguish objects from values ... A *mutator* [is an operation such that it's] possible to observe its effect on some object.

Observe that:

- The phrase "the object that is the current value of the variable" clearly implies that an object is a value. (At least, it implies that some values are objects, and hence that some objects are values.)

- The assertion that "[we] distinguish objects from values" clearly implies that an object isn't a value. (More precisely, it implies that no objects are values, and hence that no values are objects.)

- The existence of mutators—that is, operators that have an "effect on some object," or in other words update some object—clearly implies that the object in question is a variable; so some objects, at least, are variables.

So what *is* an object? The sad fact is that the picture is not nearly as clearcut as my earlier characterizations (i.e., of mutable objects as variables and immutable ones as values) would suggest. For this reason, I recommend in all sincerity that if you ever find yourself embarking on a discussion of objects, you should spend some time up front making sure that all parties to the discussion agree on exactly what the term "object" means. Otherwise, quite frankly, you're likely to be wasting your time.

Let me now explain my remark to the effect that the object model resembles assembler language in its lack of clarity over the "value vs. variable" distinction. For definiteness, I'll take IBM System/360 Assembler Language as the basis for my discussion. That language provides two instructions, DC and DS, that might be thought of, loosely, as "specify value" and "declare variable," respectively. But what they really do, both of them, is *allocate storage*; the only difference is that DC ("define constant") places a specified initial value in the

---

[11] I've quoted and deconstructed this text elsewhere too (in Chapter 6 of the present book in particular). Please forgive the repetition.

allocated storage area, whereas DS ("define storage") doesn't. Subsequently, however, the contents of the allocated storage area can be changed at any time, regardless of whether it was allocated via DC or DS. Once again, I think the parallels with the object model are obvious; once again, in other words, I think it's clear that the object model is closer to a storage model than it is to a data model.

Note: Assembler language and the object model do both include the notion of a *literal*, of course (called a "self-defining term" in IBM System/360 Assembler Language). But a literal isn't a value!—it's a *symbol* that *denotes* a value. Thus, to say that assembler language and some object model do at least have a clear notion of literals isn't to say that they have a clear notion of values per se (and in the case of some object models, at least, they certainly don't [4]).

A LITTLE SPECULATION

Note: The material of this section previously appeared in somewhat different form in reference [8].

Perhaps I should digress for a moment and consider the question of just why the object model and the relational model are so different—i.e., why the object model is really, as I've said, a storage model rather than a data model per se. It seems to me likely that the difference in question reflects a difference in origins: more precisely, a difference between the origins of object technology, on the one hand, and database technology on the other. That is, it seems to me that OO databases grew out of a desire on the part of OO application programmers, for a variety of application-specific reasons, to keep their application-specific objects in persistent memory. That "persistent memory" might perhaps be regarded as a database, but the important point is that it was indeed application-specific; it wasn't a shared, general purpose database, intended to be suitable for applications that might not even have been foreseen at the time when that "database" (if I might use that term) was defined. As a consequence, many features that database professionals regard as essential were simply not requirements in the OO world, at least not originally. To be specific, there was little perceived need for:

■ Data sharing across applications

- Physical data independence

- Ad hoc query

- Views and logical data independence

- Application-independent, declarative integrity constraints

- Data ownership and a flexible security mechanism

- Concurrency control

- A general purpose catalog

- Application-independent database design

These requirements all surfaced later, after the basic idea of storing objects in a database was first conceived; thus, they all constituted "add-on features" as far as the original object model was concerned. (I might mention in passing too that some of those features—for example, views and ad hoc query—turned out to be quite difficult to add to the original model. The reasons for this state of affairs are beyond the scope of the present discussion, however.)

One important consequence of all of the foregoing is that there truly is a difference in kind between an object DBMS and a relational DBMS. In fact, I don't think an object DBMS is really a DBMS at all!—at least, not in the same sense that a relational DBMS is a DBMS. For consider:

- A relational DBMS comes ready for use. As soon as the system is installed, in other words, users (both application programmers and end users) can start building databases, writing applications, running queries, and so on.

- An object DBMS, by contrast, is more like a kind of *DBMS construction kit*. When it's originally installed, it's *not* available for immediate use by application programmers and end users. Instead, it must first be tailored by suitably skilled technicians, who must define the necessary classes and methods, etc. (The system will provide a set of building blocks—class library maintenance tools, method compilers, etc.—for this purpose.) Only when that tailoring activity is complete will the system be available for use by application programmers and end users; in other words, the result of that tailoring will indeed more closely resemble a DBMS in the more familiar sense of the term.

■ Note, however, that the resultant "tailored" DBMS will be application-specific—it might, for example, be suitable for CAD/CAM applications, but be essentially useless for, e.g., medical applications. In other words, it still won't be a general purpose DBMS, in the same sense that a relational DBMS is a general purpose DBMS.

Please understand that I'd be the first to admit that the foregoing speculations might be wide of the mark. However, they do seem to me to explain some of the differences in emphasis that can be observed between the object and relational models, and between object and relational DBMSs and databases—or between what might be called the object and relational database worlds.

SUMMARY

In this chapter, I've tried to show that the object model can usefully be thought of as a storage model rather than a data model. I've also speculated on some of the reasons for this state of affairs. Among other things, I've tried to show that:

■ Although mutable objects can be thought of in some ways as variables, they also behave in other ways more like areas of storage.

■ Unlike variables (but like storage), mutable objects are nameless and so must be distinguished, or identified, by addresses (OIDs).

■ Object constructors are basically storage allocators. OIDs are addresses or pointers. Constructing an object might not even initialize that object—suggesting, again, that it's really just storage that's being "constructed" (or allocated, rather).

■ However, OIDs are logically unnecessary (as is obvious, in fact, since the relational model manages perfectly well without them).

- The object model doesn't distinguish clearly between values and variables (as is perhaps to be expected of a storage model, but not of a data model).

- The object model allows the database to contain arbitrarily complex data structures but *exposes them to the user*, thereby undermining data independence.

With respect to this last point, I have to ask (as I did earlier in connection with OIDs): What's the *logical* justification for this "anything goes" approach? In fact, let me close with one final observation that touches on this very issue (taken from a review by Adrian Larner [9] of a collection of papers on OO):

> [In a contribution to the collection,] Zdonik states, correctly, that in the OO paradigm, "data and programs are not ... separate ... they are designed, implemented, and used together." Yes: and *maintained* together, any change to shared data requiring modification of all the programs that use it, however irrelevant to them the data change might be. We were originally driven to use databases to avoid the costs of this unproductive maintenance ... *OO and database are incompatible*" (my italics).

ACKNOWLEDGMENTS

I'm grateful to Declan Brady and Hugh Darwen for their careful review of earlier drafts of the paper that gave rise to this chapter and their many helpful comments.

REFERENCES

1. Malcolm Atkinson et al.: "The Object-Oriented Database System Manifesto," Proc. First International Conference on Deductive and Object-Oriented Databases, Kyoto, Japan, 1989 (Elsevier Science, 1990).

2. Declan Brady: Private communication (July 1st, 1996).

3. Michael Carey et al.: "An Incremental Join Attachment for Starburst," Proc. 16th Int. Conference on Very Large Data Bases, Brisbane, Australia, August 13th-16th, 1990.

4. R. G. G. Cattell and Douglas K. Barry (eds.): *The Object Database Standard: ODMG 3.0*, 5th edition (Morgan Kaufmann, 2000).

5. J. Craig Cleaveland: *An Introduction to Data Types* (Addison-Wesley, 1986).

6. E. F. Codd: *The Relational Model for Database Management Version 2* (Addison-Wesley, 1990).

7. C. J. Date and Hugh Darwen: *Databases, Types, and the Relational Model: The Third Manifesto*, 3rd edition (Addison-Wesley, 2007).

8. C. J. Date: *An Introduction to Database Systems*, 8th edition (Addison-Wesley, 2004).

9. Adrian Larner: Review of Asuman Dogac et al. (eds.), *Advances in Object-Oriented Database Systems*, *BCS Computer Journal 38*, No. 10 (October 1995).

10. Jim Melton: "A Shift in the Landscape (Assessing SQL3's New Object Direction)," *Database Programming & Design 9*, No. 8 (August 1996).

11. Robert W. Sebesta: *Concepts of Programming Languages* (Benjamin/Cummings, 1989). *Note:* This book has been through numerous revisions and editions since the 1989 one mentioned here.

12. Michael Stonebraker et al.: "Third Generation Database System Manifesto," *ACM SIGMOD Record 19*, No. 3 (September 1990).

13. Stanley B. Zdonik and David Maier: "Fundamentals of Object-Oriented Databases," in Zdonik and Maier (eds.), *Readings in Object-Oriented Database Systems* (Morgan Kaufmann, 1990).

Chapter 8

Object Identifiers vs.

Relational Keys

This chapter presents further arguments in support of the position, already introduced—indeed, argued at some length—in the previous chapter, to the effect that object identifiers (aka object IDs or OIDs) have no place in an abstract data model.

Note: As in that previous chapter, I use the term "data model" here to mean an abstract, self-contained, logical definition of the data structures, data operators, and so forth, that together make up the abstract machine with which users interact; I don't use it to mean merely a model of the persistent data of some particular enterprise, or in other words the conceptual or logical design of some particular "enterprise database."

Publishing history: This is a revised version of a paper that first appeared—with the subtitle "Object IDs Considered Harmful"—in my book Relational Database Writings 1994-1997 (Addison-Wesley, 1998). This version copyright © C. J. Date 2022.

I used to teach a regular seminar on objects, relations, and object / relational databases. During one particular offering of that seminar [6], the question arose (as indeed it almost always did): What's the *logical* argument for object IDs? That is, if we try to come up with an abstract, formal, logical, rigorous, and coherent definition of some kind of "object model," what part do object IDs (OIDs for short) have to play in that model? *Do* they have a part to play?[1]

---

[1] I assume for the purposes of what follows that terms such as *object* and *object orientation* (*OO* for short) are all well defined and well understood. My reasons for often placing the term "object model" in quotation marks are explained in reference [7].

Well, it's clear that if, as many authorities believe, OIDs are effectively just pointers in another guise, then there's certainly a performance argument that can be made for them. But, of course, performance is an implementation matter, it's nothing to do with the model; in other words, the performance argument is really an argument for including OIDs, or something like them, in the implementation, not in the model. So are there any other arguments in favor of OIDs, apart from the performance one?

USER KEYS

To approach this question, let's start by thinking about how data is identified and referenced in the relational world (since, of course, identifying and referencing data is what object IDs are used for in the object world—more particularly, in the object model). Well, in the relational world we use keys as identifiers, and we use matching foreign keys as references to the data identified by those keys.[2] And since, typically, the actual values assumed by those keys and foreign keys are (a) initially assigned by human users, and (b) subsequently controlled and maintained—i.e., possibly even updated—by human users, let's call them *user keys* for short.

Now, it's well known that, at least in the absence of suitable discipline, user keys can suffer from certain problems. To be specific:

■ User keys might be "intelligent."

■ User keys might be nonuniform.

■ User keys might be subject to change.

■ User keys might be composite.

■ An "obvious" user key might not exist.

■ More than one "obvious" user key might exist.

---

[2] In practice we often use primary keys specifically, but I no longer believe in the need to choose one key out of several (when there's a choice, that is) and label it "primary," thereby somehow making it "more equal than the others." See reference [8] for further discussion.

To elaborate:

■ *User keys might be "intelligent"*: The term "intelligent key" refers to a user key that doesn't just act as a unique identifier but carries along with it certain encoded information about the thing identified. For example, the International Standard Book Number (ISBN), which might very likely serve as a user key in a bibliographic database, includes among other things (a) a publisher ID, (b) a code indicating the language in which the book is written, and (c) a variety of other information. The problem with such keys, of course, is that users can come to rely on their internal structure—possibly even on specific values of components of that structure (e.g., 2 = French) as well. Consequently, a change in either the structure or the values of such a key can lead to application program failures, or significant program maintenance efforts, or both.[3]

■ *User keys might be nonuniform*: Distinct user keys (i.e., identifiers of distinct "entity types") can be, and in fact usually are, of different types.[4] This fact can cause difficulties whenever it becomes necessary, for whatever reason, to create a relvar with an attribute containing references to entities of two or more distinct types.[5] For example, consider a relvar that gives the IDs of all components—CDs, sheet music, cassette tapes, vinyl albums, etc.—in a certain music collection.

■ *User keys might be subject to change*: The relational model deliberately includes no prohibition against updating keys, because there are occasions when such updates do have to be done. For example, it's a fact that the scientific names of plants and animals do change from time to time as classification schemes are revised; more mundanely, a person's name might have previously been recorded with an incorrect spelling; and both of these examples could lead in database terms to the need to do a key update.

---

[3] ISBNs are an example here too—they used to be ten characters long but now they're thirteen (this change occurred on January 1st, 2007).

[4] By "different types" here, I mean, very specifically, different *tuple* types. The point isn't recognized often enough (at least not explicitly) that keys are always *sets* of attributes—even if the set in question contains just a single attribute, as it often does—and hence that key values are always tuples.

[5] A relvar is a relation variable, or in other words a variable whose values are relation values. See Chapters 5 and 6 for further discussion.

The trouble is, of course, that a key update will often require one or more cascaded foreign key updates as well in order to maintain the integrity of the data, and—for a variety of reasons—those cascaded updates might not get done. As a consequence, the database can be in a state that, despite the fact that it's internally consistent (in the sense that it satisfies all system known integrity constraints), doesn't faithfully reflect reality. For example, a change to a company's product numbering scheme might cause the database to show, incorrectly, that customer C owns product Y instead of product X (I've been a victim of this particular error myself).

■ *User keys might be composite*: A composite key is a key that consists of two or more attributes. Though certainly legal—in fact , of course, they're sometimes logically necessary—such keys can give rise to a variety of problems, problems that I've discussed in detail in several other places (see, e.g., references [9] and [10]. One such problem is caused by the fact that such keys can overlap; for example, the column combinations $\{A,B\}$ and $\{B,C\}$ might each constitute a key for a given relvar, with the consequence that updating one of the two can have the side effect of updating the other as well (and side effects, of course, are generally best avoided).

■ *An "obvious" user key might not exist*: Sometimes we need to record information (possibly just existence information) for certain real world entities that don't have any "obvious" user key. For example, a person's name isn't unique, in general (nor even is the combination "name plus birth date"). What then is the "obvious" user key for identifying persons?

■ *More than one "obvious" user key might exist*: Some real world entities have more than one "obvious" user key (this problem is the inverse of the previous one, in a sense). As a trivial example, the very same entity might be identified as "C. J. Date" in some contexts and "Chris Date" in others. One consequence is that the system might not be able to recognize that two distinct key values in fact identify the same entity (hence the well known junk mail problem, in which some unfortunate person receives numerous copies of the same irritating piece of marketing material).

SURROGATE KEYS

Of course there's a way to avoid the problems associated with user keys (or many of those problems, at any rate), and that's to use *surrogate keys* (*surrogates* for short) instead. A surrogate key is still a key in the usual relational sense, but it's one that additionally has the following properties:

- It's not composite—i.e., it consists of just a single attribute, never a combination of two or more attributes.

- Its values serve *solely* as surrogates (hence the name) for the real world entities they stand for. In other words, such values serve merely to represent the fact that the corresponding entities exist—they carry no additional information or meaning whatsoever.

- When a new entity is inserted into the database, it's assigned a surrogate key value that's never been used before and will never be used again, even if the entity in question is subsequently deleted.

Also, it would be nice if the operation of assigning a surrogate key value to a new entity could be performed by the system instead of the user (i.e., at "create entity" time), in order to save the user from the burden of having to invent the necessary "meaningless" values. But whether they're generated by the system or by some user has nothing to do with the basic idea of surrogate keys as such. Though I note in passing that an argument could be made that many real world user keys are essentially just surrogates anyway—think of employee numbers, department numbers, musical opus numbers, etc.—and these particular surrogates are obviously generated by some user, not by the system.

Now let's take a look at how surrogate keys can help with the user key problems listed in the previous section:

- *Intelligent keys*: Surrogate keys aren't intelligent, so this problem goes away by definition.

   Note: As an aside, I remark that the arguments against "intelligent keys" actually apply essentially unchanged to all attributes, not just to keys. Thus, to say that "the problem goes away" with surrogate keys is a little misleading, in a sense. Further discussion of this issue would take us too far away from the main point of this chapter, however.

- *Nonuniformity*: Since surrogates aren't intelligent, there doesn't seem to be much reason to have distinct surrogate types for distinct entity types. And if we don't, then all surrogate values in the entire database will be "uniform," so the problems caused by lack of such uniformity won't arise.

- *Subject to change*: Since surrogate keys represent existence and nothing else, there's no reason ever to update them, and hence no need ever to perform cascaded updates on matching foreign keys. Thus, the problems caused by such updates don't arise. (The point here is that even if there are still user keys in the database—which, as we'll see below, there almost certainly will be in practice—those keys won't ever need to be used as foreign keys. That is, all referencing inside the database can always be done in terms of surrogates; and if it is, then there won't ever be any need to cascade a key update to a matching foreign key.)

- *Composite keys*: Surrogate keys aren't composite, so these problems go away by definition.

- *No "obvious" key*: Surrogate keys take care of this problem, obviously.

- *Too many "obvious" keys*: Surrogate keys can help with this problem as well, but only to some extent. To be specific, if (a) entity *e* is given surrogate *s*, and (b) we adopt the discipline that all foreign key references within the database to entity *e* are via surrogate *s*, then (c) the system will certainly be able to recognize that two such references do in fact identify the same entity. On the other hand, if the end user (a) asserts on one occasion that there's an entity "C. J. Date" (assigned surrogate *s1*), and (b) asserts on another occasion that there's an entity "Chris Date" (assigned surrogate *s2*), then (c) there's no way the system can tell, unaided, that *s1* and *s2* do in fact identify the same entity. But this problem is intrinsic: It's nothing to do with the question of whether we use surrogates or user keys (or OIDs, come to that!—see later).

To sum up: Surrogates are a good idea (frequently, if not invariably—see below). More specifically, surrogate keys can help avoid many of the problems that occur with ordinary undisciplined user keys. It follows that if OIDs are basically just surrogate keys, nothing more and nothing less, then there's a good prima facie case for including them in our "object model"; in other words, we'll have found some logical arguments for object IDs. So the question becomes: *Are* OIDs in fact the same thing as surrogate keys?

Before I try to answer this question, there are a few further points I'd like to clarify:

■ First, surrogates, even when they're a good thing, don't make user keys unnecessary. For one thing, even if all identification and referencing *inside the database* is in terms of surrogates, it's still typically user keys that we use *outside* the database (i.e., in the real world). So at the very least there needs to be some way of mapping between user key and surrogate values (unless those user keys are themselves the surrogates, of course, a possibility noted earlier), and of course that mapping is performed inside the system. In other words, user keys are still needed for interaction with the outside world.

■ Second, consider the case of the familiar suppliers-and-parts database. Suppose relvars S (suppliers) and P (parts) have keys {SNO} and {PNO}, respectively, as usual—but suppose also that SNO and PNO values are surrogates. Now consider relvar SP ("shipments"), which indicates which suppliers supply which parts. What's the key for SP? If we take it (as we usually do) to be the combination {SNO,PNO}, then that key, though it does *involve* two surrogates, isn't itself a surrogate key, it's a user key. As such, it might need updating!—e.g., consider what happens if all shipments from supplier S*x* are taken over by supplier S*y* instead.

    Note: Of course, there's nothing to stop us *introducing* a surrogate, SPNO say, as a key for shipments. But even if we do, it won't alter the fact that {SNO,PNO} is a key as well, and the foregoing remarks will still apply, mutatis mutandis.

■ Finally, you should be aware that there are sometimes good arguments— logical arguments, that is—for not using surrogate keys inside the database after all [9]. And it's relevant to observe that those arguments apply to OIDs also.

The whole question of user keys vs. surrogates is explored in depth in references [9] and [12].

OBJECT IDENTIFIERS

Back to our question ("Are OIDs the same thing as surrogate keys?"). Well, here are some logical differences between the two concepts (this might not be a complete list):

- Surrogates in a relational database are represented the same way as everything else: namely, as values of attributes in relations. By contrast, OIDs in an object database are represented *differently* from everything else, with the result that—by definition, and regardless of the advantages, if any, that might accrue from that difference—there's the inevitable *dis*advantage that object data is more complicated than relational data, involving as it does at least one additional concept.

- As a consequence of the previous point, access to relational data by surrogate is performed in exactly the same way as access by anything else: namely, associatively. By contrast, access to object data by OID is quite different from access by anything else (if indeed access by anything else is even supported, which in practice it might not be). In other words, surrogates are visible to the user, but OIDs aren't (that is, the user never sees OID values, and OID "attributes"—if I might be permitted to use such a term—don't behave at all like regular attributes).

- Following on from the previous point: In fact, of course, OIDs are really *values of type address*—in other words, they're *pointers*—and object databases necessarily support the data type *address*. Relational databases don't. *Note:* By *address* here, I don't necessarily mean a hardware address, of course. The idea is simply that every object can be thought of as having a location of some kind, and that location in turn has some kind of unique identifier which we call the OID of the object in question, and which we use to distinguish that object from all others. In other words, we can certainly *think* of that OID as an address, in the usual sense of that term, regardless of how OIDs might be implemented. That's the object model.

- It follows from the previous point that the object model fundamentally requires two operators, usually called referencing and dereferencing, that the relational model doesn't need. The *referencing* operator takes an object and returns its address (OID). The *dereferencing* operator takes an address (OID) and returns the object addressed by that OID. Incidentally, note that while these two operations are very much the kind of thing we expect programmers to be able to deal with, they're very much *not* the kind of thing we expect end users to be able to deal with (or perhaps even understand). *Note:* In practice the referencing and/or dereferencing operations might be performed implicitly—but if so, then in my opinion that just makes an already bad situation worse.

■ Indeed, OIDs really are pointers, at least conceptually. And one problem with pointers is that they *point*; that is, they have *directionality*, and they have a single, specific target. Surrogates, by contrast, are *regular data values*: A given surrogate is simultaneously connected, logically speaking, not only to the entity in question but also to all entities that reference that entity, no matter where in the database the representatives of those referencing entities might happen to be found. In other words, surrogates (like all values in a relational database, but unlike pointers) are "multiway associative." As a simple example of this latter point, the department tuple for department *d* is logically connected to all employee tuples for employees in department *d*, and each of those employee tuples is logically connected to all of the others and also to the department tuple for department *d*.

■ To repeat, OIDs really are pointers, at least conceptually. And so we have here a major difference between the object model and the relational model. When Codd first defined the relational model, he very deliberately excluded pointers. To quote reference [4]:

> It is safe to assume that all kinds of users [including end users in particular] understand the act of comparing values, but that relatively few understand the complexities of pointers. The relational model is based on this fundamental principle ... [The] manipulation of pointers is more bug-prone than is the act of comparing values, even if the user happens to understand the complexities of pointers.

To be specific, pointers lead to pointer chasing, and pointer chasing is notoriously error prone. Indeed, it's this aspect of object systems that gives rise to the criticisms sometimes heard to the effect that such systems "look like CODASYL warmed over."

In other words, OIDs do perform some of the same functions as surrogates, but they're most certainly not just "surrogates pure and simple"—they carry a lot of additional baggage with them. Furthermore, I don't think anyone can seriously argue with the claim that the baggage in question is motivated by performance considerations (i.e., by considerations that are more properly part of the implementation, not the model). And so we're still faced with our original question: What's the *logical* argument for object IDs?

IDENTITY vs. EQUALITY

One answer sometimes offered in response to this latter question is that OIDs allow us to make a distinction between *identity* and *equality*. Two objects are said to be identical if and only if they have the same OID (in other words, if and only if they're in fact the very same object); two objects are said to be equal if and only if they have the same value, regardless of whether they have the same OID. Note that by these definitions identity implies equality, while the reverse implication doesn't hold.

Note added in this rewrite: I think I understand the foregoing answer (and can see what's wrong with it!) better now than I did and could when I first encountered it. More generally, this whole area is one where my own understanding has, I hope and do believe, improved considerably over the years. All of which is just a way of saying I no longer agree—if I ever really did—with the claims of that previous paragraph. My current take goes like this:

1. Two **values** are *equal* if and only if they're the very same value; otherwise they're *distinct*.

2. Two **values** are *identical* if and only if they're equal. In other words, I consider identity and equality to be one and the same thing (identical concepts, in fact).

3. Two **values** can be distinct and yet *equivalent*, given some appropriate definition of equivalence. For example, two distinct pennies would usually be regarded as equivalent (note in particular that they're almost certainly

interchangeable). For another example, two distinct copies of the same book might be regarded as equivalent, in appropriate circumstances.

4. Two **variables** are equal if and only if they're the very same variable.

5. The previous point notwithstanding, testing two **variables** to see if they contain the same value is usually described as testing to see if they're equal. But I hope you can see that what that sloppy mode of expression really means is: The variables in question are being tested to see if they're *equivalent*—i.e., if they satisfy a certain criterion of equvalence—where the kind of equivalence we're talking about is precisely "having, or containing, the same value."

6. Turning now to the OO world, it seems to me there's some—presumably unintentional—sleight of hand going on ... In fact, it seems to me, somewhat ironically, that in OO "identity" doesn't quite mean identity! To be specific, the notion of two **objects** being identical (i.e., equal) is interpreted in OO as "having the same OID." Perhaps more to the point, the notion of "*not* being identical" is interpreted as "*not* having the same OID." And since an object's OID is distinct from the object as such, two objects can in fact have the same value—thereby corresponding to the same entity in the real world—and yet not be identical as far as OO is concerned.

Well ... let me restate the message of the foregoing paragraph in more conventional terms (as always, what's really going on becomes so much clearer if we talk in terms of values and variables instead of "objects)":

6a. *"Objects being identical" is interpreted as "having the same OID":* "Objects" here has to be understood as meaning variables (since OIDs are addresses and it's variables, not values, that have addresses). And yes, two variables are identical (unsurprisingly) if and only if they have the same address—i.e., if and only if they're the same variable.

6b. *"Objects not being identical" is interpreted as "not having the same OID":* OK, two variables are distinct if and only if they have different addresses (again unsurprisingly). But distinct variables can be "equivalent," in the sense that they have the same value!—i.e., they can "compare equal," to use the common but sloppy way of describing such a situation.

But this is all screamingly obvious! So why all the fuss? What's the big deal? One of the attendees on that original seminar of mine [6], Tony Blair (not his real name), posted a couple of questions to this effect on the Internet that evening, and I'd like to present, and offer some comments on, the responses he got. First let's take a look at the exact form of those questions.

BLAIR'S QUESTIONS

Here's the text of Blair's original message:

> The primary difference between OIDs and relational keys seems to be that OIDs allow one to make a distinction between object equivalence and object identity. I have two questions:
>
> 1. Of what logical significance is such a distinction?
>
> 2. Of what practical significance is such a distinction?
>
> Thanks for any and all opinions.

These questions drew responses from two well known figures in the object world, both of them members of the Object Data Management Group, ODMG. I'll refer to them as Member X and Member Y, respectively. The next two sections below consist largely of text from those responses, together with comments of my own, so labeled. *Note:* Members X and Y were both male, incidentally, which accounts for my occasional use of male pronouns in what follows.

RESPONSE BY ODMG MEMBER X

Member X's response begins thus:

> To make sure we're using words the same way, relational keys can be used as a secondary data structure, managed by the user, with (very slow) joins to find related rows. The relationship is by values stored in the rows.

Comment: I don't know what Member X means when he says "keys can be used as a secondary data structure"—especially when he says they *can* be used that way; how else does he think they "can" be used? Also, joins aren't necessarily "very slow," even in today's possibly somewhat limited SQL products; in fact, such a claim betrays confusion over model vs. implementation (but then such confusion is probably to be expected, given that the object model itself confuses the two). To spell the point out, there's absolutely no reason why, if we accept for the sake of the argument that "pointers are fast," joins can't be *implemented* by pointers. As I've written elsewhere:

> ... (1) implementing [joins] by pointers is very different from (2) exposing such pointers in the data model. The fact that (1) might be a good idea doesn't imply that (2) is a good idea, and of course it categorically isn't. We *must* keep logical and physical concepts distinct, and not get confused over the two levels in our debates.

Be that as it may, Member X continues:

> OIDs are system-created and -managed (unlike keys), are independent of values of the object (unlike keys), and of the location / address of the object, and relate objects (rather than rows ... often an application's object, to be force-fitted into tables, will be split into multiple rows). Also they're much faster (than joins), sometimes orders of magnitude.

Comment: "Independent of the location / address of the object"? I think all this claim means is that OIDs aren't hardware disk addresses (i.e., there's a level of indirection between the two, such as is classically provided by "page and offset" addresses). I still think OIDs are essentially just pointers—because if they're not, then the performance claims ("much faster than joins") don't make much sense.

I also object (pun intended) to the claim that "often an application's object, to be force-fitted into tables, will be split into multiple rows." The problems that design theory (normalization and the rest) is intended to address don't magically go away just because we're dealing with objects instead of relations.

Member X then goes on to offer the following responses to Blair's first question ("Of what logical significance is the distinction between equivalence and identity?"):

> [OIDs] can connect higher-level abstractions (objects, not rows).

Comment: There seems to be some confusion here over what "higher level" means. Surely objects are at a lower level of abstraction than rows (or tuples) are, not a higher level one, since they correspond (loosely speaking) to *components* of a row (or tuple). What's more, those components are "connected" (indeed, connected very simply) by the very fact that they're all part of the same tuple—it's the tuple that's doing the "connecting." See reference [5], where this position is articulated and substantiated in detail.

[OIDs] can maintain an identity concept independent of value and location.

Comment: "Independent of value"? This just means that OIDs can be thought of (in part) as surrogates. "Independent of location"? Well, user keys are at least as "independent of location" as OIDs are, and quite possibly more so.

[OIDS] are automatically managed.

Comment: "Automatic management" is an implementation detail, which in any case might equally well apply to surrogates too, as noted earlier.

[OIDs] are always present, and therefore can be relied upon for other parts of the DBMS or application.

Comment: I'm not entirely sure what Member X means here. However, a colleague, Declan Brady, makes the possibly relevant observation in reference [2] that "it's a fundamental mistake not to bother to distinguish objects *logically* just because the system does it *physically* ... [The object community] fails to take account of how *users* distinguish objects" (somewhat paraphrased). In other words, how does the user—the real user, that is, who has no knowledge whatsoever of OIDs—distinguish between two objects that are equal in all respects except for having different OIDs?

Member X then offers the following responses to Blair's second question ("Of what practical significance is the distinction between equivalence and identity?"):

[OIDs are] faster (sometimes orders of magnitude).

Comment: Faster than what? Keys, presumably. If so, then this response again betrays confusion between model and implementation (quite apart from the fact that it seems to have nothing to do with Blair's question, which, to repeat, was about equivalence vs. identity, not OIDs vs. keys).

[OIDs] often support many-to-many relationships.

Comment: So do keys. I think they do it better, too. (By the way, what exactly does that "often" mean? Is Member X just saying OIDs *can* be used to support such relationships? If so, why didn't he say so?)

[OIDs] often support bidirectional relationships.

Comment: So do keys. I think they do it better, too. *Note:* Actually I'm not sure I agree with Member X's claim here anyway, given that (as I put it earlier) pointers *point*—that is, they have *directionality*, and they have a single, specific target (meaning that one "bidirectional relationship" has to involve two distinct OIDs). And again I have to wonder about that "often."

[OIDs are] easier to use (no need to create, insert, manage foreign keys, do joins, write stored procedures for referential integrity, etc.).

Comment: I dispute these claims, very strongly! See Chapter 23 ("A Cradle-to-Grave Example") of my book *An Introduction to Database Systems* [8] for evidence in support of my position here.

[OIDs] allow direct mapping of software objects to real world entities that have identity (customers, products, etc.).

Comment: I dispute the suggestion that (e.g.) customers have identities, if by "identities" Member X means anything resembling an OID. To quote Brady again [2]: "I for one don't know where the chassis number is stamped on a human being!"

[OIDs] form the basis of several other features often found in ODBMSs, including:

    a. Distribution (transparent access to objects in any database on any server, even as objects are moved)

Comment: Keys support distribution too, and I think they do it better.

b.   Relationships (see above)

Comment: Keys support relationships too, and I think they do it better.

c.   Versions (the entire concept of versioning is to take an application-meaningful unit, or object, and track the changes of its state ... so it requires a concept of identity independent of state)

Comment: I would have said rather that the concept of versioning depends on a clear concept of *time*, together with (of course) support for that concept. The versioning issue is orthogonal to the question of OIDs vs. keys (and orthogonal to the question of objects vs. relations, come to that).

d.   Composite objects (multiple objects, linked by relationships, that act as a single object)

Comment: The idea of treating combinations (of objects or tuples or whatever) as a single aggregate construct might certainly be useful in certain contexts, but (again) it's orthogonal to the question of OIDs vs. keys. In fact, I think, once again, that keys do it better.

e.   Schema evolution (essentially versioning of types, plus migration [of] instances)

Comment: "Schema evolution" is not only considerably more complex in the object world than it is in the relational world, it's more of a *requirement* [14]. It's more complex because the schema itself is more complex; it's more of a requirement because of the model vs. implementation confusion. Thus, the suggestion that OIDs are somehow more suited to supporting such evolution is founded on a faulty premise.

[OIDs] can provide integration across the features above (e.g., behavior of relationships as one of the objects versions) and with traditional database capabilities (e.g., management of relationships or composites across recovery, concurrency, etc.).

Comment: I have nothing to say here, since I can't make head or tail of what's being claimed.

Well, it seems to me that Member X nowhere answers either of Blair's questions! (Actually Member X seems to interpret those questions as referring to the distinction between OIDs and keys, not to that between equivalence and identity. For that reason many of my comments on Member X's responses were framed in terms of that interpretation, as you might have noticed.)

RESPONSE BY ODMG MEMBER Y

In contrast to Member X, Member Y does at least try to answer the questions Blair asked. (Whether he succeeds in his attempt is another matter.) His response begins thus:

> Great question.

> When considering this problem ... [we called it] the "starry, starry night problem." Consider: You are a painter and you paint a picture of a starry, starry night. Someone comes along and puts it on the copying machine and creates 100 identical copies of it. How do you distinguish the original from the copies? And what value is placed on being able to identify the original from the copies? When is it useful?

Comment: Distinguishing the original from the copies in this example is trivial, of course (unless you think the copying machine produces paintings, not photocopies). The more interesting question is: How do you distinguish one copy from another? Or, rather, *can* you distinguish one copy from another? (The answer to this question, of course, is *yes*—for otherwise you couldn't possibly know you have 100 of them! Quite apart from anything else, in order to count them you'd need to be able to distinguish those you've already counted from those you haven't.) And—pardon the pun—this observation is the key to answering Member Y's last two questions also. Though I feel bound to add, with respect to those questions, that Member Y seems to be getting confused over the logical difference between interchangeability and indistinguishability. Just because two things are *interchangeable*, it doesn't mean they're *indistinguishable*—and in fact they can't be, because you'd have to recognize that they're distinguishable (i.e., distinct from one another) before you could even begin to think about whether they might be interchanged. Think of two pennies, for example.

Anyway, Member Y continues:

> Couldn't some collection of properties of the picture identify it as unique? Or is there some "starry, starry night" essence that makes one unique and the other [*sic*] copies (and thus each copy also unique)? Some people argued that if a value-based comparison of all the properties is done and they are all equal they are equivalent, and if they are equivalent, what matter is it if they are unique—you can't tell them apart anyways!!! If you changed one of the properties, e.g., changed a color of a star from white to yellow, then it wouldn't be equivalent and each could be distinguished. So what is identity anyway? What makes "that copy," "that copy"? Thus, this question of Object Identity and its value is one of the oldest in the OO domain ...

Comment: There seems to be considerable confusion here. First of all, the fact that indeed we *can* distinguish, somehow, between distinct copies as here claimed (and as previously discussed) means, by definition, that each copy certainly does have its own identity. At the same time, however, those copies are all equivalent to one another in a certain sense (and so Member Y is, perhaps, beginning to get at the distinction between equivalence and identity that I discussed earlier). The question is, in just what sense are they equivalent? In order to answer this question, what we need is some *criterion* of equivalence: a criterion, that is, by which we can determine whether or not two given objects are equivalent. That is, there's no such thing as *absolute* equivalence![6] For example, are or are not the following equivalent to one another?—

```
  6    6.0    VI    six    6E0    2+4
```

(etc.)? I hope it's obvious that, given any two of these, it would be possible to define one "criterion of equivalence" according to which they'd be equivalent and another according to which they wouldn't be.

(Perhaps a more telling example is the following. Let object *a* be "ODMG Member Y in 2021" and object *b* be "ODMG Member Y in 2022." Are objects *a* and *b* equivalent or aren't they?)

---

[6] Unless, I suppose you might argue, "absolute equivalence" is just another term for identity, or equality. *Note:* At the risk of confusing you, let me repeat something I said a few pages back—viz., that I do regard identity and equality as one and the same thing. In other words, I regard those concepts themselves as identical, or equal. They're also equivalent, if the criterion for such equivalence is, precisely, identity, or in other words "being the same thing as."

Anyway, Member Y continues:

The theory is: that an OID is independent of the data contained in the object. It provides the unique identity for the object independent of the characteristics or specific properties of any instance. Regardless of how the object changes or even "dies" (is deleted) the OID is never changed and never reused. If two OIDs are compared and are the same then the two objects are said to be identical. If they don't but the contents of the objects are the same, then the objects are said to be equivalent (this distinction is for the readers as you already know this ...).

Comment: Regarding this portion of Member Y's response, Brady [2] offers the following observation (slightly paraphrased here):

I remain unable to reconcile the two ideas that (a) objects correspond closely to the real world and (b) objects have identity independent of their characteristics. In the real world, an object's identity *is* one of its characteristics. Also, in the relational model, we can easily cope with the idea of not updating identifier attributes—just because it's *possible* to update an attribute doesn't mean we have to.

Member Y continues:

The theory for keys is: A key is a unique value or values that when taken together uniquely identify the entity. Now note that I didn't identify tuples or objects, because in fact you can have keys for both ... (a point to discuss in a moment). A key can either be natural and implicit to the data (e.g., a social security number) or can be generated (e.g., department number). OIDs are always generated by the "system" but are "natural" and "implicit" to the object.

   In the relational model the values must be a column or a series of columns which form a compound key. Thus in the relational model, the actual key is physically derived from the properties (columns) of the tuple. Contrast this with an OID, which in every object database, is independent of the contents of the object. This is a critical point. In a relational database, a key is actually used for two things: relationship and, possibly, identity. Two keys (or more specifically a key and a foreign key) can be compared to determine if there is a relationship between the two rows. However, it is also possible, and in fact quite common, that two rows in the same table will have the same key value. If two rows in the same table have the same key but different other columns they are not identical, nor are they equivalent, but they have the same key. If the keys are rich enough compound keys and the data normalized enough, then possibly you can also use the key to uniquely identify a specific tuple. OIDs don't have this problem.

Because they are a separate entity but implicit to the object OIDs can be used for identification, for establishing uniqueness, and for creating direct relationships.

Comment: Actually I find this extract extremely difficult to follow. Let me take it one piece at a time and see if I can make some sense of it.

■ The theory for keys is: A key is a unique value or values that when taken together uniquely identify the entity. Now note that I didn't identify tuples or objects, because in fact you can have keys for both ... A key can either be natural and implicit to the data (e.g., a social security number) or can be generated (e.g., department number). OIDs are always generated by the "system" but are "natural" and "implicit" to the object.

"A key is a value or values that identify [some] entity": Actually it isn't; in the relational world, at any rate, a key is a subset of the heading of some relvar, or in other words a set of attributes of the relvar in question. It's the *value* of a given key that identifies something. Moreover, the "something" that a given key value identifies is a *tuple*: specifically, a tuple in the relation that's the value of the relvar in question. That tuple might indeed correspond to some "entity" in the real world (but it also might not!)[7]—but any such correspondence, or mapping, is necessarily outside the scope of the model as such. And everything I've just said applies, mutatis mutandis, to the object world as well.

Now, you might think the foregoing is just quibbling—but "when transcendental questions are under discussion, be transcendentally clear" (see Chapter 4). All logical differences are big differences.

To continue with the analysis: "I didn't [say whether keys] identify tuples or objects, because in fact you can have keys for both:" Well, it's true, modulo the foregoing criticisms, that "you can have keys for both"— but that's not the point! The point is that, regardless of whether objects have keys, they *always* have OIDs (and it's OIDs that lead to the distinction that's drawn in the object world between equivalence and identity, and it's that distinction that we're trying to understand here). Whether objects also have keys is neither here nor there.

"A key can either be natural and implicit to the data (e.g., a social security number) or can be generated (e.g., department number)": I find the

---

[7] Consider, e.g., the tuples in the result of projecting the relation that's the current value of the employees relvar on just the department number and salary attributes. What "entities in the real world" do those tuples correspond to?

examples cited a little strange (social security numbers are natural?), but all I think Member Y is doing here is confirming that a key can be either a user key or a surrogate. "OIDs are always generated by the system but are natural and implicit to the object": I agree with the first part of this sentence, but the second part, to the extent I understand it, doesn't seem to make any sense at all.

■ In the relational model the values must be a column or a series of columns which form a compound key. Thus in the relational model, the actual key is physically derived from the properties (columns) of the tuple. Contrast this with an OID, which in every object database, is independent of the contents of the object. This is a critical point.

The first sentence here is very sloppy, but I can agree with the intended sense, which I take to be: "In the relational model, a key is a set of attributes (or columns). If that set contains two or more attributes, the key is said to be compound." But "the actual key is physically derived from the properties (columns) of the tuple"—? What Member Y probably means by this rather appallingly written text is that the key value for a given tuple is, precisely, the value of the set of key attributes within the tuple in question—though that tuple does need to be a tuple within the current value of some relvar for that interpretation to make sense.

   "[An] OID ... is independent of the contents of the object": I think there's a tacit assumption here that "object" means a "mutable" object (i.e., a variable) specifically—because "contents of the object" is surely just a sloppy way of saying "value of the object," and "value of a variable" makes sense, and "value of a value" doesn't. But surely a much more straightforward and understandable way of saying what the writer seems to be trying to say would simply be: "The OID of a mutable object is the address of that object."

   "This is a critical point": Agreed.

■ In a relational database, a key is actually used for two things: relationship and, possibly, identity. Two keys (or more specifically a key and a foreign key) can be compared to determine if there is a relationship between the two rows.

Once again the wording is poor—in fact, very poor (at the very least "relationship and, possibly, identity" should be replaced by "identity and, possibly, relationship")—but I can agree with what I take to be the general sense here.

■   However, it is also possible, and in fact quite common, that two rows in the same table will have the same key value.

Astoundingly wrong!—it's not possible, and a fortiori not common. "Two rows in the same table" will *never* have "the same key value" in a relational database (and two rows in the same table will never have the same key value in an SQL database either), because "duplicate key values" is simply a contradiction in terms.

   Note: Of course, SQL databases aren't relational anyway, unless some appropriate discipline is being followed [11], but I'm prepared to overlook that point here—except for the fact that what Member Y *might* have meant by his claim (viz., that two rows in the same table might have the same key value) is merely that a table in an SQL database might not have a key at all. But that's not what he said.

■   If two rows in the same table have the same key but different other columns they are not identical, nor are they equivalent, but they have the same key.

I've no idea what Member Y is trying to say here, unless perhaps he's claiming that—in his hopelessly muddled perception of what relational databases are all about!—it's possible that neither equivalence nor identity applies. But if so, then he clearly doesn't know what he's talking about. In particular (and to say it again), "two rows in the same table" simply *can't* "have the same key [i.e., key value]," by definition—and this is true of SQL databases as well as relational ones.

■   If the keys are rich enough compound keys and the data normalized enough, then possibly you can also use the key to uniquely identify a specific tuple.

I'm getting very close to giving up. The muddle just gets worse and worse. What we have here, in fact, is a prize example of why it's so difficult to have a sensible conversation with OO aficionados.

■   OIDs don't have this problem. Because they are a separate entity but implicit to the object OIDs can be used for identification, for establishing uniqueness, and for creating direct relationships.

Perfectly clear, right? I'm not even going to attempt to make sense of these remarks.

Well, I think I could stop my analysis of Member Y's text right here—but I won't, because there are some further points I need to make; so here goes. That text continues:

> In fact, in either model, you could determine equivalence by comparing all the properties or columns of two objects and rows respectively. That is useful in some applications, especially where value-based comparison is required (lots of queries are exactly that). So now we get into that "starry, starry night" question above (is there a value in identity?) but from a pragmatic side: can you compare "all" the properties— how long will that take? Space and time (performance) are issues in the nontheoretical world.

Comment: Of course I agree performance is an issue, but I certainly don't agree it's an issue only in "the nontheoretical world"! The relational model as such quite deliberately doesn't address the performance issue, but much of the rest of relational theory does (think of optimization theory in particular). In other words, there's much more to relational theory than just the relational model, and some of that additional theory is aimed specifically at the performance question. However, the whole point—or a large part of the point, anyway—of the model vs. implementation separation is precisely to keep performance issues where they belong: namely, out of the model and in the implementation.

Furthermore, I have to say that expressions like "the nontheoretical world" really make me gnash my teeth ... "Nontheoretical" is presumably intended as a synonym for "practical," and is presumably chosen to stress the point that (in the writer's opinion) "theoretical" means "not practical." Indeed, the sentence overall is intended, I'm quite sure, as a putdown. But just because something's theoretical doesn't mean it's not practical! Indeed, in the particular case we're talking about (viz., relational theory), I would argue that theory is very practical indeed. After all, what we have now is an entire industry, worth many billions of dollars a year, totally founded on one great theoretical idea! Every detail of that theoretical idea is there for very solid practical reasons. In fact I'd go further; I'd argue that SQL databases in particular are at their least attractive—and give rise to genuine practical problems—precisely where they depart from the underlying theory.

In this connection, I'd like to offer the following wonderful quote from Leonardo da Vinci's *Notebooks*:

> Those who are enamored of practice without theory are like a pilot who goes into a ship without rudder or compass and never has any certainty where he [*sic*] is going. Practice should always be based upon a sound knowledge of theory.

Anyway, back to Member Y. He continues as follows:

> While in a relational database you're not supposed to change key values, you can and often need to in order to change the relationship. In an object database, you can't change the OID and generally don't want to anyway. Relationships are expressed and changed in a different manner. Keys, however, cannot distinguish identity per se. That depends on how well you normalize the data.
>
> In an [*sic*] object model, you can also create keys for objects based on unique properties. This is very useful, especially for value-based processing (comparing) of object instances (by their properties). The same rules apply for objects as for keys, and a similar object-like "join" can be performed over the values. So one pragmatic difference is that OIDs are largely used for relationship and identity processing and keys are largely used for relationships.

Comment: There are numerous things I could say here, but I'm getting tired ... Just one point: I find it interesting that Member Y refers to the possibility of joining objects. Well, objects belong to "classes"; what class does the result of such an "object join" belong to? Also, classes have "methods" or operators; what methods apply to that result? And what's the OID of that result?

Member Y continues:

> The value of OIDs is:
>
> 1. Objects can directly refer to or reference other objects by knowing their OID or storing it as a value for a property. One side effect of this is that no intermediate entities (tables, objects, etc.) [are required] to define the relationship and no additional processing [is] required to compute what it relates to. Relationships between objects can be "navigated" by following the chain of properties and OIDs contained in them. Overall, for multivalued relationships, and in navigation in general, the performance is orders of magnitude faster than using keys and joins. This reduces space (no intermediate tables), improves performance (especially in highly interrelated or "complex"—that is usually what complex means—models),

and enhances understanding of the relationships (they can be more easily visualized). This is a practical and fundamental point.

2. Only one copy of the specific object exists. Thus if we are talking about the "Tony Blair person instance" there is only one of it, and all objects will refer to that one instance. It is semantically accurate: "that one!" "not this one!" This ... improves model accuracy, reduces data redundancy, eliminates most if not all of the normalization process (as there is in the relational model—all data, no context ...). It also lines up with how we think about people in the real world: There is only one instance of Tony Blair; when he dies there won't be another exactly like him.[8]

3. Having a notion of unique identity in the software model seems natural, as it seems to correspond to the same notion that we have about things in the real world. Object identity is an abstraction. It allows us to easily, naturally, and directly map real-world entities to ... some entity we're modeling in software. This has great value: ease of programming, simplicity of expression, comprehension, enhanced communication, and more accurate software models.

Comment: I'm very tempted to offer a small prize to the reader who finds the most instances of muddled thinking in the foregoing. As for myself, I've already given up on trying to formulate a blow by blow response, as you know ... However, I'd like to comment briefly on the remarks concerning navigation.

Navigation, as that term is being used here, means pointer chasing, and pointer chasing means we're talking about programmer access, not end user access. What the object community seems so often to overlook is that databases aren't supposed to be built for the convenience of programmers but rather for the convenience of end users (who are, I'm tempted to say, the *real* users).

Member Y concludes:

Value-based comparisons are still required and valid for determining a different kind of relationship (e.g., all RED cars) not based on unique identity. OIDs guarantee unique identity. Keys do not.

Comment: More evidence, if you weren't already convinced, that Member Y simply doesn't understand the relational key concept.

---

[8] I have absolutely no comment on this sentence.

In conclusion: At the beginning of this section I said that, in contrast to Member X, Member Y "does at least try to answer the questions Blair asked, concerning equivalence vs. identity. As I think you'll agree, however, he doesn't seem to answer those questions very satisfactorily; in fact, he very quickly veers off course and (like Member X) gets into a series of arguments regarding the alleged superiority of OIDs over keys, arguments that I for one find muddled and unconvincing.

CONCLUDING REMARKS

If the responses by ODMG Members X and Y can be considered indicative of what the object community at large has to say in defense of OIDs, I think we can safely conclude that there *is* no logical argument for them. Given this state of affairs, I'd like to quote some remarks I made on this topic in another paper [7]:

> [It's] curious that so many people seem to regard OIDs as the sine qua non of the object model. For example, *The Object-Oriented Database System Manifesto* [1] says "Thou shalt support object identity"—but it doesn't give any logical justification for such an edict. Likewise, Jim Melton [13] says "References in the form of object identifiers are the key [*sic!*] to the object-oriented paradigm," but he provides no evidence in support of this strong claim. And in a useful annotated and comprehensive anthology of writings on the subject [3], compiled by Declan Brady [and] containing "the substance of everything I've managed to unearth on the [subject] of OIDs," numerous similar assertions can be found. So far as I can see, however, none of those assertions is accompanied by any logical supporting arguments.

I think it's time to remind you of the finding (reported in Chapter 1 of this book's companion volume) that *OIDs and a good model of type inheritance are fundamentally incompatible.*[9] In other words, not only does there seem to be no logical argument in defense of OIDs, there actually seems to be a strong logical argument against them. I rest my case.

---

[9] My book *Type Inheritance and Relational Theory: Subtypes, Supertypes, and Substitutability* (O'Reilly, 2016) explains this finding in detail.

ACKNOWLEDGMENTS

I'd been meaning to write something on the topic of OIDs vs. keys for a long time, but it was Tony Blair's questions on the Internet, and the responses to those questions from ODMG Members X and Y, that finally made me get down to producing something concrete. So I'm grateful to those three individuals for providing the necessary impetus. I'd also like to thank Declan Brady for his helpful comments on the original responses by ODMG Members X and Y, and Declan Brady again and Hugh Darwen for their careful review of earlier drafts of this chapter.

REFERENCES

1. Malcolm Atkinson et al.: "The Object Oriented Database System Manifesto," Proc. First International Conference on Deductive and Object Oriented Databases, Kyoto, Japan, 1989 (Elsevier Science, 1990).

2. Declan Brady: Private communication (May 23rd, 1997).

3. Declan Brady: Private communication (July 1st, 1996). See also Declan Brady: "Relational vs. Object Oriented Database Systems: An Approach to Rapprochement," MSc thesis, School of Computer Applications, Dublin City University, Ireland (January 1997).

4. E. F. Codd: *The Relational Model for Database Management Version 2* (Addison-Wesley, 1990).

5. C. J. Date and Hugh Darwen: *Databases, Types, and the Relational Model: The Third Manifesto*, 3rd edition (Addison-Wesley, 2007).

6. C. J. Date: Live presentation, Washington DC (April 7th-8th, 1997).

7. C. J. Date: "Why the Object Model Isn't a Data Model," Chapter 7 of the present book.

8. C. J. Date: "Primary Keys Are Nice but Not Essential," in *Database Design and Relational Theory: Normal Forms and All that Jazz*, 2nd edition (Apress, 2019).

9. C. J. Date: "Composite Keys," in *Relational Database Writings 1989-1991* (Addison-Wesley, 1992).

10. C. J. Date: "Composite Foreign Keys and Nulls," in *Relational Database Writings 1989-1991* (Addison-Wesley, 1992).

11. C. J. Date: *SQL and Relational Theory: How to Write Accurate SQL Code*, 3rd edition (O'Reilly, 2015).

12. P. Hall, J. Owlett, and S. J. P. Todd: "Relations and Entities," in G. M. Nijssen (ed.): *Modelling in Data Base Management Systems* (Elsevier, 1975).

13. Jim Melton: "A Shift in the Landscape (Assessing SQL3's New Object Direction)," *Database Programming & Design 9*, No. 8 (August 1996).

14. C. M. Saracco: "Writing an Object DBMS Application," Part 1, *InfoDB 7*, No. 4 (Winter 1993/1994); Part 2, *InfoDB 8*, No. 1 (Spring 1994).

Chapter 9

Don't Mix

Pointers and Relations!

It's sometimes suggested that relational databases should be allowed to include pointers to data as well as data per se. This chapter argues against that idea, strongly. To elaborate: When Hugh Darwen and I first started working on The Third Manifesto, one of our goals was to call the community's attention to what we called the **Great Blunder***: viz., the idea of using the obviously wrong equation "relvar = class" as a basis on which to build an object / relational DBMS. That equation was widely regarded as correct at the time, and so I'm glad to be able to report that—by the time they came to market, at any rate—most O/R products did manage to avoid that blunder after all. (Whether that positive outcome had anything to do with our efforts I really don't know, though I tend to doubt it.)*

Subsequently, however, we came to realize there was a ***Second Great Blunder*** *as well, one that was at least as serious as the first: viz., mixing pointers and relations. And it looked as if just about every DBMS on the market was about to commit that one, even if it hadn't committed the first! Indeed, that second blunder has—most unfortunately, in my opinion—subsequently become enshrined in the SQL standard. So my objective with this chapter isn't the same as the one I had in mind when I wrote the original papers on which the chapter is based. At that time I was doing my best to persuade the industry at large not to go down that mistaken path. Clearly, however, I was unsuccessful in that aim, and so my goal now has to be different: To be specific. it has to be just to advise users not to "take advantage" of this unfortunate and widespread misstep on the industry's part.*

> *Publishing history: What follows first saw the light of day as two separate papers, "Don't Mix Pointers and Relations!" and a sequel, "Don't Mix Pointers and Relations—Please!" The first was originally published in InfoDB 10, No. 6 (April 1997), and was then republished in my book Relational Database Writings 1994-1997 (Addison-Wesley 1998). The second was originally published in that same book. This version copyright © C. J. Date 2022.*

The idea that databases should be allowed to contain pointers to data as well as data per se has been around for a long time. Certainly it was a sine qua non in the old prerelational world of IMS and CODASYL (i.e., hierarchic and network databases); and, in the shape of OIDs or object IDs, which as far as I'm concerned are just pointers by another name [4], it permeates the object world as well. What's more, despite the fact that Codd very deliberately excluded pointers from the relational model when he first defined it, the same idea also rears its head from time to time in the relational world. One of the most recent manifestations of that idea in a relational (or would-be relational) context occurs, not surprisingly, in connection with current attempts to extend the SQL standard to include support for objects.[1] In this chapter, I want to explain why, in my opinion, mixing pointers and relations—if I might be allowed to characterize the scheme in such a manner—is a very bad idea.

Note: One point that's worth making right up front is this. Given that there are no pointers in the relational model, it follows that databases that contain pointers (pointers that re visible to the user, that is) are by definition not relational. So what are they? Well, I couldn't really say; but I do think, to repeat, that the databases in question—and the pertinent DBMSs also, of course—have thereby forfeited any right they might once have had to call themselves relational.

Prerequisites: In order to understand the technical discussions to follow, you need to be familiar with all of the following:

■   The logical difference between values and variables in general

---

[1] As indicated in the preamble, those attempts were successful, inasmuch as the standard does now include support for various OO features, and hence for pointers in particular. Now, whether that support looks exactly like the hypothetical SQL extensions described in what follows I neither know nor care; in fact, it almost certainly doesn't, not in detail. But even if it doesn't, the overall message of the chapter remains the same.

- The logical difference between relation values and variables in particular

- The logical difference between referencing and dereferencing

I've discussed values vs. variables in general, and relation values vs. relational variables in particular, in many other writings (see, e.g., references [5] and [6]), and I won't repeat that material here—except to remind you that I usually abbreviate the term "relation value" to just *relation*, unqualified, and the term "relation variable" to *relvar*. (Actually I won't be using either of these abbreviations very much in this chapter, anyway.) I will, however, say a little more about referencing vs. dereferencing, in case those concepts aren't familiar to you. See the section immediately following.

REFERENCING AND DEREFERENCING

Many programming languages support pointers. That is, they recognize that the concept of a variable is really an abstraction of the concept of a *location in storage*; accordingly, they recognize that variables have *addresses*; they therefore support address, or pointer, values and variables (in other words, they support an address or pointer *type*). Thus, a pointer value is an address, and a pointer variable is a variable whose permitted values are addresses.

Note: By *address* here, I don't necessarily mean a physical or hardware address. The idea rather is just that every variable does have a location of some kind, and of course the address of that location is independent of the current value of the variable in question—it stays constant while the value of the variable changes. Some writers use the term *reference* for this concept, but I find that term too broad (not to say misleading),[2] and prefer the more suggestive term *address*.

The type *address* has two fundamental operators associated with it, usually called *referencing* and *dereferencing*:

- *Referencing*: Given a variable V, the referencing operator applied to V returns the address of V. Here by way of illustration is the syntax used for the referencing operator in C, Pascal, and PL/I:

---

[2] Especially as it already has a logically different meaning in the relational world in connection with foreign keys. That is, the term *reference* is generally understood in the relational world as referring to [*sic!*] some value of some foreign key.

```
C          &V
Pascal     ^V
PL/I       ADDR(V)
```

For example, the following PL/I code fragment has the effect of assigning the address of the integer variable N to the pointer variable P:

```
DECLARE N INTEGER ;
DECLARE P POINTER ;

P = ADDR ( N ) ;
```

Or if you prefer C:

```
INT N ;
INT *P ;

P = &N ;
```

Note carefully that the argument to the referencing operator must be specified as a variable, not as a literal or more general expression. The reason is, of course, that literals and more general expressions denote values, and values don't have addresses, variables do. Thus, for example, ADDR (3) and ADDR (N+1) are both illegal in PL/I. (After all, if they were legal, the best the system could do with them would be to return the address of the system generated temporary variable that holds the result of evaluating the ADDR argument expression—not a very useful thing to do from the user's point of view.)

■ *Dereferencing*: Given a variable P of type address, the dereferencing operator applied to P returns the variable V whose address is currently contained in P. Here's the syntax for dereferencing in C, Pascal, and PL/I:

```
C          *P
Pascal     P^
PL/I       P -> V
```

For example, the following PL/I code fragment has the effect of assigning the integer value 3 to the integer variable N that pointer (or address) variable P currently points to:

```
P -> N = 3 ;
```

C analog (note, incidentally, that the variable that's actually being assigned to isn't explicitly mentioned in this C example):

```
*P = 3 ;
```

Note carefully that the dereferencing operator returns a variable, not a value. The reason is, again, that values don't have addresses, variables do. (Of course, if the dereferencing operation occurs in a source position instead of a target position—in particular, if it occurs on the right side instead of the left side of an assignment—it can be regarded, harmlessly, as returning the value of the variable in question instead of returning that variable per se. The point isn't very important for the purposes of the present discussion, however.)

Before going any further, I have to say that personally I find the "referencing and dereferencing" terminology quite confusing. For example, I think it would be very reasonable to regard the PL/I expression

```
P -> N
```

as *referencing* (i.e., referring to) the particular integer variable N that pointer variable P currently points to; yet as we've seen, that expression is really an example of *de*referencing. For such reasons, I'll use the referencing / dereferencing terminology as little as possible in what follows. (I should mention too that several languages, PL/I included, support *implicit* dereferencing, which can serve to make the concepts even more confusing to the uninitiated. In what follows, all dereferencing will be explicit.)

THE BASIC IDEA

Now I can begin to examine the central issue of this chapter. As already noted, there are those who think that "relational" databases should be allowed to include pointers to data as well as data per se. For example, the SQL standard supports a data type called REF,[3] which—loosely speaking—allows a column in one table

---

[3] It would be more accurate to describe REF as a type *generator*, but calling it a type, unqualified, will suffice for present purposes.

to contain values that are addresses of rows in another table (or possibly in the same table).[4] As already indicated, I refer to this scheme as "mixing pointers and relations." Is it a good idea? Can it be made to work?

Well, let's look at an example. Fig. 1 shows what such a scheme might look like in the case of an employees-and-departments database. Note in particular the EMP column DADDR, which I presume has been defined to be of type REF (or POINTER, or ADDR, or something else of that same general nature)—probably with the additional constraint that values in that column must be, not just addresses ("references"), but addresses of DEPT rows specifically.

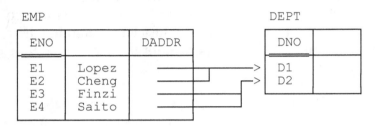

Fig. 1: Mixing pointers and relations (example)

As you can see, the EMP rows for employees E1 and E2 in the figure each contain a pointer to the DEPT row for department D1—so those two pointers are in fact equal—and the EMP rows for employees E3 and E4 likewise each contain a pointer to the DEPT row for department D2 (so those two pointers are equal too).

Now let's consider some sample queries involving this database. *Note:* Naturally I assume for the moment that the database makes sense, and therefore that queries and other operations involving it make sense too. In my opinion, however, they *don't* make sense, and the examples that follow don't stand up to careful scrutiny. But my objective for the moment is simply to give an idea of what the "mixing pointers and relations" scheme might look like in practice, in order that I might have a concrete target for subsequent analysis and criticism. Note too that (for familiarity) I use an SQL-like syntax for my examples, even though it's not to my own taste.

---

[4] Although my concern in this chapter is really with the relational model, not SQL, most if not all of my examples will be SQL examples specifically, and so I'll tend to favor the SQL terms *table*, *row*, and *column* over the relational terms *relation*, *tuple*, and *attribute*.

Example 1: Get the department number for employee E1.

```
SELECT  ex.DADDR -> DNO
FROM    EMP ex
WHERE   ex.ENO = 'E1'
```

Note the dereferencing operation in the SELECT clause (the expression *ex*.DADDR → DNO returns the DNO value from the DEPT row that the DADDR value in question points to). Note too the slightly counterintuitive nature of the FROM clause—the DNO value to be retrieved comes from DEPT, not EMP, but DADDR values come from EMP, not DEPT. I suppose we might extend the FROM clause, harmlessly, to mention DEPT as well as EMP, thus:

```
FROM EMP ex , DEPT dx
```

Though if we did, we might want to specify DISTINCT in the SELECT clause as well. (Or would we?)

By the way, it's interesting to note that the very same query can logically be formulated in terms of referencing in the WHERE clause rather than dereferencing in the SELECT clause:

```
SELECT  dx.DNO
FROM    DEPT dx
WHERE   ( SELECT  ex.ENO
          FROM    EMP ex
          WHERE   ex.DADDR = ADDR ( dx ) ) = 'E1'
```

Here I've assumed that the referencing operator invocation ADDR (*dx*) in the inner SELECT expression returns the address of the DEPT row *dx* that's currently being processed by the outer one.

Yet another formulation, again using referencing rather than dereferencing, might look like this:

```
SELECT  dx.DNO
FROM    EMP ex , DEPT dx
WHERE   ex.ENO = 'E1'
AND     ex.DADDR = ADDR ( dx )
```

Note: SQL has long been known for, and criticized for, supporting many different ways of doing the same thing [3]. In the case at hand, however, the fact that there are so many possible formulations is due, at least in part, not to the idiosyncrasies of SQL per se, but rather to the basic idea of mixing pointers and relations in the first place. To be specific (albeit simplifying somewhat), the expressions

```
ex.DADDR -> DNO
```

and

```
dx.DNO WHERE ex.DADDR = ADDR ( dx )
```

(where *ex* and *dx* represent a particular EMP row and a particular DEPT row, respectively) are logically equivalent by definition, and hence lead to distinct formulations of the same query.

Now let's look at an example illustrating *de*referencing in the WHERE clause.

Example 2: Get employee numbers for employees in department D1.

```
SELECT  ex.ENO
FROM    EMP ex
WHERE   ex.DADDR -> DNO = 'D1'
```

Note: The following expression, using referencing rather than dereferencing, might possibly be thought to be an alternative formulation of this query:

```
SELECT  ex.ENO
FROM    EMP ex
WHERE   ex.DADDR = ADDR ( SELECT  dx.*
                          FROM    DEPT dx
                          WHERE   dx.DNO = 'D1' )
```

The thinking behind this putative formulation is that the ADDR invocation in the outer WHERE clause will return the address of the DEPT row for department D1. But of course that thinking is mistaken! The expression in parentheses, though it might be thought of informally as returning the DEPT row for department D1, doesn't actually do that—in effect, it returns a new copy of that row instead.[5] As explained in the section "Referencing and Dereferencing" earlier, the expression denoting the argument to an ADDR invocation must always be a simple variable reference specifically, not a more general expression.

---

[5] More precisely, of course, it returns *a table containing* that copy.

Thus, the ADDR invocation just shown is illegal, and so therefore is the overall expression.

Example 3: What does the following expression return?

```
SELECT  ex.DADDR
FROM    EMP ex
WHERE   ex.ENO = 'E1'
```

Presumably it returns the DADDR value (that is, an *address*) for employee E1. What does this address look like if it's returned to the user? Do we have to support address literals of some kind? (The answer to this question is yes, of course. After all, if it were no, then certain *relations*—namely, those that contain addresses—wouldn't be expressible as *relation* literals!)

Here's another example of a query that returns an address:

```
SELECT  ADDR ( dx ) AS DADDR
FROM    DEPT dx
WHERE   dx.DNO = 'D1'
```

To close out this section, here are a couple of update examples.

Example 4: Insert an employee.

```
INSERT INTO EMP ( ENO , DADDR )
       VALUES ( 'E5' , ( SELECT ADDR ( dx )
                         FROM    DEPT dx
                         WHERE   dx.DNO = 'D2' ) ) ;
```

If, as the example suggests, DADDR values are provided by the user by means of ADDR invocations instead of by means of address literals or variables, then presumably it won't be possible to insert an EMP row that points to a nonexistent DEPT row—a state of affairs that might, I suppose, be claimed as an advantage of using pointers instead of foreign keys. What do you think?

Example 5: Delete a department.

```
DELETE
FROM    DEPT dx
WHERE   dx.DNO = 'D1' ;
```

Clearly, we'll need some rules—of the form either ON DELETE CASCADE or ON DELETE NO CASCADE, I presume—to cater for the possibility that there might be pointers elsewhere in the database to the row(s) being deleted.[6] Note, however, that since EMP rows point to DEPT rows and not the other way around, we can't just chase pointers from the DEPT row to find the pertinent EMP rows in such a situation. (What can we do instead? In fact, what do we have to do instead? And is what we have to do made better or worse by the fact that we're using pointers instead of foreign keys?)

A CLOSER LOOK

Having sketched the basic idea of mixing pointers and relations, I now want to ask the question: Does that idea really stand up? Let's take a closer look.

First of all, note that (as I've said several times already) values don't have addresses, variables do. It follows that, e.g., the addresses in column DADDR in the example of Fig. 1 must be addresses, not of row *values*, but of row *variables*. *But there's no such thing as a row variable in the relational model.* The relational model deals with relation values, which are (loosely speaking) sets of row values, which are in turn (again loosely speaking) sets of scalar values. It also deals with relation variables, which are variables whose values are relations. However, it does *not* deal with row variables (variables whose values are rows) or scalar variables (variables whose values are scalars). In other words, the *only* kind of variable included in the relational model is, very specifically, the *relation* variable. *It follows that the idea of mixing pointers and relations constitutes a **major** departure from the relational model, introducing as it does an entirely new kind of variable.*

Why exactly would the introduction of row variables constitute such a major departure? Well, orthogonality would dictate that we'd have to allow such variables to appear in the database as well as relation variables. And then we'd have to define a whole new query language for rows—that is, a set of row operators (a "row algebra"?) analogous to the operators already defined for relations (viz., the relational algebra). We'd also have to define row level update operators, analogous to the existing relational ones. We'd have to be able to define row level integrity and security constraints, and row level views. The catalog would have to describe row variables as well as relation variables. (And

---

[6] Do you think any analogous rules are needed for UPDATE? Justify your answer!

what would the catalog itself consist of?—row variables? or relation variables? or a mixture?) We'd need a row level design theory, analogous to the existing body of relational design theory. We'd also need guidelines as to when to use row variables and when relation variables. And so on (I'm sure this list of issues isn't exhaustive).

The net of all this is:

■ Assuming that a "row algebra" can be defined, and all of the other questions raised in the previous paragraph answered satisfactorily, now we'll have two ways of doing things where one sufficed before. In other words, adding a new kind of variable certainly adds *complexity*, but it doesn't add any *power* (there's nothing useful that can be done with a mixture of row and relation variables that can't be done with relation variables alone).

■ Thus, the user interface will now be more complex and involve more choices—most likely without good guidelines as to how to make such choices.

■ As a direct consequence, database application, including in particular general purpose applications or "front ends," will become more difficult to write and more difficult to maintain.

■ Those applications will also become more vulnerable to changes in the database structure. That is, some degree of logical data independence will be lost (consider what happens, for example, if the representation of some piece of information is changed from relation variables to row variables, or the other way around).

In my opinion, the foregoing arguments should be sufficient to stop the "mixing pointers and relations" idea dead in its tracks.[7] Nevertheless, there are several further criticisms of the idea that are also worth articulating. Before I can get to those, however, I want to take a look at one suggestion that's sometimes made in an attempt to rescue the basic idea.

---

[7] In place of "should be sufficient" I suppose I now have to say "should have been sufficient, but weren't." However, I do want to mention the point (indeed, I want to stress it) that precisely analogous arguments apply to the idea of introducing *any* new kind of variable into the relational model. Would-be "extenders of the relational model" please note!

CAN THE IDEA BE RESCUED?

The suggestion I refer to is as follows: Instead of insisting that addresses such as those in column DADDR in the example of Fig. 1 must point to row variables per se, can't we think of them as somehow pointing to *components* of *relation* variables—thereby retaining relation variables as the only kind of variable permitted in the model? In PL/I, for example, the expression ADDR (S.C), where S is a structure variable and C is a component of S, is perfectly legitimate. As another example, the PL/I expression ADDR (A(3)), where A is an array variable and that 3 is a subscript, is likewise perfectly legitimate. So why not dispose of the row variable argument in the same kind of way? Let's examine this idea.

- First of all, of course, those "component pointers" (meaning pointers to components of some relation variable) obviously can't be absolute addresses, for all of the usual reasons.

- Nor can they be relative or "offset" addresses, because of course a given relation variable contains different rows at different times; thus, even if it contains "the same" row at different times, there can be no guarantee that the offset remains the same, because of insert / delete activity. (Note carefully that this argument doesn't apply to the PL/I examples mentioned above.)

- Hence, they must be purely symbolic, or associative, in nature. In other words, they must be key values! (or something logically indistinguishable from key values)—where by *key* I mean, of course, some key of the relation variable in question. In which case the "pointers" we're dealing with are really nothing but conventional foreign keys in a different guise.

If we adopt the "component pointers" suggestion, in other words, we're not really dealing with pointers, in the generally accepted sense of that term, at all. As a consequence, the entire idea of mixing pointers and relations reduces to nothing more than a different syntax for something the relational model already gives us—namely, keys and foreign keys, together with certain foreign key rules such as ON DELETE CASCADE—and is therefore fundamentally uninteresting from a logical point of view.[8] (Not to mention the fact that using keys to implement pointers seems 100% backward: indeed, perverse in the extreme. By contrast, the inverse idea—i.e., using pointers to implement keys—could sometimes be useful, as I've indicated elsewhere [4].)

As an aside, let me point out that the discussions of this section go some way toward explaining (a) why, contrary to what's sometimes claimed, foreign key values aren't pointers, and (b) why, unlike the proposed pointer mechanism, foreign keys don't violate the spirit of the relational model.

FURTHER ISSUES

From the discussions of the previous section, I conclude that the pointers that people—at least, some people—want to mix with relations really are genuine pointers and really do point to variables (albeit variables that are somehow "contained within" other variables, despite the fact that this latter notion makes no sense, logically speaking). In this section I want to point out a number of further implications of this state of affairs.

More on Values vs. Variables

Regardless of whether we agree that the idea of relation variables containing row variables makes no sense, we must surely agree that *values* can't contain variables, and hence that relation values in particular can't contain variables (not row variables, and not any other kind either). It follows that the pointers we're talking about always "point into" relation variables specifically, not into relation values. As a consequence, we're dealing with a system in which certain operators work for variables but not for values![9] Consider the following example, which is intended to show an SQL-like representation of what we might call—since it's based on matching pointer (i.e., address) values—a *pointer join* (more precisely, a projection of such a join).

---

[8] It's not a very nice syntax, either, because of the asymmetry inherent in referencing vs. dereferencing. In the case of those pointers from EMP to DEPT, for example, the process of stepping from EMP to DEPT is quite different, both syntactically and semantically, from that of stepping from DEPT to EMP. Contrast the situation with key value matching, where no such asymmetry arises.

[9] Of course, this remark is already true of update operators. But the operators I'm talking about here aren't update operators, they're read-only operators.

Example 6: For all employees, get the employee number and corresponding department number.

```
SELECT  ex.ENO ,  dx.DNO
FROM    EMP ex , DEPT dx
WHERE   ex.DADDR = ADDR ( dx )
```

EMP and DEPT here are relation variables, and the pointer join works just fine. But suppose we were to replace the reference to DEPT by a relation literal, representing the current value of that relation variable, as follows (note the use of the SQL VALUES construct, which—among other things—allows us to write such literals):

```
SELECT  ex.ENO ,  dx.DNO
FROM    EMP ex , ( VALUES ( 'D1' , ... ) , ( 'D2' , ... ) )
                                        AS dx ( DNO , ... )
WHERE   ex.DADDR = ADDR ( dx )
```

This expression will fail at compile time, because the expression denoting the ADDR argument isn't just a simple variable reference. [10]

If you're having difficulty appreciating the significance of this point, the following analogy might help. Let X and Y be variables of type INTEGER, with current values 4 and 5, say. Then it's as if the "+" operator for integers were defined in such a way that the expression X + Y gives 9, but the expression X + 5 fails! (The expressions X + (Y + 1), and X + (Y + 0), and even X + (Y), will all have to fail too, presumably.)

A related point—perhaps it's the same point in a different guise—is the following. The operators of the relational algebra are defined to work on *relations* (that is, relation *values*); in particular, of course, they work on the values that happen to be the current values of relation *variables*. But none of those operators works on relation variables specifically; that is, none of those operators *requires* some operand to consist of a relation variable specifically. The "pointer join," by contrast, certainly does require one operand (the "pointed to" operand) to be a relation variable specifically. *And so we're talking about another major departure from the classical relational model.* To spell it out:

---

[10] Analogous remarks would apply if we were to replace that VALUES literal by a more general relational expression, representing (say) the join of two other relations. *Note:* If the expression didn't fail at compile time after all, then it would presumably have to return an empty result, because the ADDR invocation would then have to refer to the system generated temporary relation variable *dx* that contains the result of evaluating the VALUES expression, while DADDR values refer to the relation variable DEPT (and the comparison in the WHERE clause thus couldn't possibly evaluate to *true*).

The classical relational algebra has no concept of a relation variable at all; the "pointer join," by contrast, necessarily does.[11]

Yet another related point is as follows. When people talk of "pointers to rows in relations," it's quite clear that what they mean is pointers to rows in *base* relations specifically. (I deliberately blur the values vs. variables distinction here.) In other words, they forget about *derived* relations! As I've argued elsewhere, this is a mistake of the highest order, because the question as to which relations are base and which derived is, in a very important sense, arbitrary. For further discussion of this issue, see reference [2] or—for a more in-depth examination of the issues involved—my book *View Updating and Relational Theory: Solving the View Update Problem* (O'Reilly, 2013).

More on the Pointer Join

Let's take another look at the original pointer join example from the previous subsection:

```
SELECT  ex.ENO , dx.DNO
FROM    EMP ex , DEPT dx
WHERE   ex.DADDR = ADDR ( dx )
```

Observe now that of course each EMP row has just one corresponding DEPT row (the DADDR value in any given EMP row obviously points to just one DEPT row); in other words, the pointer join is inherently a many to one operation. What happens if the situation changes, such that the same department can be represented in several DEPT rows?—for example, if departments are spread across several locations, and DEPT contains one row for each valid DNO / LOCATION combination? Clearly, the pointer join operation won't work any more—or rather (and more fundamentally) the database design won't be valid any more. By contrast, the conventional relational design, in which EMP contains a DNO column instead of a DADDR column, would still be valid after the change, and the conventional relational join—

```
SELECT  ex.ENO , dx.DNO
FROM    EMP ex , DEPT dx
WHERE   ex.DNO = dx.DNO
```

---

[11] You might find this remark surprising, but it's true. Relation variables, as opposed to relation values, become significant from the point of view of the relational model only when we begin talking about update operations or, more specifically, relational assignment—and relational assignment, though it's certainly part of the relational model, isn't part of the relational algebra as such.

—would still work.

Orthogonality

If we're allowed to deal with addresses of row variables, orthogonality dictates that we should be allowed to deal with addresses of other kinds of variables too. And since the "mixing pointers and relations" idea certainly does entail at least one other kind of variable—viz., relation variables—it follows that we should be able to write expressions of the form

```
ADDR ( R )
```

and

```
P -> R
```

where *R* is a relation variable. I certainly haven't explored all of the implications of this point, but I'd be willing to wager that some of them, at least, are undesirable.[12]

INTERMISSION

The first of the two papers on which the present chapter is jointly based closed with the following discussion and acknowledgments, which I repeat here for the record despite the fact that this isn't the end of this combined version of those two papers.

Discussion

Where did this strange idea of mixing pointers and relations come from? It seems to me that what we have here is (as so often) *a fundamental confusion between model and implementation.* To be specific, it has been observed that certain SQL products don't perform very well on certain joins, and it has further

---

[12] One implication—I suspect, though I haven't been able to find a logician who can either confirm or refute this suspicion on my part—is that the system will now have to deal with second order logic, whereas the relational model is founded on conventional first order logic.

been conjectured that performance would be improved if we could follow a pointer instead of doing a join. As I've written elsewhere [4], however, such thinking is seriously confused:

> ... (1) implementing [joins] by pointers is very different from (2) exposing such pointers in the data model. The fact that (1) might be a good idea doesn't imply that (2) is a good idea, and of course it categorically isn't. We *must* keep logical and physical concepts distinct, and not get confused over the two levels in our debates.

Of course, I'm aware that another driving force behind the idea of exposing pointers in the model is a desire to bring object and relational technologies closer together. In itself, this is a worthy objective.[13] However, as Hugh Darwen and I have argued elsewhere [7], there's a right way and a wrong way to approach such a goal. The wrong way, which we refer to as **The Great Blunder**,[14] involves a mistaken understanding of the true nature of objects—relations too for that matter—and seems to lead inevitably to the heresy of mixing pointers and relations. And I believe the analysis of this chapter up to this point tend to reinforce our position that **The Great Blunder** certainly deserves to be so called ... By contrast, in *The Third Manifesto* [7], we've tried to show what would be involved in approaching this same goal in the "right" way, which (among other things) doesn't lead to that same heresy.

Acknowledgments

I'm grateful, first of all, to Don Chamberlin, whose original question "So what's wrong with having pointers in a relational database?"—I'm quoting from memory—led me to write the original paper on which the chapter up to this point is based.[15] I'd also like to thank Nelson Mattos for his more detailed explanation of the "REF type" idea. I'm also grateful to Hugh Darwen for numerous discussions, for his careful review of an earlier draft of that original paper, and for providing me with a copy of the relevant SQL documentation. Finally, I'm

---

[13] At least, let's assume it is for the sake of the present discussion.

[14] As noted in the preamble to this chapter, we now regard it as the *first* great blunder. Mixing pointers and relations is the second.

[15] I should make it clear that this wasn't just an idle question on Chamberlin's part; au contraire, he was actively involved—possibly the lead player—at that time in the whole business of adding pointers to SQL.

grateful to my other reviewers Declan Brady and Don Chamberlin (again) for further helpful comments.

WHAT HAPPENED NEXT

As noted above, I wrote the first of the two papers on which the present chapter is based as a response to a question from Don Chamberlin—and of course I sent a draft to Chamberlin before it was published, in order to give him a chance to respond. Which he did, and my paper and his reply [1] were published alongside one another in the same issue of *InfoDB*. So reference [1] was Chamberlin's response to some of my arguments. The remainder of the present chapter consists of an edited version of my response to that response. *Note:* Reference [1] isn't being republished here, of course, but in any case I believe my response to it stands on its own.

First off, I have to say that my original paper and Chamberlin's response to it didn't just disagree, they seemed to be at complete cross purposes. In my original (in the section "Can the Idea Be Rescued?"), I explained that the idea of mixing pointers and relations could be interpreted in two quite different ways, which might loosely be characterized as follows:

- *Interpretation 1*: The pointers are really just keys.

- *Interpretation 2*: The pointers are really pointers, not keys.

If Interpretation 1 is the correct one, then we're not really talking about pointers at all, we're just talking about a syntactic shorthand, and the whole debate becomes a nonissue (at least from a logical point of view, though there are certainly some psychological questions that need to be addressed—I'll get to those later). In other words, Interpretation 2 is the interesting one. In my original paper, therefore, I assumed for the most part that we were talking about Interpretation 2, and I tried to explain why I thought it would be a mistake for the industry to embrace such a radical idea.

In his response, however, Chamberlin incorrectly assumed that my principal concern was with Interpretation 1. Noting that he accuses my original paper of containing a number of red herrings, therefore, I think that, on the contrary, his entire response is one huge red herring! Nevertheless, I also think that many of the points he raises do need to be refuted. Now read on ...

RED HERRINGS?

Chamberlin's incorrect assumption that I was addressing Interpretation 1 is, I believe, the main reason why he thinks some of my points are red herrings. I claim, contrariwise, that the points in question are both germane and important. Let me address some of Chamberlin's specific comments in this regard.

> One [red herring] is the observation that the ADDR operator ... is not meaningful when applied to a constant or an expression. This is an unremarkable fact, and has a direct analogy in every programming language that has a similar operator ... So we should not be surprised that if a similar operator is introduced into SQL, it is undefined for constants and expressions—indeed, we should be surprised if this were not the case.

Well, I'm sorry, but the fact is *not* unremarkable! Rather, the point is that "every programming language that has a similar operator" also has *variables*, and the operand to ADDR is required to be a variable specifically. Thus, when we talk of the ADDR of a "row," we have to mean, specifically, the ADDR of a row variable. The relational model doesn't have row variables, and neither does SQL. So we're talking about a major departure from precedent, or in other words a major extension!—and in my analysis I showed that the extension in question has a number of undesirable consequences.

As for "we should not be surprised that if a similar operator is introduced into SQL, it is undefined for constants and expressions": What should surprise us is the idea that someone might suggest introducing such an operator into a language that doesn't include the kind of thing the operator needs to operate on. Chamberlin's second and third sentences are the real red herrings here.

By the way: Statements like "[the ADDR operator] is undefined for constants and expressions" illustrate the difficulty of talking about these matters with clarity and precision, and the consequent difficulty of getting the language specifications right (whatever "right" might mean in the present context).[16] After all, the SQL standard certainly does say we can write something like ADDR (*x*), and *x* here is certainly an expression (a simple variable name is certainly an

---

[16] What Chamberlin should have said rather is that the only thing the expression denoting the ADDR argument can be is a simple variable reference (it can't be a literal, nor can it be a more general expression). By the way, note that there's a logical difference (one that Chamberlin seems confused about) between a constant and a literal—a constant is a value, a literal is a "self-defining term" that denotes such a value.

expression, albeit a special case). In other words, ADDR *does* apply to expressions; the question is rather, which ones?

And by the way again: Note that, as far as SQL's concerned, the *x* in ADDR (*x*) is required to denote a row specifically (SQL actually uses the syntax REF ROW *x* in place of my ADDR (*x*), which makes this point a little more explicit). I observe, however, that once the idea of "addressing" or "referencing" or "pointing" is introduced—no matter what term or syntax we use—then, as I said previously, orthogonality would surely dictate that it be available for all variables, of all kinds. But it isn't, in SQL.

> In Example 2 [Date] writes a putative formulation [of a certain query] which applies ADDR to an expression, which is invalid in SQL and has never been proposed by anybody.

I've already noted that in fact ADDR does apply to expressions (by which I mean its operand is *denoted by* an expression); what Chamberlin means is that the particular expression I was using wasn't valid in that context. True enough; but all I was trying to do was draw the reader's attention to a trap that SQL users in particular might be likely to fall into. The query was "Get employee numbers for employees in department D1," and the "putative formulation" included the following ADDR invocation (slightly simplified here):

```
ADDR ( SELECT * FROM DEPT WHERE DNO = 'D1' )
```

As I tried to explain in connection with that example, the (incorrect) thinking here is that the ADDR invocation will return the address of the DEPT row for department D1. This thinking is incorrect because, as already discussed, the operand expression in an ADDR invocation must be a variable reference specifically, not a more general expression. The point I was trying to make, though, is that SQL users in particular might be likely to fall into this trap (as indeed I did myself, on my first attempt!), because SQL already makes the mistake of regarding an expression such as

```
SELECT * FROM DEPT WHERE DNO = 'D1'
```

as denoting a row rather than a table—very likely a *base* row at that, meaning a row within a base table and not just a copy of such a row—in certain contexts. To elaborate:

- ■ If the expression appears in a row subquery, it effectively denotes a row. (More precisely, it denotes a table of one row, and that table then gets implicitly converted, or *coerced*, to the row in question.)

- ■ If the expression appears in a cursor declaration, it effectively denotes a base row specifically. (More precisely, it denotes a table of one row, and the row in question can then be directly retrieved, updated, or deleted via that cursor. The fact that it can be updated or deleted in this way effectively means the row in question must be a base row specifically.)

Since the expression can be certainly regarded as denoting a row (and a base row at that) in some contexts, I stand by my contention that users might reasonably think an ADDR invocation is one such context, and be surprised when they discover it isn't.

> In Example 6 [Date] attempts to apply ADDR to a constant relation ... [and] then writes that the failure ... to produce any meaningful result is as if the "+" operator were defined ... in such a way that the expression X + Y [where X and Y have current values 4 and 5, respectively] gave 9, but the expression X + 5 failed. This analogy is clearly invalid, since "+" is defined for both variables and constants but ADDR is not.

Here Chamberlin misses my point. The analogy isn't between "+" and ADDR, it's between "+" and *join*. The "+" operator is indeed defined "for both variables and constants" (as Chamberlin puts it), *and so is join*—at least, the join that's part of the relational algebra. But the operator I called for want of a better term "pointer join" *doesn't* work "for both variables and constants," it works for variables (that is, relation variables) only. The relational algebra doesn't have relation variables. So we're talking about another departure from precedent, and another major extension—this time, to the relational algebra.

Incidentally, the foregoing criticism applies regardless of whether we're talking about Interpretation 1 or Interpretation 2.

> [Date observes that] the classical relational algebra has no concept of a relation variable. The consequences of this argument are interesting to consider. The concept of a relation variable (or table, as it is called in SQL) is, of course, essential to INSERT, DELETE, UPDATE, and any other operation that modifies the database. While it is true that these operations are missing in the classical

relational algebra, I believe that they have proved their worth to the database industry.

Again Chamberlin has missed my point. My observation that the relational algebra has no concept of a relation variable isn't an "argument," it's a fact. I'm certainly not trying to suggest—though the functional programming community might!—that we don't *need* relation variables and update operators; rather, I'm saying that we shouldn't muddy up the relational algebra per se with such concepts. The operators of the relational algebra are (by definition) *read-only* operators, and they operate on values; operators such as INSERT, UPDATE, and DELETE are, by contrast (and again by definition), *update* operators, and they operate on *variables*—and, to spell the point out, they're not part of the algebra. But (and again regardless of whether we're talking about Interpretation 1 or Interpretation 2, incidentally) the idea of mixing pointers and relations introduces a totally new kind of construct: namely, an operator, ADDR, that, though (like the algebraic operators) read-only, nevertheless requires its operand to be a variable, not a value. I claim, therefore, that this construct introduces muddle where there was none before.

By the way: Unlike the relational algebra, SQL does include the concept of a relation variable, of course. However, I observe that, in most languages, the syntax for the operation that returns the value of a given variable, be it a relation variable or any other kind, consists simply of the name of the variable in question; thus, e.g., we write the expression V to refer to the value of the variable V. But this simple convention is violated in SQL! In SQL, in order to refer to the value of relation—or table—variable T, we usually have to write an expression of the form SELECT * FROM T (or something along such lines). This fact, I believe, lends additional weight to my earlier contention that people might easily, albeit incorrectly, expect certain SELECT expressions to be a valid way of denoting an ADDR operand.

And by the way again, I have to ask: If as Chamberlin says the SQL term for "relation variable" is *table*, then what's the SQL term for "relation value"?

SQL EXTENSIONS

In a section of reference [1] entitled "Reality" (!), Chamberlin describes Interpretation 1 (or, rather, his interpretation of Interpretation 1) by sketching certain "small extensions" to SQL that are currently proposed as part of the SQL standard. [17] He claims, essentially, that those SQL proposals correspond to Interpretation 1—though he isn't quite correct in this claim, as I'll show. [18]

Chamberlin's first extension is really two separate extensions rolled up into one: namely, "the idea of a system generated unique identifier for a row," and "a syntax that can be used to refer to this identifier." I'll come back to that syntactic extension later. Regarding the "system generated unique identifiers" extension: I have no objection to the basic idea of system generated identifiers, if done properly—in fact, I think they could be very useful [4]—so long as:

1. In accordance with Codd's *Information Principle*, those identifiers aren't hidden from the user.

2. In accordance with *The Principle of Interchangeability*,[19] they're available for derived rows as well as base ones.

However:

1. In SQL, those system generated identifiers can be hidden from the user.[20] Chamberlin says such hiding is "much like hiding a column by a view" (slightly paraphrased). No, it isn't! The analogy is a complete red herring! If the identifiers for table *T* are hidden, then it's not as if the "column" that contains those identifiers is somehow "hidden"; rather, *no such column exists* (i.e., the identifiers aren't in a column at all). And there's fundamentally only one way those identifiers can be accessed: namely, via the new SQL "reference operator" REF ROW *T*. And there's simply no way such an expression can be regarded as syntactic shorthand for anything already available in SQL.

---

[17] When I wrote the papers on which this chapter is based, pointers hadn't actually been included the standard, they were merely proposed for such inclusion. This state of affairs accounts for some of the wording in this section, regarding "proposed extensions" and the like.

[18] Pointer support as it appeared when it finally made its way into the actual standard wasn't identical to the version that Chamberlin describes here, but the differences aren't important.

[19] *The Principle of Interchangeability* can be stated (*very* loosely!) thus: To the user, views should look just like base tables.

[20] Not true in the final version of the standard. This is one of the details that changed after I wrote the papers this chapter is based on. I decided to leave my original text essentially unchanged, though, because the arguments as such are still valid, and they'd need to be invoked again if—as could easily happen—someone tried to reintroduce the notion of hidden identifiers. In fact I believe such things (i.e., hidden identifiers) are already supported in some products.

In case the point isn't clear, let me elaborate briefly. "Hiding a column by a view" doesn't mean the information in that column has to be accessed by some new and special operation like REF ROW *T*; it merely means the information can't be accessed via the view in question. Of course, that information *can* be accessed via the pertinent underlying table(s), and that access is performed by means of conventional SQL operations.

In other words. and contrary to Chamberlin's repeated assertions, what's being proposed here is *not* mere syntactic shorthand (i.e., it's not just Interpretation 1). And yes, it does violate the *Information Principle*. In particular, it means that two rows that are in fact distinct might appear to the user to be duplicates (e.g., in a display of the table in question).

I note in passing too that if, e.g., department (DEPT) identifiers are hidden, then the column of the employees table (EMP) that contains DEPT "references" (addresses) can't be defined as a foreign key. As a consequence, referential actions such as ON DELETE CASCADE can't be specified for that column, either. Implications of this fact are left as something for you to meditate on.

2. In SQL, those system generated identifiers apply to base tables only. To repeat something I said earlier, this is a mistake of the highest order, because the question as to which tables are base and which derived is, in a very important sense, arbitrary [2]. I note in passing that this particular issue is one of several originally raised by me that Chamberlin doesn't address at all.

As a matter of fact, I do have another objection to the idea of system generated identifiers—at least, to the specific manner in which that idea is currently realized in SQL. The point is, those system generated identifiers involve a brand new data type, called a "REF type" in SQL (and so it isn't possible to request, e.g., system generated identifiers of type INTEGER). This fact means, again, that what's being proposed for SQL isn't mere syntactic shorthand (again, it's not just Interpretation 1); there's no way those system generated identifiers, or references to them, can be expressed in terms of existing SQL constructs.

I now move on to Chamberlin's next extension, which is "a phrase [*i.e., mere syntax again*] that is used [to declare that a] column is defined on the same domain as the [system generated identifiers] of some target table." Again I have no major problems with the basic idea here, but:

1. I claim once again that it's a big mistake to introduce arbitrary distinctions, as this extension does, between base tables and derived ones.

2. It's also a big mistake to permit base table *T2* to include a column *C*, as this extension does, that's "defined on the same domain as" the system generated identifiers of some base table *T1* if those identifiers are "hidden" in *T1*. Note in particular that we can't perform a join of *T2* and *T1* on the basis of column *C* and those hidden identifiers.

3. I remark in passing that the term *domain* as used by Chamberlin here must be understood in its relational sense, not its SQL sense.

4. I remark further that the domain in question must be, not just any domain but, very specifically, one whose values are values of the new REF type.

5. Chamberlin notes in passing (not in the text cited) that the actual syntax proposed for SQL in this connection is awkward. Here I agree with him, though my reasons are probably not the same as his.

Chamberlin's final extension is the dereferencing operator, which he says is:

> ... nothing more than a syntactic shortcut ... If column D contains references to [rows within] the DEPT table, then [the dereferencing operation]

```
D -> LOCATION
```

is defined [to be equivalent to] the following scalar subquery:

```
( SELECT LOCATION FROM DEPT X WHERE ADDR ( X ) = D )
```

Well, yes, the SQL dereferencing operator might be just shorthand, but only for another new construct—it's not shorthand for anything that can be expressed in any previous version of SQL, because of the reliance already noted on the new REF type. Moreover—perhaps precisely because it *is* supposed to be shorthand for a "scalar subquery" specifically—an expression such as D → LOCATION can't appear in a target position in UPDATE. Thus, e.g., the following is illegal:

```
UPDATE ...
SET    D -> LOCATION = 'New York'
WHERE  ... ;
```

By contrast, most other languages, if they support dereferencing at all. certainly do permit it in target positions. I gave this PL/I example earlier:

```
P -> N  =  3 ;
```

("assign the value 3 to the variable N that pointer variable P currently points to"). This omission in SQL looks like a serious lack of orthogonality to me.

Oddly enough, SQL apparently does permit the following *sequence* of operations:[21]

```
SELECT  ex.DADDR
INTO    D
FROM    EMP ex
WHERE   ex.ENO = 'E1' ;

SET D -> LOCATION = 'New York' ;
```

(The SELECT statement assigns the address of a certain DEPT row to the pointer variable D, and the SET operation then assigns the value "New York" to the LOCATION component of the row that pointer variable D points to.) The fact that the SET operation in particular is legal here suggests that perhaps dereferencing isn't just shorthand for a scalar subquery after all!—and so, once again, we're not really talking just about Interpretation 1. *Note:* SQL defines the effect of the SET operation in the foregoing example to be equivalent to that of the following UPDATE:

```
UPDATE DEPT
SET    LOCATION = 'New York'
WHERE  REF ROW DEPT = D ;
```

Of course, the possibility that the database might be updated by means of a simple assignment (i.e., SET) operation raises all kinds of additional questions!

---

[21] No longer true. This is another SQL detail that changed after this text was first written. Again I decided to leave the original unchanged, however, for essentially the same reasons as before (see footnote 20).

However, further discussion of those questions would take us much too far away from the topic at hand; I'll have to leave them for another day.

Chamberlin goes on to accuse me of objecting to the idea that dereferencing might be just a shorthand:

> The introduction of an operator that is defined in terms of other operators is presented by Date as a disadvantage, since it conflicts with the idea that there should be One True Way to formulate each query. But redundant operators can be found in almost all languages ... Modern database optimizers often take advantage of this fact to transform queries into equivalent forms that they find more manageable.

Well, I've never argued that there should be just "One True Way" to formulate a query, nor do I necessarily believe we can design languages that meet such a goal. However, I do think the goal is worth striving for as an ideal. I think we should try to design languages, as far as possible, in such a way as to exclude features with overlapping functionality—except where a feature is *expressly defined* to be shorthand for some other combination of features. In other words, I have nothing against syntactic shorthands per se, so long as they're properly defined to be such shorthands. As I've already pointed out, however, SQL's referencing operator is not so defined, and now it seems its dereferencing operator isn't, either.

As an aside, I feel bound to observe that the SQL already has far too many constructs (e.g., EXISTS, GROUP BY, HAVING, range variables, and many others) that weren't originally defined to be shorthands but later turned out to be redundant [3]. As a result, saying just what it is that might be equivalent to such constructs—thereby showing that the construct in question is indeed redundant—can certainly be done, but at the same time the process can be messy. Surely it would have been better to define a kernel language with as little redundancy as possible first, and then define appropriate shorthands, in a systematic manner, later.[22] Because this procedure wasn't followed with SQL, however, the business of "optimizers [transforming] queries into equivalent forms that they find more manageable" is made *much* more difficult than it ought to have been; indeed, numerous transformations have appeared in the literature that have turned out on closer inspection to be incorrect. References [8], [9], [10], and [13] provide several (inadvertent!) illustrations of this point.

---

[22] In other words, abide by *The Principle of Syntactic Substitution.* See Chapter 7 ("Some Principles of Good Language Design") in this book's companion volume.

Chamberlin also asks, rhetorically: "If ADDR (*x*) is an operator [invocation] that returns a system generated key [value], what is *x?*" And he answers, in effect, that *x* is the name of a range variable, and states perfectly correctly that range variables are an integral part of the relational calculus. True enough; but they're not part of the relational algebra, and in fact (as noted in the previous paragraph) they're 100% redundant in SQL today. So something that's redundant and unnecessary in SQL today might become nonredundant and necessary in SQL in the future!—a state of affairs that should, I think, give us some pause.

One last point on SQL: As already indicated, Chamberlin sees his extensions as a realization of Interpretation 1—but I'm not sure the SQL committee members see them the same way. Indeed, it's quite clear that at least some of those members see them as a vehicle for introducing "true object orientation" into SQL (see, e.g., references [11] and [12]; the fact that the extensions under discussion have been moved into a separate part of the specification with the suggestive name *SQL/Object* is relevant here, too).[23] And "true object orientation" strongly implies, at least to me, that what those committee members really want to do is make SQL a realization of Interpretation 2, With All That That Entails. Indeed, this objective probably accounts for the introduction of the new REF data type; REF values look suspiciously like what the object community calls object IDs. Given all of these points taken together, it follows that I reject the arguments Chamberlin propounds in the final section ("What About Objects?") of his response.

REFERENTIAL INTEGRITY

Under this heading, Chamberlin points out, again correctly, that the proposed new SQL-style "references" provide strictly less functionality than foreign keys (a strange argument, to my mind, for wanting to support them!). And he takes me to task for "confusion" over the differences between such SQL-style references, on the one hand, and the familiar relational concept of referential integrity on the other.

Well, I plead guilty as accused ... but such confusions seem to me inevitable, given the considerable overlap in functionality and the unfortunate terminological clashes (note that the very term *reference* itself now means two

---

[23] That name was later dropped, I don't know why. Though I might make a guess.

quite different things!). Whoever was it who thought it would be a good idea to introduce a new feature whose functionality duplicates so extensively that of something that already exists? Whoever was it who took the familiar relational term "reference" and gave it this brand new (additional, but overlapping) meaning? How many times will similar confusions arise in the future? How many *people* will get confused? Has any thought been given to the concomitant problems of teaching, and learning, and communication, and documentation (and on and on)?

Under the same heading, Chamberlin also criticizes another of my examples. The example in question involves the following expression (which makes use of a "pointer join"):

```
SELECT  ex.ENO , dx.DNO
FROM    EMP ex , DEPT dx
WHERE   ex.DADDR = ADDR ( dx )
```

In my original text, I noted the reliance here on the fact that each EMP row had just one corresponding DEPT row, and asked what would happen if the situation changed, such that the same department were now represented in several DEPT rows (e.g., if departments were spread across several locations, and DEPT had one row for each valid DNO / LOCATION combination). I claimed that after such a change, the pointer join wouldn't work any more—or, rather (and more fundamentally), the database design wouldn't be valid any more. I also claimed that, by contrast, the conventional relational design, in which EMP contains a DNO column instead of a DADDR "reference," would still be valid after the change, and the conventional relational join would still work (it would now be a many to many join instead of a many to one join, of course). Here are Chamberlin's comments on this example:

> After [the] change, each reference [i.e., DADDR] value in EMP will still identify a single row in DEPT, perhaps representing the department and location of the given employee. Joining a row of the EMP table to the DEPT row that represents the employee's department and location is a perfectly reasonable thing to do, and there's nothing about Date's example query that won't work any more.

Well, let me just observe that this approach of Chamberlin's:

■ Involves a mass update to EMP to change all EMP.DADDR values appropriately (I'll be charitable and assume no similar mass update is required to DEPT, though in practice I think this assumption probably wouldn't be valid)

- Makes an unwarranted semantic assumption (viz., that each employee has just one corresponding department location)

- Changes the semantics of EMP (or at least of EMP.DADDR)

None of these actions and assumptions would be necessary if the design were based on regular column values instead of "references."

WHY WE DON'T NEED "REFERENCES"

Chamberlin says (in a section titled "Why Do We Need References?"):

> *The Information Principle* ... has served us well over the years. [It] is not compromised by the introduction of [system generated identifiers].

(Yes, it is, if those identifiers are hidden.) And he goes on to say:

> I believe [the sole purpose of] references [is] to simplify the expression of an important class of queries.

In support of this position, he presents two examples, one involving outer join (which I don't propose to discuss here at all because I think it's a major red herring), and the other the well known query "Find names and salaries of employees who make more than their managers." Here's Chamberlin's "references"-style formulation of this latter query:[24]

```
SELECT  ex.NAME , ex.SALARY
FROM    EMP ex
WHERE   ex.SALARY > ex.DEPTREF -> MANAGER -> SALARY
```

But—my goodness!—if that's what all the fuss is about (viz., merely simplifying the formulation of certain queries), well, we can surely achieve that

---

[24] I deliberately leave it as an exercise to figure out the precise semantics of Chamberlin's formulation.

objective without all this baggage of a new data type and "references" (or pointers, or addresses, or whatever you want to call them). Let me illustrate.

First, let's revert to a conventional relational design (i.e., one not involving any SQL-style "references" at all). Thus, let's assume that table DEPT has a conventional key column called DNO; also, let's replace the "references" columns EMP.DEPTREF and DEPT.MANAGER by conventional foreign key columns EMP.DNO and DEPT.MGRNO, respectively. Now consider the following expression:

```
SELECT  ex.NAME , ex.SALARY
FROM    EMP ex
WHERE   ex.SALARY > ex.DNO ▶ DEPT.MGRNO ▶ EMP.SALARY
```

I've just invented this syntax, and I make no great claims for it, and it probably has problems, but I'd be willing to wager I could clean it up satisfactorily. Anyway, for what it's worth, I explain it as follows. First, let *ex* denote some row within the current value of relation variable EMP. Then the expression

```
ex.DNO ▶ DEPT
```

returns the unique row within the current value of relation variable DEPT that's referenced by the value of the DNO foreign key in that EMP row *ex*. Let's call that DEPT row *dx*. Then the expression on the right hand side of the ">" comparison in the WHERE clause is logically equivalent to the expression

```
dx.MGRNO ▶ EMP.SALARY
```

which means, analogously (more or less), the SALARY value in the unique row in the current value of relation variable EMP that's referenced by the value of the MGRNO foreign key in the DEPT row *dx*.

In other words, we don't need pointers as such (or a new REF data type, or SQL-style "references") in order to achieve the desired simplification of expressions; all we need is an operator ("▶") that represents traversal of the relationship between a foreign key and matching target key. I suppose—if you really insist, though I don't think I'd recommend it—I might even let you use the arrow syntax "→" instead of my "▶" notation, but (again) we certainly don't have to buy into the whole pointers idea just to use that syntax!

Let me close by taking this syntactic shorthand issue just a tiny bit further. Don't you think it's odd that even though the SQL syntax is supposed to be "just shorthand" (at least, that's what Chamberlin claims), the whole business of referencing and dereferencing applies only to tables that are *defined in a certain special way*? I complained earlier that it applied only to base tables and not to derived ones; now I observe (and complain further) that it doesn't even apply to all base tables, but only to certain special ones—basically those that are defined to make use of the new REF type (the exact details are a little complex and not too relevant to the overall message of this paper). In other words:

- As I said earlier, I don't think Interpretation 1 is all that interesting.

- On the other hand, I don't have major objections to it, either.

- But I do think that if we decide to go for it, then it should be done properly.

- And it *isn't* being done properly in SQL!

And here's how I closed the original version of my response:

> Don't let the SQL committee do this to us! Let's stop this crazy idea before it's too late!

Well, I tried.

ACKNOWLEDGMENTS

As before I'm grateful, first of all, to Don Chamberlin for forcing me to get my thinking straight on this subject and to get that thinking down on paper. I've always had the greatest respect for Don personally and for his very great contributions to our field, and I hope nobody will take my criticisms as any kind of ad hominem attack. I'm also grateful to Declan Brady and Hugh Darwen for their comments on my original draft.

REFERENCES

1. Donald D. Chamberlin: "Relations and References—Another Point of View," *InfoDB 10*, No. 6 (April 1997).

2. C. J. Date: *SQL and Relational Theory: How to Write Accurate SQL Code*, 3rd edition (O'Reilly, 2015).

3. C. J. Date: Chapter 4 ("Redundancy in SQL") of *Stating the Obvious, and Other Database Writings: Still More Thoughts and Essays on Database Matters* (Technics Publications, 2020).

4. C. J. Date: "Object Identifiers vs. Relational Keys," Chapter 8 of the present book.

5. C. J. Date: "Types, Values, and Variables" (in two parts), Chapters 5 and 6 of the present book.

6. C. J. Date: "Some Principles of Good Language Design," Chapter 6 in the companon volume to the present book.

7. C. J. Date and Hugh Darwen: *Databases, Types, and the Relational Model: The Third Manifesto*, 3rd edition (Addison-Wesley, 2007). See also the website *www.thethirdmanifesto.com*.

8. Richard A. Ganski and Harry K. T. Wong: "Optimization of Nested SQL Queries Revisited," Proc. 1987 ACM SIGMOD Int. Conf. on Management of Data, San Francisco, Calif. (May 1987).

9. Werner Kiessling: "On Semantic Reefs and Efficient Processing of Correlation Queries with Aggregates," Proc. 11th Int. Conf. on Very Large Data Bases, Stockholm, Sweden (August 1985).

10. Won Kim: "On Optimizing an SQL-Like Nested Query," *ACM TODS 7*, No. 3 (September 1982).

11. Jim Melton: "A Shift in the Landscape," *Database Programming & Design 9*, No. 8 (August 1996).

12. Jim Melton: "The What's What of SQL3," *Database Programming & Design 9*, No. 12 (December 1996).

13. Karel Youssefi and Eugene Wong: "Query Processing in a Relational Database Management System," Proc. 5th Int. Conf. on Very Large Data Bases, Rio de Janeiro, Brazil (September 1979).

Chapter 10

Multiple Assignment

Part 1

To targets properly defined
Separate values are assigned;
Disbelief we can suspend—
Constraints are checked at statement end.

—Anon:
Where Bugs Go

Chapter 1 of this book's companion volume referred in passing to
the concept of multiple assignment, which is something I now
consider to be a sine qua non of the relational model—see, e.g., the
section titled "The Relational Model Defined" in Chapter 1 of my
book E. F. Codd and Relational Theory, Revised Edition (Technics
Publications, 2021). Together this chapter and the next explain that
concept in detail and show why it's so important.

Publishing history: This is a revised version of a paper by
Hugh Darwen and myself that was originally published in my book
Date on Database: Writings 2000-2006 (Apress, 2006). I've divided
it into two parts in order to make it a little more digestible. This
version copyright © C. J. Date 2022.

Assignment per se is the only update operator that's logically necessary. This
fact—I'd like to say, this well known fact, but I'm not sure it's really as well

known as it ought to be—is explained in detail in many places, by other writers as well as myself; for example, it's discussed in my book *Using SQL Relationally: How to Write Accurate SQL Code,* 3rd edition (O'Reilly, 20015). As those various writings all show, other update operators are just shorthand for certain assignments (and this is true of the familiar relational INSERT, DELETE, and UPDATE operators in particular). From the point of view of the underlying model, therefore, assignment is the only update operator we need—and in the case of the relational model in particular, this state of affairs is recognized explicitly. However, it's my thesis in these two chapters that the assignment operator in question does need to be a multiple form of that operator, not the more conventional single form we're all familiar with.

So what does multiple assignment mean? Loosely speaking, it means we can assign to several different variables simultaneously. Here's a trivial example:

```
X := 1 , Y := 2 ;
```

The comma separator means the individual or constituent assignments (to variables X and Y, respectively, in the example) are bundled up into a single statement, or in other words into a single, atomic, "unit of execution." Here's a slightly more precise definition of the term *statement* as I'm using it here:

Definition (programming language statement): A construct that causes some action to occur, such as defining or updating a variable or changing the flow of control. All such statements are "atomic," in the sense that no statement—no multiple assignment statement in particular—is ever allowed to fail in the middle (unless explicitly otherwise indicated, of course); in other words, a statement in general either executes in its entirety or has no effect at all, except possibly for raising an exception.

Note that there's an important logical difference between a statement and an expression. Here's a definition of this latter concept:

Definition (programming language expression): A read-only operator invocation; a construct that denotes a value; in effect, a rule for computing, or determining, the value in question. Every expression is of some type— namely, the type of the value it denotes. Literals, constant references, and variable references are all considered to be read-only operator invocations and thus all constitute legal expressions.

Before I go any further, let me also give a precise definition of what I mean by the term *assignment*:

Definition (programming language assignment): A statement consisting of one or more individual assignments, where each individual assignment is an operator that assigns a value (the source, denoted by an expression) to a variable (the target, denoted by a variable reference—syntactically, just a variable name); also, the operation performed when that statement is executed. Each source must be of the same type as the corresponding target, and the operation overall is required to abide by (a) *The Assignment Principle* (always), as well as (b) **The Golden Rule** (if applicable).

Note: The foregoing definition explicitly does *not* incorporate the idea, supported by certain object languages, that "assigning *V1* to *V2*" causes the *address*, not the value, of *V1* to be assigned to *V2*. (Note too that *V1* here would have to be a variable specifically for the foregoing interpretation even to make sense.)

Subsidiary definitions, included here mainly just for completeness:

Definition (*The Assignment Principle*): After assignment of value *v* to variable *V*, the comparison $v = V$ is required to evaluate to TRUE.

Definition (The Golden Rule): No database is ever allowed to violate any integrity constraint.

To get back to the example: The particular multiple assignment shown in that example isn't all that interesting—certainly it fails to convey any hint of the importance that attaches to multiple assignment in general—because even though it's atomic, its effect is equivalent, more or less, to that of the following sequence of two separate single assignments:

```
X := 1 ; Y := 2 ;
```

As we'll see, however, that qualifier "more or less" is definitely needed. To be more specific:

■ With the two separate assignments, a certain notion of *betweenness* exists; that is, we can sensibly talk about the state of affairs that holds after the first assignment has been executed and before the second has. In particular, we can sensibly ask what the values of X and Y are between the two single assignments.

■ By contrast, with the multiple assignment—more specifically the *double* assignment, in the example under discussion—there's no such notion; the concept of there being some intermediate state between the two constituent assignments has no meaning, and in particular we can't sensibly ask what the values of X and Y are "after the first assignment and before the second."

Let me now give a slightly more convincing example:

```
X := Y , Y := X ;
```

This statement has the effect of interchanging the values of X and Y. Without multiple assignment, we can achieve this effect only indirectly, by introducing an intermediate variable (TEMP, say), like this:

```
TEMP := X ; X := Y ; Y := TEMP ;
```

What's more, there are some things that can't be done at all without multiple assignment, as we'll see later. In other words, multiple assignment truly is a primitive (and, to repeat, atomic) operator.

A LITTLE HISTORY

I'll begin by briefly reviewing the concept of single assignment (which is just a special case of multiple assignment, of course). What exactly do I mean by the term "single assignment"? Well, we can surely agree that any assignment, be it single or multiple, involves *sources* and corresponding *targets*, where the sources are values and the targets are variables[1]—and such is the case even if the assignment is specified in terms of INSERT, DELETE, UPDATE, or some other shorthand. Each source is denoted by an expression; each target is denoted by a variable reference (syntactically just a variable name); and there's a one to one correspondence between sources and targets. In practice, of course, there's usually just one source and just one target, but the whole point of the present

---

[1] Or *pseudovariables*—but I'll ignore pseudovariables until further notice.

discussion is to argue in favor of dropping this limitation. For the sake of definiteness, then, I'll say an assignment is *single* if and only if it involves exactly one source and exactly one target.

Now, all imperative programming languages include support for single assignment, though the syntax varies considerably from language to language. Here are some examples of the various syntactic styles currently in use:

```
Algol:      X := Y
APL:        X <- Y
COBOL:      MOVE Y TO X
Fortran:    X = Y
POP-2:      X -> Y
SQL:=       SET X = Y
```

All of these examples (even the POP-2 one) have the effect of assigning the value denoted by the expression Y to the variable denoted by the variable reference X. *Note:* I've deliberately omitted from the foregoing examples all of the usual statement terminators (new line, semicolon, period, etc.) that are typically needed in practice. For definiteness, though:

■ When I do need to show an explicit terminator symbol later (especially in SQL contexts), I'll use a semicolon, as I did in the examples in the previous section.

■ For the assignment operator as such I'll use the Algol symbol (":="), except when I'm explicitly giving an example in some language that uses some different syntax.[2]

Turning now to semantics, the effect of the single assignment

```
target := source
```

is defined as follows: First, the expression *source* on the right side is evaluated; second, the result of that evaluation—i.e., the value denoted by that expression—is assigned to the variable *target* on the left side. In accordance with the definition given earlier, moreover, I assume throughout what follows that *target* and *source* are of the exact same type. In other words, I ignore:

---

[2] As a matter of interest (probably only very slight interest!) I note that the syntax originally proposed for Algol was actually the reverse of what we see today. Thus, the assignment "X := Y" (for example) would originally have been written "Y =: X" instead.

a. The possibility that the value denoted by *source* might be implicitly converted ("coerced") to the declared type of the variable denoted by *target*

b. The possibility that the value denoted by *source* might be of some proper subtype of the declared type of the variable denoted by *target*

Neither of these simplifying assumptions has any significant impact on the discussions to follow.

As noted previously, I also assume that all assignments abide by *The Assgnment Principle*, viz.: After assignment of value *v* to variable *V*, the comparison *v* = *V* is required to evaluate to TRUE. Of course, this principle is so obvious (even trivial) that it might hardly seem worth stating, let alone dignifying with such a grand name. But it's violated so ubiquitously!—especially in SQL. For example:

a. Let X be an SQL variable of type CHAR(3), and let Y be the string 'AB' (of length 2, observe, not 3). After the (legitimate!) assignment SET X = Y, then, the comparison X = Y does *not* necessarily evaluate to TRUE. To be precise, it evaluates to TRUE if PAD SPACE applies to the pertinent "collation," but to FALSE otherwise. See Chapters 1 ("Equality") and 2 ("Assignment") of my book *Stating the Obvious, and Other Database Writings* (Technics Publications, 2020) for a detailed explanation of this bizarre state of affairs.

b. Let X be an SQL variable of any type, let Y be an SQL variable of the same type as X, and let Y currently "be null." After the assignment SET X = Y, then, the comparison X = Y certainly doesn't evaluate to TRUE (in fact it evaluates to UNKNOWN).

That said, however, I should say too that *The Assignment Principle* isn't particularly relevant to the discussions to follow—at least, not explicitly.

For the remainder of this section, the unqualified term "assignment" should be understood to mean single assignment specifically, barring explicit statements to the contrary.

Nonscalar Assignment

Now, assignment as originally defined in most languages was always a *scalar* operator, meaning the source was a scalar value (denoted by a scalar expression) and the target was a scalar variable (denoted by a scalar variable reference). Subsequently, however, various languages introduced various kinds of nonscalar assignments. For example, in PL/I (which uses the same syntactic style as Fortran for assignment), the following code fragment is valid:

```
DECLARE H(10) INTEGER ;
DECLARE K(10) INTEGER ;

H = K ;
```

Explanation: H and K here are one-dimensional array variables of ten (integer) elements each, and the assignment assigns the current value of K to H. But that assignment is really just shorthand—its overall effect is defined to be equivalent to that of the following loop:

```
DO I = 1 TO 10 ;
   H(I) = K(I) ;
END ;
```

The fact that such assignments are just shorthand leads to complications, however. Suppose we revise the example thus:

```
DECLARE H(10) INTEGER ;
DECLARE K(10) INTEGER ;

H = K + H(1) ;
```

The first thing that happens in the expanded form of the assignment here is that a new value is assigned to H(1). But what happens next? To be more specific, in the implicit assignments to H(2), H(3), ..., and H(10), which value of H(1) is used—the old one or the new one? To put it another way, which of the following PL/I code fragments more accurately represents the semantics of the original array assignment?

```
DO I = 1 TO 10 ;              TEMP = H(1) ;
   H(I) = K(I) + H(1) ;       DO I = 1 TO 10 ;
END ;                            H(I) = K(I) + TEMP ;
                              END ;
```

Consideration of examples such as the foregoing quickly leads to the conclusion that nonscalar assignment needs to be properly defined as such—namely, as a "lock, stock, and barrel" assignment of a certain *single* (albeit nonscalar) value to a certain *single* (albeit nonscalar) variable. In the example, the effect of such a definition would be as follows (conceptually, at any rate):

- First, a new array value *v*, say, would be computed in which for all I (I =1, 2, ..., 10) the element *v*(I) is equal to the sum of K(I) and H(1).

- Second, that new array value *v* would then be assigned to the array variable H.

In other words, the overall assignment would really just be a new kind of single assignment.[3]

Pseudovariables

Another extension to assignment as originally defined involves the use of *pseudovariables* (this term is taken from PL/I; *virtual variables* might be a little more apt). Pseudovariables are discussed at length in Chapter 5 of the present book, so I'll content myself here with a very brief review of a few salient points from that chapter.

Essentially, a *pseudovariable reference* consists of an operational expression that appears in the target position of an assignment (i.e., on the left side, in my preferred syntax). Consider the following PL/I code fragment:

```
DECLARE VC CHAR(6) ;

VC = 'Middle' ;
SUBSTR ( VC , 2 , 1 ) = 'u' ;
```

Variable VC here is defined to contain character strings of length exactly six characters. After the first assignment, that variable has the value 'Middle'; after the second, it has the value 'Muddle'—the effect of that second assignment is to "zap" the second character position within the variable, replacing the *i* by

---

[3] Just for the record, the original IBM version of PL/I and the ANSI standard version of that language differ on this issue. In terms of the example, the IBM version would indeed use the new value of H(1) in the implicit assignments to H(2), H(3), ..., and H(10), but the ANSI standard version wouldn't.

a *u*. The expression on the left side of that second assignment is a pseudovariable reference.

Now, it should be clear that the second assignment in the foregoing PL/I example is really shorthand for the following longer one:

```
VC = SUBSTR ( VC , 1 , 1 ) || 'u' || SUBSTR ( VC , 3 , 4 ) ;
```

Here the left side is a simple variable reference, as is normally (and fundamentally!) required for assignment. As for the right side, the expression on that side denotes the character string obtained by concatenating, in left to right order, the first character of the current value of VC, the character *u*, and the last four characters of the current value of VC. It follows that the overall assignment has the effect already explained.

Note carefully that the foregoing—viz., the fact that the original assignment in the example is really just shorthand for some longer assignment—isn't just a fluke; rather, it's *always* the case that an assignment that involves a pseudovariable reference is logically equivalent to one that doesn't. Thus, pseudovariables aren't logically required (they're only shorthand); however, they can be extremely useful in practice, for reasons of "user friendliness" if not for any others.

Recall now *The Third Manifesto*, by Hugh Darwen and myself, and the language **Tutorial D** that Darwen and I use to illustrate the concepts espoused by our *Manifesto* (refer to the preface to this book if you need to refresh your memory concerning these matters). One form of pseudovariable that in the *Manifesto* we regard as particularly important makes use of what we call *THE_ operators*. Consider the following code fragment, expressed in **Tutorial D**:

```
TYPE POINT /* geometric points in two-dimensional space */
    POSSREP CARTESIAN { X RATIONAL , Y RATIONAL } ;

VAR P POINT INIT CARTESIAN ( 0.0 , 0.0 ) ;

THE_Y ( P ) := 5.0 ;
```

Explanation: Values of type POINT can "possibly be represented"—see the POSSREP specification in the POINT type definition—by cartesian coordinates X and Y, each of which is a rational number. Variable P is declared to be of type POINT and has initial value the origin—i.e., the point whose cartesian coordinates X and Y coordinates are both 0.0 (see the INIT specification). The assignment statement then sets the Y coordinate of P to the value 5.0 (speaking a trifle loosely). And as you can see, the target of that assignment is a pseudovariable.

However, the assignment statement in this example, which involves a pseudovariable, is defined to be shorthand for the following, which doesn't:

```
P := CARTESIAN ( THE_X ( P ) , 5.0 ) ;
```

The expression on the right side here is a *selector invocation*; to be specific, it's an invocation of that unique selector that corresponds to the CARTESIAN possible representation, as declared for type POINT. In general, a selector is an operator that's used to "select," or specify, values of some specified type; every type has exactly one selector for each possible representation that's declared for the type in question, and every selector has the same name as the possible representation it corresponds to. In the example, therefore, the CARTESIAN selector invocation selects exactly that point whose X coordinate is that of the point value contained in variable P and whose Y coordinate is 5.0. (As a matter of fact, we've already seen another example of a CARTESIAN selector invocation: namely, the expression CARTESIAN (0.0,0.0), which appears in the INIT specification in the definition of variable P.)

For further explanation of possible representations, selectors, THE_ operators, and related matters, please refer to Chapter 5.

ASSIGNING TO SEVERAL VARIABLES AT THE SAME TIME

Now (at last!) I can begin to discuss multiple assignment as such. Earlier, I characterized multiple assignment, loosely, as an operator that lets us assign to several variables simultaneously. Well, the idea of assigning to several variables simultaneously is far from new—many languages provide some such facility already. For example, the following is a valid Algol statement:

```
A := B := C := D ;
```

The effect of this statement is to assign the value of the source expression D to each of the target variables A, B, and C. More precisely, the statement is defined to be shorthand for a sequence of statements along the following lines:

```
A := D ;
B := D ;
C := D ;
```

In effect, therefore, the source expression D is evaluated just once, and the result of that evaluation is then assigned to each of the target variables A, B, and C in sequence. (Actually there's a slight complication here if any of the target variables happens to be subscripted, but we can safely ignore the details of that complication for present purposes.)

Analogously, in PL/I we can say:

```
A , B , C = D ;
```

Again the effect is to assign the value of D to each of A, B, and C.[4] *Note:* The same complication regarding subscripts applies here as well. But there are additional complications in the PL/I case that I don't think apply to the Algol counterpart. For example, what does the following do?

```
SUBSTR ( VC , 1 , 2 ) , SUBSTR ( VC , 2 , 2 ) = 'co' ;
```

But, again, such complications need not concern us here.

Next, some languages also support certain nonscalar assignments, as we already know. If those assignments are regarded as, in effect, assigning to several scalar variables at the same time, they might be thought of as another kind of multiple assignment. As I've already said, however, I believe they should *not* be so regarded but should rather be defined as true nonscalar assignments, in which case they aren't multiple assignments at all but single assignments instead.

Third, in his book *A Discipline of Programming* (Prentice-Hall, 1976), Edsger W. Dijkstra briefly discusses what he calls a *concurrent* form of assignment, according to which, e.g., the statement

```
X , Y := Y , X ;
```

has the effect of interchanging the values of X and Y. (Near the beginning of this chapter, I used a statement of the form

```
X := Y , Y := X ;
```

---

[4] As a matter of fact PL/I even uses the term *multiple assignment* for such a construct. By contrast, Robert W. Sebesta (in the 1989 edition of his book *Concepts of Programming Languages*, published by Benjamin/Cummings) calls it *multiple target assignment*, which in some respects is actually a better term, inasmuch as "multiple" target variables are assigned the same source value.

to achieve the same effect.) In other words, the syntax of Dijkstra's concurrent assignment looks something like this:

```
target-commalist := source-commalist ;
```

The two commalists must contain the same number, n say, of sources and targets, and the semantics are as follows: First, all of the n sources are evaluated; second, the result of evaluating the ith source is assigned to the ith target ($i = 1$, 2, ..., n). Note carefully, however, that the targets must all be distinct. As Dijkstra puts it, "it would be foolish to attach to a statement such as

```
X , X := 1 , 2 ;
```

any meaning other than *error*." *Note:* I've reworded Dijkstra's remarks just slightly here (more to the point, I'm going to disagree with them later).

Last, consider the following SQL UPDATE statement:

```
UPDATE EMP
SET    SALARY = 1.1 * SALARY ,
       BONUS = SALARY
WHERE  DEPT = 'Programming' ;
```

The effect of this UPDATE is, for every employee in the programming department, (a) to set the bonus equal to the current salary and (b) to increase the salary by ten percent. It might be claimed, therefore, that we have here yet another example of multiple assignment: The UPDATE shown assigns to several portions of several rows "at the same time" within table EMP.[5] Such an UPDATE resembles Dijkstra's concurrent assignment in that:

a. All of the expressions on the right sides of assignments in the SET clause are evaluated before any of those assignments are performed.

b. No two of those assignments are allowed to specify the same target column. (Actually I'm simplifying matters just slightly here. See the appendix at the end of the next chapter for further discussion.)

---

[5] In this chapter and the next, I use the terms *relation*, *tuple*, and *attribute* in relational contexts but the terms *table*, *row*, and *column* in SQL contexts.

Please note, however, that I said "it might be claimed" that the foregoing UPDATE statement constitutes an example of multiple assignment. I definitely wouldn't make such a claim myself, though! Note in particular that in order for the idea of assignment to rows (or portions of rows) to make any sense, the "rows" in question must be row variables specifically. But SQL tables are *not* collections of row variables, any more than, e.g., arrays are collections of element variables (see the section "A Little History," earlier). To spell the point out in detail, therefore: UPDATE in SQL—and UPDATE in a relational language like **Tutorial D**, come to that—is best understood as shorthand for assigning *a single value* (namely, a table or relation value) to *a single variable* (namely, a table or relation variable); in other words, it's really another case of single (but nonscalar) assignment. Analogous remarks apply to INSERT and DELETE, of course.

To summarize, there are at least four constructs already described in the literature that might lay some claim to being called "multiple assignment," as follows:

1. An assignment that assigns the same source value (more precisely, the result of evaluating the same source expression) to several targets

2. Nonscalar assignment

3. Dijkstra's concurrent assignment

4. SQL's UPDATE statement

However, the kind of multiple assignment we need, and the kind I'll be talking about from this point forward, is different from all of these! Dijkstra's notion of concurrent assignment is, perhaps, closest to what we need and what I'll be discussing. Unlike Dijkstra, however, I won't require that the target variables all be distinct; in some cases, in fact, the ability to assign to the same target variable more than once turns out to be positively desirable, for reasons that should, I hope, soon become clear.

AN EXAMPLE

At this point, it would be nice if I could explain exactly what my preferred version of multiple assignment looks like. As you might guess, however, the fact that we sometimes need to be able to specify the same target variable more than once causes complications, and I'm not yet in a position to explain just what those complications are. Until further notice, therefore, I'll focus not so much on what the operator actually is, but rather on why we need it and why systems should support it—and I hope the examples will be sufficient, for now, to give some idea as to how it's supposed to work.

As a basis for my first example, consider the usual suppliers-and-parts database, with definition and sample value as shown in the preface. (Recall too that the objects in that database labeled S, P, and SP are relation variables or *relvars*). Suppose that database is subject to the admittedly rather contrived, but possible, constraint that supplier S1 and part P1 must never be in different cities. Here's a **Tutorial D** formulation of this constraint:

```
CONSTRAINT S1_P1_COLOCATED
      COUNT ( ( S WHERE SNO = SNO ('S1') ) { CITY }
                UNION
              ( P WHERE PNO = PNO ('P1') ) { CITY } ) ≤ 1 ;
```

Paraphrasing: If relvars S and P contain tuples for supplier S1 and part P1, respectively, then those tuples must contain the same CITY value (if they didn't, the COUNT invocation would return the value two); however, it's legal for relvar S to contain no tuple for S1, or relvar P to contain no tuple for P1, or both.

Given the sample database value shown in the preface, then, each of the following UPDATEs will fail:

```
UPDATE S WHERE SNO = SNO ('S1') : { CITY := 'Paris' } ;

UPDATE P WHERE PNO = PNO ('P1') : { CITY := 'Paris' } ;
```

By contrast, the following UPDATE will succeed (note the comma separator):

```
UPDATE S WHERE SNO = SNO ('S1') : { CITY := 'Paris' } ,
UPDATE P WHERE PNO = PNO ('P1') : { CITY := 'Paris' } ;
```

Explanation: Of course, UPDATE is really assignment, and the various UPDATE statements in this example are basically all assignment statements. For example, the statement

```
UPDATE S WHERE SNO = SNO ('S1') : { CITY := 'Paris' } ;
```

(the one that attempts to move supplier S1 to Paris) is shorthand for something like the following:

```
S := ( S WHERE SNO ≠ SNO ('S1') )
        UNION
      ( EXTEND S WHERE SNO = SNO ('S1') :
                          { CITY := 'Paris' } ;
```

It follows that the successful UPDATE in the example is indeed a multiple assignment; in fact, it involves precisely two target variables, relvar S and relvar P, and it assigns one value to one of these variables and another to the other. By contrast, the UPDATEs that failed were both single assignments. And so we have here our first example of a multiple assignment that can't be simulated by a sequence of single assignments. As I claimed earlier, in other words, there are some things that can't be done at all without multiple assignment, and multiple assignment thus truly is a new primitive operator.

Let's get back to the example. As that example suggests, and correctly suggests, it's the fact that *certain constraints are in effect* that makes it impossible for certain multiple assignments to be replaced by a sequence of single assignments. As you might have realized, however, I'm making a tacit assumption here: viz., that all constraint checking is immediate, meaning that it's done "at end of statement" or, loosely, "at semicolons." Thus, you might be thinking that if such checking were deferred instead—specifically, deferred to "end of transaction"—then there wouldn't be any need for multiple assignment after all, at least as far as the example under discussion is concerned. And indeed you'd be right in thinking so. But there are very good reasons for insisting that checking never be deferred in the foregoing sense, reasons I've explained in detail elsewhere (see, e.g., my book *SQL and Relational Theory: How to Write Accurate SQL Code*, 3rd edition, O'Reilly, 2015). And multiple assignment is required—in the example under discussion, at any rate—as a logical consequence of this state of affairs.

Incidentally, the foregoing discussion serves to highlight a significant difference in emphasis (not the only one) between multiple assignment as proposed here and Dijkstra's concurrent assignment. *The main reason for wanting to be able to perform several separate—though presumably interrelated—assignments as a single operation is to ensure that no integrity checking is done until all of the assignments in question have been executed.* This emphasis on the importance of integrity checking is surely understandable, given the context (viz., database management). By contrast, Dijkstra's language presumably didn't support integrity constraints, in the usual database sense, at all; hence, the problems that multiple assignment is intended to address presumably just didn't arise.

To say it again, therefore: If constraint checking is immediate, there's no way the multiple assignment in the foregoing example can be simulated by any sequence of single assignments, and so multiple assignment really is a new primitive operator. But let me add a small historical note here: The fact is, multiple assignment is trickier than it looks. Darwen and I first proposed such an operator in *The Third Manifesto*, but we didn't get it quite right—in fact, we got it wrong twice, in two different ways. I'll elaborate on these matters in the section on semantics in the next chapter.

WHY WE NEED MULTIPLE ASSIGNMENT

I showed in the previous section that one important reason why we need multiple assignment is that we need to be able to perform several individual assignments without checking any constraints until all of the assignments in question have been executed. Indeed, that particular reason is easily the most important one— but there are others, and this section discusses some of them.

Convenience

The multiple assignment

```
X := Y , Y := X ;
```

is surely more convenient (more user friendly, and possibly less error prone too) than its single assignment counterpart

```
TEMP := X ;   X := Y ;   Y := TEMP ;
```

Note: This first argument is perhaps not very compelling; however, it does become a little more so if the variables X and Y are nonscalar. Consider what happens if they're array variables, for example, when even just having to declare the auxiliary variable TEMP becomes a little painful.

Assigning to Several Attributes at the Same Time

Suppose supplier S5 acquires a new name (Clark) and a new status (45) and moves to Paris. Then the statement

```
UPDATE S WHERE SNO = SNO ('S5') :
     { SNAME := 'Clark' , STATUS := 45 , CITY := 'Paris' } ;
```

is preferable for several reasons to the following sequence of statements:

```
UPDATE S WHERE SNO = SNO ('S5') : { SNAME := 'Clark' } ;

UPDATE S WHERE SNO = SNO ('S5') : { STATUS := 45 } ;

UPDATE S WHERE SNO = SNO ('S5') : { CITY := 'Paris' } ;
```

Note: Considered as an argument in favor of multiple assignment, the foregoing argument, like the previous one, isn't very compelling—but the reason it isn't is that it isn't actually an argument for multiple assignment at all! Indeed, the given example doesn't involve any multiple assignment.[6] Au contraire, in fact: Each of the four UPDATEs shown, including the first one in particular, is a *single* assignment—each one assigns a single relation value to a single relation variable (or relvar), viz., the suppliers relvar S. In other words, to think of the first of those UPDATEs in particular as somehow being a "multiple" assignment, with targets the "variables" SNAME, STATUS, and CITY, is strictly incorrect.

On the other hand, however, UPDATE does share with multiple assignment the property that all of the source expressions are evaluated before any updating is done, a fact that can be significant if any of those source expressions includes a reference to any of the target attributes. Not to mention the fact that UPDATE is, of course, an atomic operation, which implies that there's certainly a semantic difference between the first of the UPDATEs in the foregoing example and the sequence consisting of the other three.

---

[6] Compare the SQL UPDATE example discussed in the section "Assigning to Several Variables at the Same Time," earlier.

Assigning to Several Relvars at the Same Time (I)

Suppose we want to enforce a "cascade delete" rule that says that when a supplier is deleted, all shipments for that supplier must be deleted too. For example:

```
DELETE S  WHERE SNO = SNO ('S1') ,
DELETE SP WHERE SNO = SNO ('S1') ;
```

Of course, we might expect the system to perform such "compensatory actions" on our behalf, automatically;[7] but even so, the implication is only that multiple assignment is needed by the system as well as by the user—under the covers, as it were, as well as above them.

Assigning to Several Relvars at the Same Time (II)

Consider the following database definition:

```
VAR EMP RELATION
   { ENO ENO , ENAME CHAR , DNO DNO , ... }
     KEY { ENO }
     FOREIGN KEY { DNO } REFERENCES DEPT ;

VAR DEPT RELATION
   { DNO DNO , DNAME CHAR , ENO ENO , ... }
     KEY { DNO }
     FOREIGN KEY { ENO } REFERENCES EMP ;
```

The semantics are that (a) every employee works in exactly one department and that (b) every department has exactly one manager (where attribute ENO in relvar DEPT identifies the manager in question). Observe, therefore, that each of EMP and DEPT includes a foreign key that references the other (in other words, there's a "referential cycle" involved). As a consequence, the multiple assignment

---

[7] By "automatically" here, I mean the following. First, the cascade delete rule should be specified declaratively, not procedurally (presumably as part of the declaration of the fact that {SNO} in relvar SP is a foreign key matching the key {SNO} of relvar S). Second, the user should only have to request a DELETE on relvar S, and the necessary compensatory DELETE on relvar SP should be done implicitly by the system. *Note:* Even if such compensatory actions are indeed performed automatically, however, users will still have to be aware of them, in general (and they will be, thanks to those declarative specifications).

```
INSERT EMP  RELATION { TUPLE { ENO ENO ('E1') ,
                               DNO DNO ('D1') } } ,
INSERT DEPT RELATION { TUPLE { ENO ENO ('E1') ,
                               DNO DNO ('D1') } } ;
```

might well succeed, whereas the following pair of assignments will fail (no matter which is executed first):

```
INSERT EMP  RELATION { TUPLE { ENO ENO ('E1') ,
                               DNO DNO ('D1') } } ;

INSERT DEPT RELATION { TUPLE { ENO ENO ('E1') ,
                               DNO DNO ('D1') } } ;
```

Assigning to Several Relvars at the Same Time (III)

Consider the suppliers-and-parts database once again. Our usual design for that database assumes that every part has a color. Suppose, however, that for some parts the property of having a color doesn't apply, while for others the color is relevant but unknown. Then—ignoring part names, weights, and cities for simplicity—the following alternative design is preferable:[8]

```
VAR P RELATION          /* master parts list */
  { PNO    PNO }
    KEY { PNO } ;

VAR PCOL RELATION       /* parts with known color */
  { PNO    PNO ,
    COLOR COLOR }
    KEY { PNO }
    FOREIGN KEY { PNO } REFERENCES P ;

VAR PNCOL RELATION      /* parts with no color */
  { PNO    PNO }
    KEY { PNO }
    FOREIGN KEY { PNO } REFERENCES P ;

VAR PUCOL RELATION      /* parts with unknown color */
  { PNO    PNO }
    KEY { PNO }
    FOREIGN KEY { PNO } REFERENCES P ;
```

---

[8] I've discussed the advantages of such a design in may places—most extensively in Chapter14 of my book *Database Design and Relational Theory: Normal Forms and All That Jazz*, 2nd edition (Apress, 2019), also in Chapter 2 of my book *Fifty Years of Relational, and Other Database Writings* (Technics Publications, 2020).

Of course, the foregoing definitions ought also to include an explicit constraint to the effect that every part number appearing in relvar P must also appear in exactly one of the other three. I omit the details of that constraint for simplicity (though I do assume it's being enforced). It should be clear, then, that, e.g., "inserting a new part" will require two updates to be performed at the same time: one on relvar P, and one on one of the other three relvars. (The situation is similar but not identical to that illustrated by the EMP / DEPT example above— the difference is that there's no foreign key, as such, from relvar P to any of the other three relvars in this design.)

View Updating

Consider a view V defined as, e.g., A JOIN B or A UNION B for some A and B. Without going into details, it should be clear that an update to V will require updates to both A and B, in general, and hence that such an update to V is really shorthand for some multiple assignment (perhaps under the covers again).

Performance

Strictly speaking I shouldn't even be mentioning this point, since my primary concern is—as always—with getting the model right first before worrying about the implementation. But it does seem reasonable to expect that executing a multiple assignment will often be more efficient than executing an equivalent sequence of single ones (not to mention the fact that such an equivalent sequence might not even exist). In particular, such an expectation seems reasonable if the same target variable is specified more than once. For if the same target variable, V say, is specified n times in a given multiple assignment, it's surely reasonable to see the implementation to update V just once, while n separate single assignments will probably involve n separate updates. In fact, the formal definition of multiple assignment effectively requires just a single update in such a situation!—which brings me to the next section.

ASSIGNING TO THE SAME VARIABLE MORE THAN ONCE

Recall that assignment to a THE_ pseudovariable (like assignment to any pseudovariable, in fact) is really shorthand for a longer assignment that doesn't involve pseudovariables at all. In the case of type POINT, for example (see the section "A Little History," earlier), the assignment

```
THE_Y ( P )  := 5.0 ;
```

is shorthand for the following expanded form:

```
P := CARTESIAN ( THE_X ( P ) , 5.0 ) ;
```

Suppose now that the initial value of the variable P is the origin (0.0,0.0), and consider the following multiple assignment:

```
THE_X ( P )  := 7.0 , THE_Y ( P )  := 5.0 ;
```

If we simply expand the two constituent assignments individually, we obtain this:

```
P := CARTESIAN ( 7.0 , THE_Y ( P ) ) ,
P := CARTESIAN ( THE_X ( P ) , 5.0 ) ;
```

What are the semantics of this latter statement (which is still, please observe, a multiple assignment)? Well, suppose we apply the usual rule: namely, we evaluate all of the right sides first (i.e., before doing any assignments), and then we go on to perform the actual assignments in sequence. Then:

- The expression CARTESIAN (7.0, THE_Y (P)) in the first of the two constituent assignments returns the point value (7.0,0.0).

- The expression CARTESIAN (THE_X (P), 5.0) in the second of the two constituent assignments returns the point value (0.0,5.0).

The net result is thus that P is assigned the point value (0.0,5.0)—*not* the point value (7.0,5.0), as presumably required; in other words, the assignment to THE_X has had no lasting effect. (To be more precise, it does have an effect in the first of the two constituent assignments, but the second of those assignments then causes the result of the first to be overwritten.)

Clearly, what we need to do is collect together the two constituent assignments somehow, such that the result of the first is *combined* with that of the second instead of being overwritten by it. I'll show how this can be done in the next chapter. First, however, I want to say a little more regarding the foregoing example specifically. That example consists of a multiple assignment in which the same variable, P, appears as a target more than once—which is reasonable on the face of it, because that's what we want; I mean, we do want to assign to the same variable more than once, albeit to different portions of that variable in different constituent assignments (speaking a trifle loosely). Thus, while I might agree with Dijkstra that a multiple assignment of the form

```
X := 1 , X := 2 ;
```

doesn't make a lot of sense,[9] I don't agree that assigning to the same variable more than once is always an error. And I definitely don't want to impose a syntax rule to that effect, therefore.

Let's look at a couple more examples. First, here's one involving arrays:

```
VAR A ARRAY INTEGER [5]
    INIT ARRAY INTEGER [ 1 , 2 , 3 , 4 , 5 ] ;

A[4] := 0 , A[2] := 8 ;
```

Observe first that, logically speaking, expressions A[4] and A[2] on the left sides of the constituent assignments here are in fact pseudovariable references, and so we're definitely talking about pseudovariables once again. Expanding each of those constituent assignments individually yields:

```
A := ARRAY INTEGER [ A[1] , A[2] , A[3] , 0 , A[5] ] ,
A := ARRAY INTEGER [ A[1] , 8 , A[3] , A[4] , A[5] ] ;
```

The constituent assignments here both involve the same target variable—namely, the array variable A—and the effect of the foregoing "expanded" statement overall is to set A to the array value A [1,8,3,4,5] (again, the first of the constituent assignments has no lasting effect). Clearly, however, what we'd like is for the original multiple assignment to be treated as equivalent to the following:

```
A := ARRAY INTEGER [ A[1] , 8 , A[3] , 0 , A[5] ] ;
```

Again, I'll explain how this effect can be achieved in the next chapter.

---

[9] But not no sense at all. That is, there's a definite meaning that can or at least could be ascribed to it, even if that meaning might not be particularly useful in practice.

For a final example, I return to suppliers and parts. Suppose that for some (bizarre!) reason, relvar S is subject to the constraint that suppliers S2 and S3 must always have total status 40. Then each of the following single assignments will fail (I use the UPDATE shorthand for convenience):

```
UPDATE S WHERE SNO = SNO ('S2') : { STATUS := 15 } ;

UPDATE S WHERE SNO = SNO ('S3') : { STATUS := 25 } ;
```

But the following multiple assignment will succeed (again I use the UPDATE shorthand):

```
UPDATE S WHERE SNO = SNO ('S2') : { STATUS := 15 } ,
UPDATE S WHERE SNO = SNO ('S3') : { STATUS := 25 } ;
```

Again both of the constituent assignments involve the same target variable, here relvar S. *Note:* This time I'll leave the desired single assignment equivalent as a (somewhat nontrivial) exercise.

Chapter 11

Multiple Assignment

Part 2

For a description of the background to this chapter, please see the preamble to Chapter 10. This version copyright © 2022 C. J. Date.

SEMANTICS

The previous chapter should be sufficient to hint at some of the complications involved in getting the semantics of multiple assignment right; indeed, in our work on *The Third Manifesto*, Darwen and I got them wrong twice, as I've said. Partly because I think that examining blind alleys can be instructive, however (and partly just for the record), I summarize our failed attempts below. Let multiple assignment *MA* consist of single assignments, in sequence, *A1*, *A2*, ..., *An*. Then:

- In the first (1998) edition of our *Manifesto* book, we simply defined *MA* to be equivalent to executing *A1*, *A2*, ..., *An* in sequence (except that no constraint checking was done until the very end, of course). This definition didn't work because it meant (for example) that the assignment

    ```
    X := Y , Y := X ;
    ```

    would fail to interchange the values of X and Y (it would set X equal to Y but then leave Y unchanged).

■ In the second (2000) edition of our book, by contrast, we required all of the right sides to be evaluated first; then we required *A1*, *A2*, ..., *An* to be executed in parallel (followed by the constraint checking). This definition didn't work because it meant (for example) that the assignment

```
X := Y , X := Z ;
```

would have an unpredictable effect.

And in the book *Temporal Data and the Relational Model*, by C. J. Date, Hugh Darwen, and Nikos A. Lorentzos (Morgan Kaufmann, 2003), we got the semantics wrong *again* ... To be specific, we required all of the right sides to be evaluated first, and then we required *A1*, *A2*, ..., *An* to be executed in sequence instead of in parallel (followed by constraint checking as usual). This definition didn't work because it meant (for example) that the assignment

```
THE_X ( P ) := 7.0 , THE_Y ( P ) := 5.0 ;
```

would have no effect on THE_X(P), as explained in the final section of the previous chapter.

Here then is my, and our, current last word (!) on the subject. Again, let *MA* be the multiple assignment

```
A1 , A2 , ... , An ;
```

Then the semantics of *MA* are defined by the following pseudocode (Steps 1-4):

1. For $i = 1, 2, ..., n$, expand any syntactic shorthands involved in *Ai* (in other words, replace assignments to pseudovariables by appropriate assignments to variables as such). After all such expansions, let *MA* take the form

```
B1 , B2 , ... , Bz ;
```

for some $z \geq n$, where for all i $(1 \leq i \leq z)$ *Bi* is of the form

```
Vi := Xi
```

such that:

a.   *Vi* (*i* = 1, 2, ..., *z*) is the name of some declared variable (not a pseudovariable) not defined in terms of any others.

   Note: That qualifying phrase "not defined in terms of any others" is intended to take care of assignment to views. Views are variables that *are* defined in terms of others; thus, assignments to views are replaced by assignments to the relevant view defining expressions,[1] and those assignments in turn are then replaced by assignments to the relvars in terms of which the views are defined. This process is repeated until all of the assignments have base relvars as their targets.

b.   *Xi* (*i* = 1, 2, ..., *z*) is an expression whose declared type is the same as that of *Vi*.

   Note: The declared type of an operational expression is the declared type of the result of the outermost operator involved in that expression.

2.   Let *p* and *q* (1 ≤ *p* < *q* ≤ *z*) be such that *Vp* and *Vq* are identical and there's no *r* (*r* < *p* or *p* < *r* < *q*) such that *Vp* and *Vr* are identical. Replace *Bq* in *MA* by an assignment of the form

```
Vq := WITH ( Vq := Xp ) : Xq
```

and remove *Bp* from *MA*. Repeat this process until no such pair *p* and *q* remains. Let *MA* now consist of the sequence

```
U1 := Y1 , U2 := Y2 , ... , Um := Ym ;
```

where each *Ui* is some *Vj* (1 ≤ *i* ≤ *j* ≤ *m* ≤ *z*).

3.   For *i* = 1, 2, ..., *m*, evaluate *Yi*. Let the result be *yi*.

4.   For *i* = 1, 2, ..., *m*, assign *yi* to *Ui*.

Let me elaborate briefly on Step 2, since the implications of that step might not be immediately apparent. Consider again the following multiple assignment from the final section of the previous chapter:

---

[1] Note that updating a view is, logically, an assignment to a pseudovariable.

```
THE_X ( P ) := 7.0 , THE_Y ( P ) := 5.0 ;
```

In accordance with Step 1, we first expand the two constituent assignments, to obtain:

```
P := CARTESIAN ( 7.0 , THE_Y ( P ) ) ,
P := CARTESIAN ( THE_X ( P ) , 5.0 ) ;
```

Now we have two assignments with the same target. In accordance with Step 2, therefore, we remove the first and replace the second by:

```
P := WITH ( P := CARTESIAN ( 7.0 , THE_Y ( P ) ) ) :
            CARTESIAN ( THE_X ( P ) , 5.0 ) ;
```

This latter assignment in turn is equivalent to:

```
P := CARTESIAN
        ( THE_X ( CARTESIAN ( 7.0 , THE_Y ( P ) ) ) , 5.0 ) ;
```

And *this* assignment is equivalent to:

```
P := CARTESIAN ( 7.0 , 5.0 ) ;
```

The desired result is thereby attained.

By way of another example, suppose type POINT corresponds to points in *three*-dimensional space and can thus "possibly be represented" by cartesian coordinates *x*, *y*, and *z*, and consider the multiple assignment:

```
THE_X ( P ) := 7.0 ,
THE_Y ( P ) := 5.0 ,
THE_Z ( P ) := 6.0 ;
```

(where P is, of course, a variable of type POINT once again). Step 1 yields:

```
P := CARTESIAN ( 7.0, THE_Y ( P ) , THE_Z ( P ) ) ,
P := CARTESIAN ( THE_X ( P ) , 5.0, THE_Z ( P ) ) ,
P := CARTESIAN ( THE_X ( P ) , THE_Y ( P ), 6.0 ) ;
```

Step 2 then yields:

```
P := WITH
   ( P := CARTESIAN ( 7.0 , THE_Y ( P ) , THE_Z ( P ) ) ) :
      WITH
   ( P := CARTESIAN ( THE_X ( P ) , 5.0 , THE_Z ( P ) ) ) :
          CARTESIAN ( THE_X ( P ) , THE_Y ( P ) , 6.0 ) ;
```

This assignment in turn is equivalent to:

```
P := CARTESIAN
       ( THE_X ( CARTESIAN
                   ( THE_X ( CARTESIAN ( 7.0 ,
                                         THE_Y ( P ) ,
                                         THE_Z ( P ) ) ) ,
                     5.0 ,
                     THE_Z ( CARTESIAN ( 7.0 ,
                                         THE_Y ( P ) ,
                                         THE_Z ( P ) ) ) ) ) ,
         THE_Y ( CARTESIAN
                   ( THE_X ( CARTESIAN ( 7.0 ,
                                         THE_Y ( P ) ,
                                         THE_Z ( P ) ) ) ,
                     5.0 ,
                     THE_Z ( CARTESIAN ( 7.0 ,
                                         THE_Y ( P ) ,
                                         THE_Z ( P ) ) ) ) ) ,
         6.0 ) ;
```

And *this* assignment—if you analyze it carefully!—turns out to be equivalent to just:

```
P := CARTESIAN ( 7.0 , 5.0 , 6.0 ) ;
```

SYNTAX

In this section I summarize the syntax I've been using in examples thus far. The syntax is based on that of **Tutorial D** but is deliberately, and considerably, simplified for present purposes. In particular, I've tried to choose names for syntactic categories in this simplified grammar that are suggestive of the intended semantics, and I've therefore felt free to omit numerous rules that would need to be included, perhaps in prose form, in a more complete definition. I've included a few explanatory comments, however.

```
<assignment>
   ::=   <assign> [ , <assign commalist> ] ;
```

Comment: I reject the "obvious" syntax of Dijkstra's concurrent assignment (which uses a source commalist, a target commalist, and a single assignment symbol between them) because that syntax doesn't work very well when some of the constituent assignments (or "<*assign*>s") are expressed in the form of INSERT or DELETE or UPDATE shorthands. In any case, **Tutorial D** as a general rule spurns reliance on ordinal position as a basis for pairwise matching; left to right ordering of attributes of relations is expressly prohibited in the relational model, and it seemed to us—i.e., Darwen and myself—a good design principle to apply the same rule to other constructs in the language.[2]

```
<assign>
    ::=   <scalar assign>
        | <nonscalar assign>

<scalar assign>
    ::=   <scalar target> := <scalar exp>
```

Comment: We could if we wanted—and in fact we do—include another form of <*scalar assign*>, viz., <*scalar update*>, parallel to and somewhat along the lines of <*relation update*>. See the next section for further details.

```
<scalar target>
    ::=   <scalar var ref>
        | <pseudo scalar var ref>
```

Comment: A <*scalar var ref*> is just a scalar variable name. I omit further details of <*pseudo scalar var ref*>s.

```
<nonscalar assign>
    ::=   <relation assign>
```

Comment: The only kind of nonscalar assignment I discuss here is relational assignment, but we could clearly include other kinds if we wanted (e.g., <*tuple assign*>, <*array assign*>, and so on), and **Tutorial D** in fact does.

---

[2] More specifically, we wanted the semantics of a commalist to be independent, as far as possible, of the sequence in which the elements of that commalist happen to be specified. However, we did depart from this goal in certain contexts. One important case occurs in connection with prefix operator invocations—if the operator in question is defined in terms of two or more parameters, then (as in many other languages) invocations of that operator use ordinal position to match up arguments and parameters.

```
<relation assign>
   ::=    <relation target> := <relation exp>
          | <relation insert>
          | <relation delete>
          | <relation update>

<relation target>
   ::=    <relation var ref>
          | <pseudo relation var ref>
```

Comment: A *<relation var ref>* is just a relvar name. I omit further details of *<pseudo relation var ref>*s.

```
<relation insert>
   ::=    INSERT <relation target> <relation exp>

<relation delete>
   ::=    DELETE <relation target> [ WHERE <bool exp> ]
```

Comment: The *<bool exp>* is allowed to include an *<attribute ref>*, q.v., wherever a literal would be allowed. An analogous remark applies to the production rule immediately following as well.

```
<relation update>
   ::=    UPDATE <relation target> [ WHERE <bool exp> ] :
                 { <attribute update>
                         [ , <attribute update commalist> ] }

<attribute update>
   ::=    <attribute target> := <exp>
```

Comment: The *<exp>* is allowed to include an *<attribute ref>* wherever a literal would be allowed.

```
<attribute target>
   ::=    <attribute ref> | <pseudo attribute ref>
```

Comment: An *<attribute ref>* is just an attribute name. I omit further details of *<pseudo attribute ref>*s.

BUT WHAT ABOUT TYPE CONSTRAINTS?

I have a significant piece of unfinished business to attend to. Suppose we're given a type ELLIPSE, defined as follows:

```
TYPE ELLIPSE
    POSSREP ( A INTEGER , B INTEGER , CTR POINT )
            CONSTRAINT A ≥ B ;
```

Explanation: I assume for simplicity that:

- Ellipses can "possibly be represented" by their major semiaxis *a*, their minor semiaxis *b*, and their center *ctr*.

- The semiaxes are just integers, and the center is a point in two-dimensional space.

- Since the specified possible representation has been given no explicit name of its own, it and the corresponding selector are both given the type name— viz., ELLIPSE—by default.

Note: For brevity, I'll refer to the semiaxes and the center of a given ellipse as its *components*. Please note immediately, however, that this usage is more than a little sloppy; the components in question aren't really components of the ellipse as such, they're components of the specified possible representation of that ellipse. But the usage is convenient, and I'll stay with it in this section.

Observe now that ellipses are subject to a *type constraint*: namely, the constraint that *a* must not be less than *b*. (It's the presence of that type constraint that makes this example different in kind from the POINT examples I've been using earlier, in both this chapter and its predecessor.) Now let E be a variable of declared type ELLIPSE—

```
VAR E ELLIPSE ;
```

—and consider the following multiple assignment:

```
THE_A ( E ) := 7 , THE_B ( E ) := 3 ;
```

The intended effect, presumably, is to make the current value of E an ellipse with $a = 7$, $b = 3$, and center unchanged (i.e., the center should be the same as it was before the assignment). In other words, we want to "zap" the *a* and *b* components of E while leaving the center component alone. But what actually happens? Well, let's expand the two constituent assignments:

```
E := ELLIPSE ( 7 , THE_B ( E ) , THE_CTR ( E ) ) ,
E := ELLIPSE ( THE_A ( E ) , 3 , THE_CTR ( E ) ) ;
```

Now we remove the first assignment and replace the second by:

```
E := WITH
   ( E := ELLIPSE ( 7 , THE_B ( E ) , THE_CTR ( E ) ) ) :
           ELLIPSE ( THE_A ( E ) , 3 , THE_CTR ( E ) ) ;
```

Suppose the previous value of E had $a = 10$ and $b = 4$; then this assignment will work perfectly and will have the desired effect. But suppose the previous value of E had $a = 10$ and $b = 8$. Then the expression in the WITH clause—

```
ELLIPSE ( 7 , THE_B ( E ) , THE_CTR ( E ) )
```

—will raise a run time error! To be specific, it'll attempt to produce an ellipse with $a = 7$ and $b = 8$, thereby violating the type constraint on ellipses to the effect that a must not be less than b. To elaborate: That expression in the WITH clause is a selector invocation once again. As you'll recall, selectors are operators that are used to select, or specify, values of some specified type. By definition, such operators *cannot* yield a value that violates whatever type constraint applies to the type in question. Type constraints are thus an exception to the general rule that constraint checking is done at end of statement ("at semicolons"); we can *never* tolerate the existence of a value that's in violation of the pertinent type constraint, because such a value is a contradiction in terms (i.e., it's simply not a value of the pertinent type). And since, ultimately, the *only* way a value of any kind can be introduced into any computational context whatsoever is by means of some selector invocation,[3] it follows that type constraint checking has to be done as part of such an invocation.

Now, we could avoid the problem in the specific case at hand by simply interchanging the two constituent assignments, thus:

```
E := ELLIPSE ( THE_A ( E ) , 3 , THE_CTR ( E ) ) ,
E := ELLIPSE ( 7 , THE_B ( E ) , THE_CTR ( E ) ) ;
```

But this solution clearly won't always work (consider what would happen if the previous value of E had $a = 2$ and $b = 1$, for example). Another approach— and this one does always work—consists in replacing the original multiple

---

[3] Do you agree with this claim?

assignment by a *single* assignment, which in the case at hand would look like this:

```
E := ELLIPSE ( 7 , 3 , THE_CTR ( E ) ) ;
```

This approach is still unattractive in general, however (imagine a type with a possible representation involving hundreds of components). In **Tutorial D**, therefore, we offer another solution—in syntactic terms, an additional form of *<scalar assign>*—that looks like this:[4]

```
UPDATE <scalar target> :
    { <assign> [ , <assign commalist> ] }
```

Within such an UPDATE, every individual *<assign>* target must be a component of the same possible representation for the declared type of the *<scalar target>*. Here's an example:

```
UPDATE E : { A := 7 , B := 3 } ;
```

This example is an assignment statement, or in other words an *<assignment>*. That *<assignment>* in turn contains just one *<assign>*—in fact, a *<scalar assign>*—and that *<scalar assign>* takes the particular form under discussion. The statement overall is shorthand for the single assignment shown earlier:

```
E := ELLIPSE ( 7 , 3 , THE_CTR ( E ) ) ;
```

More generally, the *<scalar assign>*

```
UPDATE <scalar target> :
    { <assign> [ , <assign commalist> ] }
```

is defined as follows:

■ Let the specified *<scalar target>* be *ST*; let its declared type be *T*; let the pertinent possible representation for *T* be *PR*; and let *PR* have components

---

[4] Note, however, that in the final analysis this solution is still just another shorthand. It's patterned after a construct, *<tuple update>*, that already exists in **Tutorial D**. Observe, incidentally, that we're overloading the keyword UPDATE here (in fact it was already overloaded, being used in connection with both *<tuple assign>*s and *<relation assign>*s, but now we're overloading it still further by using it in connection with *<scalar assign>*s as well).

C1, C2, ..., Cn (only). Note that the selector operator corresponding to the possible representation *PR* is also called *PR*.

■ Syntactically, the commalist of *<assign>*s appearing between the braces is itself a multiple assignment,[5] except that there is no terminating semicolon and hence no constraint checking (except for the special case of type constraints, of course).

■ The *<assign>*s are processed in accordance with Steps 1 and 2 of the definition given in the section "Semantics," earlier. After that processing is done, the resulting commalist of *<assign>*s must be such that every *<assign>* specifies some component *Ci* as its target. (Note that no two distinct *<assign>*s will specify the same target, thanks to Step 2.)

■ Then the specified *<scalar assign>* is defined to be semantically equivalent to the *<scalar assign>*

```
ST := PR ( X1 , X2 , ... , Xn )
```

The arguments *Xi* ($i = 1, 2, ..., n$) are defined as follows:

    a.   If an *<assign>* exists for *Ci*, then let the source in that *<assign>* be *X*. For all *j* ($j = 1, 2, ..., n$), replace all references in *X* to *Cj* by (THE_*C j*(*ST*)). The version of *X* that results is *Xi*.

    b.   Otherwise, *Xi* is THE_*Ci*(*ST*).

Here to close this section is a slightly more complicated example. Let variable E be of declared type ELLIPSE; recall that ellipses have a possible representation with components A, B, and CTR, this last being of declared type POINT. Then the statement

```
UPDATE E : { A := 9 , UPDATE CTR : { X := 5.0 } } ;
```

is defined to be shorthand for the following:

---

[5] But I must stress that "Syntactically" qualifier—a scalar UPDATE operation, like all other forms of *<assign>*, involves just a single target variable.

```
E := ELLIPSE ( 9 ,
                THE_B ( E ) ,
                CARTESIAN ( 5.0 , THE_Y ( THE_CTR ( E ) ) ) ) ;
```

CONCLUDING REMARKS

The fundamental purpose of multiple assignment is, in effect, to allow the checking of certain constraints to be deferred briefly, while at the same time avoiding the possibility that the user will ever see an inconsistent state of the database. However, multiple assignment does have a number of subsidiary uses as well, which these two chapters have also briefly examined.

By the way, I observe that the word *multiple*, which in practice is very often abused, is indeed the mot juste in the present context. In general, a good way to tell whether it's being used appropriately is to see whether it makes sense to replace it by, say, "double" or "triple." This simple test shows immediately that remarks such as "There are multiple reasons to vote for bright orange buffoons" are badly formulated ("double reasons"?). By contrast, "double assignment" is a perfectly reasonable construction, and so are "triple assignment," "quadruple assignment," and, more generally, "multiple assignment."

APPENDIX: MULTIPLE ASSIGNMENT IN SQL

The SQL standard includes several features that can reasonably be regarded as multiple assignment support in some shape or form. Some of the features in question were introduced in SQL:2003, the version of the standard that was current when the paper on which these chapters are based was first written; others go all the way back to the very first version of that standard (SQL:1986, *aka* SQL/86); the rest were introduced at various points along the way. This appendix briefly surveys the features in question.

One point that's worth making right away is this: As just indicated, SQL's multiple assignment features have been incorporated into the language piecemeal, and they don't seem ever to have been perceived as different aspects of the same general problem. As a consequence, they do suffer from a certain lack of orthogonality, parsimony, and consistency in their design, as will be seen. The reader—more to the point, the user—is warned.

What follows is divided into four subsections. The first gives an overview of SQL's support for assignment in general, in order to lay some necessary groundwork. The next two discuss the principal SQL assignment statement—viz., the SET statement—in detail; the first covers single assignment and the second multiple. The final subsection describes certain relevant aspects of the regular SQL UPDATE statement.

Overview

SQL has always supported INSERT, DELETE, and UPDATE, of course. These statements can all be characterized as table assignments, though obviously they don't use conventional assignment syntax. Moreover, they're all *single* assignments—i.e., they all assign a single source value to a single target variable (a table variable, of course, though SQL doesn't use such terminology)[6]

Second, SQL has also always supported SELECT INTO and FETCH, which are both *multiple* assignments, in general. For example, the following statement against the suppliers-and-parts database—

```
SELECT  S.STATUS , S.CITY
INTO    :XST , :XSC
FROM    S
WHERE   SNO = SNO ('S1') ;
```

—effectively assigns values to two host variables, viz., XST and XSC, simultaneously.[7]

Third, SQL also supports a variety of miscellaneous statements (e.g., GET DESCRIPTOR, GET DIAGNOSTICS) that can also be regarded as assignments of a kind. I'll ignore such statements for the remainder of this appendix, for simplicity.

Fourth and most important, SQL also now includes an explicit assignment statement called SET (first introduced in connection with the Persistent Stored Modules feature, SQL/PSM). SET as originally defined supported single assignment only, but SQL:2003 extended that support to cover multiple

---

[6] I assume here that what we're talking about is the so called "searched" form of DELETE and UPDATE. How best to characterize the "positioned" form (DELETE or UPDATE ... WHERE CURRENT OF *<cursor>*) I leave as something for you to ponder.

[7] There's a certain amount of sneakiness going on here, though; at the very least, SQL is blurring the distinction (considerably!) between a table as such, on the one hand, and what such a table contains on the other. What's really happening is this. First, the SELECT statement actually returns a table—a table, in the example, consisting of two columns and one row (it would be an error, in this context, if the table contained more than one row). Assuming it does contain exactly one row, that table is then coreced to the row in question. The two scalar values contained in that row are then extracted. Finally, those two extracted values are assigned to the pertinent host variables.

assignment as well. It also supports both scalar and certain nonscalar assignments—and "nonscalar" here includes arrays and rows, but not tables (thus SET can't be used to update the database[8]).

Fifth and last (and despite what I said previously regarding this issue near the end of the section "Assigning to Several Variables at the Same Time" in the previous chapter), SQL's regular UPDATE statement *might* be regarded as a kind of multiple assignment. Moreover, INSERT, DELETE, and UPDATE all effectively provide some implicit (albeit limited) support for multiple *table* assignment, thanks to (a) their ability to update certain views and (b) in the case of DELETE and UPDATE, their support for certain "compensatory actions," such as cascade delete. I don't want to discuss that implicit support in this appendix; however, I do want to say more regarding the UPDATE statement as such, and that's the subject of the final subsection.

The SET Statement: Single Assignment

To repeat from the body of the chapter, the single assignment version of the SQL SET statement takes the form

```
SET target = source
```

(plus a statement terminator, which I'll show as a semicolon in what follows). Exactly what constitutes a legitimate target is a rather more complicated question than I want to get into here;[9] I'll content myself with considering a few specific examples. First a simple scalar example:

```
DECLARE I INTEGER ;

SET I = 0 ;
```

Note: All DECLARE statements shown in this appendix are SQL statements specifically (i.e., they have the effect of defining some SQL variable). Like SET, DECLARE was first introduced into the SQL standard as part of the Persistent Stored Modules feature, SQL/PSM.

---

[8] Except as noted in footnote 9, q.v.

[9] Except to note that in certain kinds of triggered procedures a target can be a column (specified by means of a column reference), in which case SET can be used to achieve the effect of updating the database after all, albeit only indirectly.

Next, an array example:

```
DECLARE H INTEGER ARRAY [10] ;
DECLARE K INTEGER ARRAY [10] ;

SET H = K ;
```

Observe that the SET statement here is indeed a single assignment (see the discussion of this issue in the section "A Little History" near the beginning of the previous chapter). It's also a nonscalar assignment. *Note:* It's not very relevant to the main message of this appendix, but you should be aware that arrays in SQL are variable length; thus, the two "[10]"s in the declarations of H and K each define an *upper bound*, and those two variables can each contain any number *n* of elements ($n \geq 0$), up to but not exceeding that upper bound. So if, for example, the variable H currently contains exactly three elements, then those elements are precisely H[1], H[2], and H[3]. (Which prompts the obvious question, of course: If H does currently contains just three elements, what does the reference H[8], say, denote? *<Your answer here>*.)

Third and last, a row example:

```
DECLARE NAME ROW ( FIRST VARCHAR(25) ,
                   LAST  VARCHAR(25) ,
                   MI    CHAR(1) ) ;

SET NAME = ROW ( 'Truman' , 'Harry' , 'S' ) ;
```

Again the SET statement here is a single, nonscalar assignment (in fact it's SQL's counterpart to **Tutorial D**'s *<tuple assign>*, which was mentioned in the body of this chapter, though not discussed in detail). The expression on the right side is a *row value constructor*. The keyword ROW is optional in such constructors.

Now I turn to pseudovariables. SQL supports three kinds: elements of arrays, fields within rows, and something analogous (somewhat) to our THE_ pseudovariables. I'll consider each in turn. Here first is an example involving an array element:

```
DECLARE A INTEGER ARRAY [5] ;

SET A    = ARRAY [ 0 , 0 , 0 , 0 , 0 ] ;
SET A[4] = 8 ;
```

The first SET statement here assigns an array of five elements, all of them zero, to the array variable A—the expression on the right side is an *array value constructor* (analogous to a selector in **Tutorial D**). The second SET statement then replaces the value of the fourth element of that array variable by the value eight. Thus, that second SET statement is effectively shorthand for this one:

```
SET A = ARRAY [ A[1] , A[2] , A[3] , 8 , A[5] ] ;
```

Note: I could have replaced the first SET statement in the foregoing example by an appropriate DEFAULT clause on the array variable declaration, like this:

```
DECLARE A INTEGER ARRAY [5]
          DEFAULT ARRAY [ 0 , 0 , 0 , 0 , 0 ] ;
```

The keyword DEFAULT is a little misleading in this context, though, inasmuch as what an SQL DEFAULT clause really does is assign an *initial* value to the variable in question (just as the INIT specification does in **Tutorial D**), and that value can later be overridden.

Here now is an example involving assignment to a field within a row variable:

```
DECLARE NAME ROW ( FIRST VARCHAR(25) ,
                   LAST  VARCHAR(25) ,
                   MI    CHAR(1) ) ;

SET NAME.LAST = ROW ( 'Potter' ) ;
```

Here's the expanded form of the foregoing SET statement:

```
SET NAME = ROW ( NAME.FIRST , 'Potter' , NAME.MI ) ;
```

A note on terminology: The term *field*—referring to a component of a row type, row value, or row variable—was first introduced into SQL when explicit row type support was added, in SQL:1999. Of course, tables contain rows too, and the components of those rows were historically, and rather awkwardly, called columns. Now, however, they too are referred to as fields.

Now let's consider SQL's analog of our THE_ pseudovariables. Here first is an example:

```
CREATE TYPE POINT AS ( X REAL , Y REAL ) ;

DECLARE P POINT ;

SET P.Y = 5.0 ;
```

This SET statement expands to:

```
SET P = P.Y ( 5.0 ) ;
```

This expansion requires a certain amount of explanation, I think! To be specific.

- First, type POINT is what's called a *structured type*; it has a representation with two components, X and Y, which are called *attributes*.

  Note: That representation isn't a "possible representation" in the **Tutorial D** sense—in particular, a given type can't ever have more than one of them—and those attributes are nothing to do with attributes in the relational sense. Also, SQL requires the definition of a structured type to include a specification of whether the type is FINAL or NOT FINAL; this specification has nothing to do with the topic of this appendix, however, and I therefore omit it from the examples for brevity.

- Second, the "Y" in the expression P.Y (5.0) on the right side of the expanded form does *not* denote the Y attribute, as such, of type POINT; nor does it denote the Y attribute of the variable P; nor does it denote the Y attribute of the point contained within that variable P. Rather, it denotes a "method" of the same name as each of those attributes (where a *method* is really just a special kind of operator). Each attribute definition causes automatic definition of two methods, both with the same name as the attribute in question: viz., one "observer" method and one "mutator" method. The effect of such methods in terms of our POINT example can be explained as follows:

  a. The *observer* invocation P.Y returns the Y coordinate for the point value in the point variable P.

     Note: Possible appearances to the contrary notwithstanding, no such observer invocation appears in either of the SET statements in the foregoing example.

    b. The *mutator* invocation P.Y (5.0) returns the point whose X coordinate is that of the point value in the point variable P and whose Y coordinate is five.

          Note: The term *mutator* is thus a misnomer here, because an SQL mutator doesn't actually mutate anything—instead, it returns a value. In fact, an SQL mutator is what the object community calls an *observer* (!), or what *The Third Manifesto* calls a *read-only operator*.

The net effect of all of the above is that the original SET assignment in the example—

```
SET P.Y = 5.0 ;
```

—does achieve what it might intuitively be expected to.

Note: In addition to the observer and mutator methods as discussed above, the definition of a structured type also causes automatic definition of a (niladic) *constructor* method, with the same name as that of the type in question. Invoking that method returns that unique value of the type in question whose attributes all have the applicable default value (often null, though of course null isn't a value). For example, the expression POINT ( ) returns the point with default X and Y values (both of which are, by default, null, since we didn't explicitly specify anything different in the attribute definitions). It follows that, e.g., the following sequence of assignments—

```
SET P = POINT ( ) ;
SET P = P.X ( 7.0 ) ;
SET P = P.Y ( 5.0 ) ;
```

—will have the effect of assigning the point with X coordinate seven and Y coordinate five to the variable P. What's more, the entire sequence can be collapsed into a single assignment, thus:

```
SET P = POINT ( ) . X ( 7.0 ) . Y ( 5.0 ) ;
```

Now here again is the code from our original POINT example:

```
CREATE TYPE POINT AS ( X REAL , Y REAL ) ;

DECLARE P POINT ;

SET P.Y = 5.0 ;
```

The SQL term for an expression such as P.Y, if (as here) it appears on the left side of an assignment, is *mutator reference*[10]—and, importantly, such references can be nested.[11] For example:

```
CREATE TYPE ELLIPSE AS
            ( A INTEGER , B INTEGER , CTR POINT ) ;

DECLARE E ELLIPSE ;

SET E.CTR.Y = 5.0 ;
```

The SET statement here is shorthand for:

```
SET E.CTR = E.CTR.Y ( 5.0 ) ;
```

And this one in turn is shorthand for:

```
SET E = E.CTR ( E.CTR.Y ( 5.0 ) ) ;
```

Now, structured types in general can have user defined methods associated with them in addition to the system defined ones I've been discussing so far. I deliberately didn't include any user defined methods in the original POINT example; however, let's now define one, M say. Then a SET statement of the form

```
SET P.M = exp ;    /* for example */
```

will be legal if and only if all three of the following are true:

1. M is not a constructor method.

---

[10] Despite the fact that, as we'll see in a few moments, the method involved (Y in the example) doesn't have to be a mutator method as such, and despite the fact that such references don't cause anything to be mutated. Don't you love this language?

[11] The same is true of our own THE_ pseudovariables, though I didn't stress the point in the body of the chapter.

2. M returns a value of type POINT.

3. Exactly one parameter, of the same type as *exp*, is defined for M in addition to the distinguished parameter, SELF, that's common to every nonconstructor method.

    Note: The argument corresponding to SELF in an invocation of M is specified by the expression immediately preceding the dot preceding the method name. In the invocation P.Y (5.0), for example, the argument corresponding to SELF in the invocation of the mutator method Y is P.

In other words, SQL doesn't just support analogs of our THE_ pseudovariables—it supports what are in effect *user defined* pseudovariables as well. On the other hand, SQL's analogs of our THE_ pseudovariables are supported only for what SQL calls *structured types*; they aren't supported for other user defined types, nor for system defined types. Furthermore, they can't be used with SELECT INTO or FETCH (though elements wthin arrays and fields within rows, by contrast, can).

The SET Statement: Multiple Assignment

Now (at long last, you might be forgiven for thinking) I come to the multiple assignment version of the SQL SET operator. The syntax has the following general form:

```
SET ( target-commalist ) = row-expression
```

(plus a statement terminator). Note carefully that the right side here consists of a single (row valued) expression, not a commalist of separate expressions. The semantics are that the *i*th field value within the row denoted by that expression is assigned to the *i*th target. More precisely, let the row denoted by the expression on the right side be

```
ROW ( S1 , S2 , ... , Sn )
```

(the keyword ROW is optional, recall). Also, let the target commalist on the left side be

```
T1 , T2 , ... , Tn
```

Then the overall assignment reduces to something like Dijkstra's concurrent assignment (see the previous chapter):

```
SET ( T1 , T2 , ... , Tn ) = ( S1 , S2 , ... , Sn ) ;
```

(However, the SQL operator differs from Dijkstra's in that the targets don't all have to be distinct.) This statement SQL then defines as being semantically equivalent to the following *compound* statement (pseudocode):[12]

```
BEGIN
   DECLARE TEMP ROW ( F1 ... , F2 ... , ... , Fn ... ) ;
   SET TEMP = ROW ( S1 , S2 , ... , Sn ) ;
   SET T1 = TEMP.F1 ;
   SET T2 = TEMP.F2 ;
      .........
   SET Tn = TEMP.Fn ;
END ;
```

I'll give some examples in a moment (examples involving pseudovariables, that is—examples not involving pseudovariables are essentially trivial and are left as an exercise).

Now, the foregoing definition does at least ensure that all source expressions are evaluated before any assignments are done. Curiously, however, it fails to ensure that the overall operation is atomic—even though all that would be needed to make it so would be to add the keyword ATOMIC to the expansion, immediately following the keyword BEGIN.[13] What makes the situation even odder is that there's a workaround that not only evaluates all source expressions first but guarantees atomicity as well. For example, the statement

```
SET ( U , V ) = ROW ( 1 , 2 ) ;
```

isn't atomic by the foregoing definition, but the following statement, which has more or less the same effect, is:

```
SELECT 1 , 2
INTO   U , V
FROM   ( VALUES 0 ) AS POINTLESS ;
```

---

[12] Like SET and DECLARE, compound statements were introduced into SQL with SQL/PSM.

[13] Actually there was an error in SQL's original definition of compound statements, as a consequence of which ATOMIC actually had no effect. It's my understanding that this error has since been corrected.

(The sole purpose of the FROM clause here is to ensure that the SELECT clause operates on a table containing exactly one row. The value of that row is immaterial, because there aren't any references to it in the SELECT clause. As for the specification AS *POINTLESS*, it's pointless, but it's required by SQL's syntax rules.)

I turn now to the promised examples involving pseudovariables. First, one involving array elements:

```
DECLARE A INTEGER ARRAY [5]
         DEFAULT ARRAY [ 1 , 2 , 3 , 4 , 5 ] ;

SET ( A[4] , A[2] ) = ROW ( 0 , 8 ) ;
```

First we apply the rule for expanding multiple assignment, to obtain:

```
BEGIN
   DECLARE TEMP ROW ( F1 ... , F2 ... ) ;
   SET TEMP = ROW ( 0 , 8 ) ;
   SET A[4] = TEMP.F1 ;
   SET A[2] = TEMP.F2 ;
END ;
```

Next we apply the rule (twice) for expanding assignment to an array element pseudovariable, to obtain:

```
BEGIN
   DECLARE TEMP ROW ( F1 ... , F2 ... ) ;
   SET TEMP = ROW ( 0 , 8 ) ;
   SET A = ARRAY [ A[1] , A[2] , A[3] , TEMP.F1 , A[5] ] ;
   SET A = ARRAY [ A[1] , TEMP.F2 , A[3] , A[4] , A[5] ] ;
END ;
```

Thus, the final value of A is:

```
ARRAY [ 1 , 8 , 3 , 0 , 5 ]
```

For a second example, let P be a variable of type POINT once again, and consider the assignment

```
SET ( P.X , P.Y ) = ROW ( 7.0 , 5.0 ) ;
```

First expansion:

```
BEGIN
   DECLARE TEMP ROW ( F1 ... , F2 ... ) ;
   SET TEMP = ROW ( 7.0 , 5.0 ) ;
   SET P.X = TEMP.F1 ;
   SET P.Y = TEMP.F2 ;
END ;
```

Second expansion:

```
BEGIN
   DECLARE TEMP ROW ( F1 ... , F2 ... ) ;
   SET TEMP = ROW ( 7.0 , 5.0 ) ;
   SET P = P.X ( TEMP.F1 ) ;
   SET P = P.Y ( TEMP.F2 ) ;
END ;
```

The first assignment to P (i.e., in the second expansion) sets the X coordinate to seven, leaving the Y coordinate unchanged; the second then sets the Y coordinate to five, leaving the X coordinate unchanged. The final result is thus that P contains the point with coordinates (7.0,5.0), as desired. Note carefully that, in contrast with the analogous example in the body of the chapter, we do *not* have to "collect together" the two constituent assignments in order to achieve the desired result. Why not? Well, in order to answer this question, it helps to examine a more complex example:

```
CREATE TYPE ELLIPSE AS
         ( A INTEGER , B INTEGER , CTR POINT ) ;

DECLARE E ELLIPSE ;

SET ( E.A , E.B ) = ROW ( 7 , 3 ) ;
```

For brevity, let's combine the two expansions this time. The overall result looks like this:

```
BEGIN
   DECLARE TEMP ROW ( F1 ... , F2 ... ) ;
   SET TEMP = ROW ( 7 , 3 ) ;
   SET E = E.A ( TEMP.F1 ) ;
   SET E = E.B ( TEMP.F2 ) ;
END ;
```

Now suppose the previous value of E had $a = 10$ and $b = 8$. Then the first assignment to E yields an ellipse with $a = 7$ and $b = 8$in other words, an ellipse with $a < b$. However, this state of affairs does *not* cause a run time error (and the second assignment to E thus goes on to yield an ellipse with $a = 7$ and $b = 3$, as desired). Why isn't there any run time error? Answer: *Because SQL isn't aware of the type constraint to the effect that a must be greater than or equal to b!* (Observe that the definition of type ELLIPSE included no such constraint; in fact, SQL doesn't support the concept of type constraints at all, and we can't even state them.)

In my opinion, this lack of type constraint support on SQL's part constitutes a very serious flaw. While as we've just seen it does make it a little easier to support multiple assignment,[14] it also means there are many "real world" types that can't be properly specified in SQL. For example, suppose we want to define a type called LENGTH, with the obvious meaning. Then we might specify, say, integers as the associated representation, and of course that specification does impose an a priori constraint on the values that go to make up the type. Considered as type constraints, however, such a priori constraints are extremely weak. In the case at hand, for example, there's no way to specify that lengths mustn't be negative! As a consequence, therefore, SQL necessarily permits negative lengths, noncircular circles, nonsquare squares, and all kinds of similar nonsenses. *Note:* Likely reasons—though not in my opinion *good* reasons—for SQL's lack of type constraint support are described in detail in my book *Type Inheritance and Relational Theory: Subtypes, Supertypes, and Substitutability* (O'Reilly, 2016).

I close this subsection by noting that, owing to its lack of proper support for multiple table assignment in particular, SQL can't directly handle either (a) the example discussed in the section "An Example" in Chapter 10 or (b) the example discussed at the end of the section "Assigning to the Same Variable More than Once" at the end of that chapter. Instead, it has to use several separate assignment statements in both cases, and bundle those statements up into a transaction. It also has to make sure the pertinent constraint checking is deferred.[15]

---

[14] But it turns out that SQL still has to collect constituent assignments together anyway in another context, as we'll see in the next subsection,. Thus, the fact that it doesn't have to do so in the present context can hardly be considered a significant advantage.

[15] Yes, SQL does support "deferred constraints." For a detailed discussion of this (complicated!) aspect of SQL, I refer you to Chapter 2 ("Assignment") of my book *Stating the Obvious, and Other Database Writings* (Technics Publications, 2020).

The SQL UPDATE Statement Revisited

As noted in the previous chapter, I don't regard SQL's UPDATE statement as a true multiple assignment. However, it does have some points in common with multiple assignment, as I'll show, and in fact the SET clause in UPDATE is now permitted to include (nested) multiple assignments as such. I'll illustrate these points with a slightly abstract example. Let table T have columns C1, C2, C3, C4, and C5 (and possibly others), where C1 is of type INTEGER, C2 is of type POINT, C3 is of type INTEGER ARRAY, and C4 and C5 are of the same type as each other. Now consider the following UPDATE statement (WHERE clause omitted for simplicity):[16]

```
UPDATE T
   SET C1 = 2 ,
       C2.X = 7.0 ,
       C2.Y = 5.0 ,
       C3 [ 2 ] = 2 ,
     ( C4 , C5 ) = ROW ( C5 , C4 ) ;
```

The SET clause here is applied to each row r of T as follows:

1. Syntactic substitutions are applied until the left side of each assignment consists of a simple column reference. With one exception (having to do with the two assignments to C2—see below), these substitutions are essentially as described for the SET statement earlier in this appendix.

2. The right sides of those assignments are evaluated for that row r.

3. A row r' is formed by copying r and then replacing the values for columns C1-C5 in that copy by the corresponding results of those evaluations.

The value assigned to T is the bag of rows r' thus computed.

Now, in accordance with the substitutions as described earlier in this appendix, the original UPDATE expands to:

---

[16] I remark in passing that, while as already noted the syntax of the SET *statement* broadly follows the Dijkstra style, the syntax of the SET *clause* in the UPDATE statement is more in the style of **Tutorial D**. More evidence, if evidence is needed, of the fact that multiple assignment in general was never perceived by the SQL designers as a single generic problem, one that could benefit from a single generic solution. (But then the same is true of single assignment as well, in SQL.)

```
UPDATE T
   SET C1 = 2 ,
       C2 = C2.X ( 7.0 ) ,
       C2 = C2.Y ( 5.0 ) ,
       C3 = something complicated ,
       C4 = C5 ,
       C5 = C4 ;
```

Note: The last two assignments here really do interchange the values of columns C4 and C5, because the right sides are evaluated before any assignments are done.

The complications surrounding the assignment to the array column C3 need not concern us here (they have to do with the fact that SQL arrays are varying-length). The two assignments to C2 need further attention, however, because no column is allowed to appear as a target in any given SET clause more than once (precisely because all right sides are evaluated before any assignments are done). A further substitution therefore has to occur, according to which assignments to the same column *that have arisen thanks to the prior substitution process* are collected together. Without going into details—the process is essentially similar to the one described in the section on semantics at the beginning of the present chapter—the net effect in the example is that the two assignments to C2 are replaced by this one:

```
C2 = C2.X ( 7.0 ) . Y ( 5.0 )
```

Thus, if the "old" value of C2 is the point (2.0,3.0), then the invocation X (7.0) on that point yields the point (7.0,3.0), and the invocation Y (5.0) on *that* point then yields the point (7.0,5.0).

Finally, you might be wondering why our example included no column C6 of some row type and an assignment to some field F of that column, as here:

```
C6.F = 3
```

Columns such as C6 are indeed permitted. Sadly, however, SQL doesn't support the updating of fields within such columns in the manner suggested—i.e., it doesn't permit such an assignment in the SET clause. (At least, these observations were valid as of SQL:2003. I'll leave it as an exercise to determine whether they still are.)

Chapter 12

Database Graffiti

Part 1

Scribbles from The Askew Wall

satis eloquentia, sapientiae parvum

This chapter and the next two together consist of a series of quotations, aphorisms, and anecdotes—along with a few personal comments, here and there—that are (mostly) relevant to the general subject of database management. The material isn't meant to be technically deep, but a number of serious messages do lie not too far below the surface. My aim is partly to edify, partly just to amuse.

Note: What follows started out in life as a script for a live presentation, and for that reason is a little chattier than is normal for a technical publication (I hope you don't find it too shrill). I should mention too that portions of that script are based on various other writings of mine—a few of them writings published, or republished, in either the present book or its companion volume—so in some cases you might have heard the story before, as it were. But there's a lot that's new, too.

Publishing history: This is a greatly extended version of one of the regular columns I did for the magazine Database Programming & Design (Vol. 10, No. 3, March 1997). I included an expanded version of that original column in my book Relational Database

*Writings 1994-1997 (Addison-Wesley, 1998). What follows is a
revised and extended version of that already expanded version. I've
divided it into three parts in order, I hope, to make it a little more
digestible. This version (all three parts) copyright © C. J. Date
2022.*

Hello! I'm very pleased to welcome you to this perhaps rather self-indulgent
presentation. What I want to do is this. For many years now, I've been
maintaining a private collection of quotations, aphorisms, anecdotes, etc., that are
relevant—sometimes pretty loosely, I have to confess—to the overall subject of
database management and database technology. And today I'd like to share
some gems from that collection with you ... So this isn't exactly a technically
deep session!—though I do have some important points to make, I think. My
aim is partly to edify, partly just to amuse.

I should perhaps begin by explaining the background. Some of you will
know that some time ago I used to do a regular column in one of the trade
magazines, *Database Programming & Design*. Well, that magazine celebrated
its tenth anniversary in March 1997, and I dedicated my column in that issue to
such "gems from my collection" as a way of marking the occasion and wishing
many happy returns to the magazine on its tenth birthday. By the way, I think
you'll be getting a copy of that original column as a handout later.[1] Anyway, I
called that column "Database Graffiti" ... And this presentation is essentially a
greatly expanded version of that original column.

I must also explain my subtitle ("Scribbles from The Askew Wall"). The
term *The Askew Wall* is due to Hugh Darwen ... I presume it's pretty obvious
where he gets it from (?). As he explains:

- Basically—see the picture on the next page—the Askew Wall is an ugly
  construction that surrounds Relationland.

- And that Wall acts as a major barrier to communication between
  Relationland and the rest of the world. It really gets in the way!—people
  look for Relationland and see only the Wall.

---

[1] Not true for this incarnation, of course—but the column in question is subsumed by these three chapters
anyway.

- Because of the Wall, indeed, some people don't even realize that Relationland exists. In other words, they think the Wall, with all its warts and blemishes, is all there is—with the result, of course, that the relational model gets blamed for the shortcomings and mistakes of S-Q-L (sorry, I mean the Askew Wall).

  By the way, this one really makes me gnash my teeth!—because the biggest problem with SQL is precisely that it doesn't properly conform to the relational model. But I digress ...

- Others have tried to enter Relationland but have lost their way and become inextricably stuck inside the Wall itself.

- Still others who were once honest Relationlanders have also since become immured (I could name a few names here, but it's probably better if I don't).

Well, I don't think I'd better push this metaphor any further ... But I just couldn't resist the idea of my *graffiti* being scribbled on Hugh's *wall*.

Onward. I've divided the rest of my talk—somewhat arbitrarily in some cases—into the following sections:

- Introduction (we're in this right now)

- The prehistoric era

- Objects and objections

- Normalization, networks, and nulls

- The role of simplicity

- The joy of self-reference

- Some fundamental principles

- Relational database: further misconceptions number four

- Some *good* quotes

- Books and book reviews

- Miscellany

- The great database limerick competition

- Concluding remarks

Without further ado, let's get started. I'll begin with ancient history—that is, the world before relational databases (or at least SQL databases) became a commercial reality.

THE PREHISTORIC ERA

We're so used to relational databases these days, and think of them as so "obvious" and "natural" and "right," that I suspect many people don't even know what the database scene was like before Ted Codd published his original papers in the early 1970s. So I think it's worth taking a look ... Indeed, the obvious first quote is:

> Those who don't know history are doomed to repeat it [*George Santayana, somewhat paraphrased*].

The actual quote is: *Those who cannot remember the past are condemned to repeat it.*

Of course, some cynic did once say that the only thing we learn from history is that we learn nothing from history ...

(Actually, the cynic was Hegel. The exact quote is: *What experience and history teach is this—that people and governments never have learned anything from history, or acted on principles deduced from it.*)

Incidentally— as I expect some of you know—I do have a real concern here regarding *object databases*. The object database people really do seem to be repeating a lot of history, and a lot of bad history at that. But that's a whole separate topic!—we can't get into it now, it would take us much too far afield. Some of my other presentations do deal with this issue—e.g., my full-length seminar on object databases.[2]

Let's have a look at the historical context, then. What was going on in the database world before relational databases came along? Well, here's a quote that might give some idea:

> Logically deleting a logical child prevents further access to the logical child using its logical parent. Unidirectional logical child segments are assumed to be logically deleted. A logical parent is considered logically deleted when all its logical children are physically deleted. For physically paired logical relationships, the physical child paired to the logical child must also be physically deleted before the logical parent is considered logically deleted.
>
> *Physical Parent of a Virtually Paired Logical Child*: When ... all physical children that are virtually paired logical children are logically deleted, the physical parent segment is physically deleted.

---

[2] See also Chapters 7 and 8 in the present book.

No prizes for guessing where this deathless prose comes from! (Actually it's from the IMS/ESA Database Administration Guide.). But you see the garbage we used to have to put up with?

Mind you, I'm not sure matters have improved all that much. Here's a more recent quote:

> However, because global temporary table contents are distinct within SQL-sessions, and created local temporary tables are distinct within <module>s within SQL-sessions, the effective <schema name> of the schema in which the global temporary table or the created local temporary table is instantiated is an implementation-dependent <schema name> that may be thought of as having been effectively derived from the <schema name> of the schema in which the global temporary table or created local temporary table is defined and the implementation-dependent SQL-session identifier associated with the SQL-session [*from the 1992 version of the SQL standard, "SQL:1992"*].

I beat up on this one in the book I wrote on SQL:1992 with Hugh Darwen, *A Guide to the SQL Standard*, 4th edition (Addison-Wesley, 1997). But I certainly think it bears repeating here. The entire sentence (yes, it's all one sentence!) is taken from a section of the standard titled—and intended to explain the SQL concept of—"Tables."

I never realized tables were so complicated.

It all reminds me of that great line:

> If you're not confused by all this, it just proves you're not thinking clearly.

I don't know where this quote comes from originally, but I got it from Nagraj Alur. Or maybe it was Bill Kent?

Of course, it's not just SQL; our entire industry is plagued by bad terminology and graceless prose. By way of example, consider the following:

> I nonconcur with the subject release for announcement for the following reasons and understand that under the rules of dissent, I am obligated to escalate my nonconcurrence for a timely resolution. [*This was one of the options that used to appear—I don't know if it still does—on ANSI standard review forms.*]

To redress the balance a little, perhaps I should give an example to show that other disciplines—if I might be allowed a little poetic license in the use of such a term—can yield sentences that are just as impenetrably bad as the ones just quoted:

> For the purposes of this Act a person carries on business as a scrap metal dealer if he [*sic*] carries on a business which consists wholly or partly of buying and selling scrap metal whether the scrap metal sold is in the form in which it was bought or otherwise, other than a business in the course of which scrap metal is not bought except as materials for the manufacture of other articles and is not sold except as a by product of such manufacture or as surplus materials bought but not required for such manufacture, and "scrap metal dealer" (where the expression is used in this Act otherwise than in reference to carrying on business as a scrap metal dealer) means a person who (in accordance with the preceding provisions of this subsection) carries on business as a scrap metal dealer [*excerpt from the U.K. Scrap Metal Dealers Act of 1964, quoted in a letter to the London Times, April 5th, 1995*].

Back to databases and the historical context. In 1975, while he and I were both still in IBM, Ted Codd wrote an internal IBM memo suggesting that relational database should be seriously considered as part of IBM's long term database strategy. Here's the reply he got from the IBM manager concerned:

> My staff and I have found your comments interesting. In order to provide a more thorough and in-depth analysis on their applicability as a requirement for future database systems, we respectfully request that you provide the following:

(By the way, I love that "respectfully." It reminds me of *Yes Minister*. You know, Sir Humphrey says, "With the deepest respect, Minister," and the Minister replies "Don't use that filthy language to me!" Of course, "with the deepest respect" really means "with the deepest *dis*respect.")

1. A clear definition of relational databases: their structure, access technique, programming methods, compatibility, and comparison with our current database standard DL/I

2. Economic justification of a business case

3. Account scenarios and experience of users in today's environment, with names, descriptions, performance, and function provided

4. Account of application descriptions of users in the future, by industry and application type, if possible

5.   Description of compatibility with CODASYL

All this, in *1975* ... !

Actually, while I'm talking about history: Did you know that in fact some people dispute Ted Codd's claim to be the originator of the relational model? ... Indeed, there's considerable evidence to suggest that the true originator was William Shakespeare:

> Thy gift, thy tables, are within my brain
> Full charactered with lasting memory,
> Which shall above that idle rank remain
> Beyond all date, even to eternity;
> Or at the least so long as brain and heart
> Have faculty by nature to subsist,
> Till each to razed oblivion yield his part
> Of thee, thy record never can be missed.
> That poor retention could not so much hold,
> Nor need I tallies thy dear love to score;
> Therefore to give them from me was I bold,
> To trust those tables that receive thee more.
> > To keep an adjunct to remember thee
> > Were to import forgetfulness in me.

This is Shakespeare's Sonnet 122 (and acknowledgments here to Pam McFarland—at that time with a company called VM Software—who first brought my attention to the fact that the Bard was relational-hip).

But actually, if you take a closer look, you can see that Shakespeare isn't really making a claim to prior *ownership* of the relational model—in fact, he's *addressing* Ted, and admitting that it was all really Ted's doing all along—

Thy gift, *thy* tables, are within my brain ...

So now we've solved another mystery!—the Dark Lady of the Sonnets is obviously Ted Codd.

I'm not sure about that "beyond all Date," however!

On a more serious note—here's a quote from Maurice Wilkes (grand old man of British computing) that I really like:

I would like to see computer science teaching set deliberately in a historical framework ... Students need to understand how the present situation has come about, what was tried, what worked and what did not, and how improvements in hardware made progress possible. The absence of this element in their training causes people to approach every problem from first principles. They are apt to propose solutions that have been found wanting in the past. Instead of standing on the shoulders of their precursors, they try to go it alone [*CACM 34, No. 5 (May 1991)*].

Indeed, I do think it's sad to see how often the wheel gets reinvented in our field. I also think object databases are a case in point! As I've already suggested, there's almost nothing about them that's truly new, and much that has indeed been "tried [and] found wanting in the past." Again, however, I really don't want to get into that discussion here. Let me just say that, in my opinion, there's exactly one good idea in object databases—namely, *abstract data types*—and that's not new.

OBJECTS AND OBJECTIONS

Although I've already said I don't want to get into detail on why I think object databases are so misguided, there's just one item I would like to "share with you," as they say ... In the 6th edition of my book *An Introduction to Database Systems* (Addison-Wesley, 1995)—which was the first edition in which I had a chapter on object databases—I said this:

Caveat: Before we start getting into details, it is as well to warn readers not to expect the kind of precision they are accustomed to in the relational world. Indeed, many [object oriented] concepts ... are quite imprecise, and there's very little true consensus and much disagreement, even at the most basic level.

Of course, I wasn't all that surprised when one reviewer (an OO person, of course) complained—quite hotly!—that my characterization here was unfair. But I *was* surprised by what he actually said:

No, no, no, no, no! Object concepts aren't fuzzy and imprecise at all. It's only the definitions that are sometimes fuzzy and imprecise [*source suppressed here in order to protect the guilty*].

I'm tempted to say "I rest my case."

Though perhaps it would be more diplomatic to say, with Mark Twain, merely that:

> The logic of our adversary resembles the peace of God [*from Roughing It; Twain was quoting Thomas Fitch, editor of the Union newspaper in Virginia City, Nevada*].

A wonderful example of an insult that sounds like a compliment! Good old Sam Clemens.

More diplomatically still—or at least more charitably—I might have responded in the words of Sidney Smith, who, on seeing two women leaning out of their respective houses and arguing across the street, observed:

> Those two ladies will never agree, for they are arguing from different premises.

(And, I might add, different foundations.)

Still on objects: Despite the phenomenal success of relational technology in the marketplace, we are—predictably enough—seeing something of a "relational backlash" right now. Mind you, I'm not quite sure what the term "relational backlash" means, but it was the headline on the *Computerworld* article that I got this quote from:

> It is hard for relational advocates, having been on the leading edge for 10 to 12 years, to wake up and find that fashion has moved on to something else. The temptation is to tell the upstarts they don't know what they're talking about [*Charles Babcock, Computerworld (June 28th, 1993)*].

Babcock was referring, of course, to the wave of hype at the time regarding object systems. It all reminds of the old line "But am I paranoid if everyone really *is* out to get me?"

Talking of paranoia, by the way, here's another great quote I came across recently:

> Paranoia is having all the facts [*this one is from William Burroughs; it's kind of the flip side of "ignorance is bliss," I suppose*].

But on objects: The fact is, of course, the upstarts—the object folks—*don't* know what they're talking about, at least as regards database technology in general or relational databases in particular. Indeed, that's the problem: We've got the object community over *here* and the database community over *there*, and the two communities really don't seem to communicate with each other very well. At least I can tell you this: The object people I've spoken to do *not* understand the relational model. And it does seem to me that if you're claiming that technology *A* should be replaced by technology *B*, then it's incumbent on you to understand technology *A* first, and to show conclusively that:

- First, technology *B* can solve every problem that technology *A* can handle;

- Second, it can also solve some problem that technology *A* can't.

And in the case of objects and relations, I don't think anyone has ever shown any such thing.

Anyway, objects are indeed *fashion*—fashion really is the mot juste here—as Babcock effectively admits ("fashion has moved on"). I have a nice quote on this point, by the way; it comes from the end of a long letter that I got from a friend in the U.K., Adrian Larner, when I was learning all about objects for myself. That letter—I think it was 27 pages long—gave Adrian's own take on the subject, and this was his closing paragraph:

> I am, I regret to say, resigned to the transient triumph of object orientation: Fashion is more powerful than reason, for reason is not the property of any vested interest. We should count ourselves lucky that for some while now, fashion and reason have coincided in relational. But—once again—we have failed to learn from our successes [*Adrian Larner, private communication*].

Very elegant, and very eloquent ... But, you see, *I* am *not* so resigned! However, that's (once again) a topic for another day.

By the way, why exactly do we talk about object *orientation*? Is it because that's all it is—just an *orientation*? A *leaning*? Is this an admission that objects (unlike relations) don't rest on any solid model or theory?

While I'm on the subject of disagreements, here's another quote I like very much—a serious one again:

> Whenever you find yourself getting angry about a difference of opinion, be on your guard; you will probably find, on examination, that your belief is going beyond what the evidence warrants [*from Bertrand Russell, "An Outline of Intellectual Rubbish," in Unpopular Essays (Simon & Schuster, 1950)*].

I really wish people would take this one to heart. It reminds me of Wittgenstein, who said *Whereof one cannot speak, thereon one must remain silent*—or words to that effect.

Still on the subject of objections and disagreements, I recently came across the following beautiful excample. It's a criticism of a certain professor's work by a rival academic:

> It seems to me that [my esteemed colleague], by avoiding the issue of the concrete historical reality lying behind the various similarities between cultural forms which he seeks to recognize, has allowed himself a much freer hand and perhaps a less disciplined methodology than might have been prudent [*from Colin Renfrew, Archaeology and Language (Cambridge University Press, 1988)*].

I love this! The understatement ("allowed himself a much freer hand" ... "perhaps a less disciplined methodology" ... "than might have been prudent") is perfectly delightful.

In fact I have another (similar) example from the same source:

> The methods of comparative linguistics have much to offer in the study of these processes, but the construction of a protolexicon may not be their most important contribution.

Obviously the words "may not be their most important contribution" here really mean the work in question—i.e., "the construction of a protolexicon," whatever that might be—is complete and utter nonsense. It's the academic's way of saying "You *turkey*, how could you *possibly* believe anything so stupid" (etc., etc.).

NORMALIZATION, NETWORKS, AND NULLS

Now let me move on to some quotes that are a bit more directly relevant to modern (that is to say relational, or at least SQL) databases. They're a bit of a miscellany, but as I say they do at least have something to do with the modern database world. Well, sort of.

The first has to do with normalization. I overheard this snippet in the hallway as I was hurrying to my session at the Database and Client/Server World conference in Chicago a few years back (actually December 1995):

Well, he *said* the tables were all in fifth normal form, but I think he must have meant sixth.

I wish I'd had time to stop for further enlightenment ... I mean, we do all know that fifth is the final normal form, right? I mean, there's nowhere else to go after fifth. Right?

Note added later: Well ... as a matter of fact, I did subsequently invent a "sixth normal form" myself, in connection with the work I did wth Hugh Darwen and another colleague, Nikos Lorentzos, on temporal databases. But fifth is still "final" in the sense originally intended. I don't think this is the place to get into details, so I won't. If you want to know more, see me afterward!

When I told Hugh Darwen the foregoing story, he countered by telling me of someone he'd had dealings with in the U.K. who, on first hearing the term *normalization*, inquired:

Normalization? What's that? Is it sort of the opposite of *de*normalization?

I believe the someone in question had previously served some kind of internship with a certain well known SQL vendor who I won't name here (but the name began with O).

Anyway, all this talk of normal forms and normalization reminds me of one of my favorite definitions:

Normal: *see* abnormal [*from an early IBM PL/I reference manual, circa 1969*].

And that, of course, unavoidably reminds me of the old chestnut:

Recursion: *see* recursion.

Which reminds me in turn of the following maxim, which I first heard from Jim Gray:

Anything in computer science that's not recursive is no good.

How true!

By the way: If anyone wants to argue that *relations* are therefore no good, because they can't contain relations nested inside themselves and therefore aren't recursive, let me just say that this criticism is in fact incorrect, though it might come as a surprise to some people to hear me say this. Again I don't have time to go into detail; suffice it to say that relations *can* contain other relations, as I've explain at length elsewhere—see, for example, my paper "What First Normal Form Really Means" in the book *Date on Database: Writings 2000-2006* (Apress, 2006).

And talking of "old chestnut" definitions, it would be very remiss of me not to include this one:

> Network: Any thing reticulated or decussated, with interstices between the intersections [*from Dr Johnson's Dictionary—where else?*].

And networks bring me to distributed databases ... I hope I'm not the only one to find a small degree of humor in the next two:

> Yu, C. T., et al. 1982a. "Promising approach to distributed query processing," in ... (etc.).

> Yu, C. T., et al. 1982b. "Two surprising results in processing simple queries in distributed databases," in ... (etc.).

These two items are taken, slightly edited, from the references section of a paper on distributed query processing in *ACM Computing Surveys 16*, No. 4 (December 1984). I love that combination of "promising approach" followed by "surprising results" ... The description of some line of investigation first as promising, later as surprising, could probably be applied to a lot of research activity, if the truth be known.

While I'm on the subject of distributed databases, perhaps I should tell you the story I heard at one conference on the topic, in Paris I think it was (it's a dirty job, this business of going to conferences, but someone has to do it). The speaker was talking about having dinner at a restaurant the night before. The story went like this:

> At the next table, there was a young couple who seemed to be celebrating their engagement or something ... Anyway, every time they took a sip of wine they would clink their wine glasses first. And I got to thinking ... Two people clinking their glasses means one clink for every drink. Three people means—er—three clinks per drink. Four people means six clinks. Five means ten clinks. And so on (N people means $1 + 2 + ... + (N-1)$ clinks). So pretty soon, there's too much clinking and not enough drinking. *And that's the problem with distributed database.*

OK ... to close out this section, here are a few quotes having to do with missing information and nulls (not my favorite subject, as I expect you know):

Database management would be simpler if missing values didn't exist. [This is one of my all-time favorites!—it's from Ted Codd, in our "Much Ado about Nothing" debate, *Database Programming & Design 6*, No. 10 (October 1993), in a rebuttal to one of my rebuttals to one of his rebuttals to an original article of mine on the subject.][3]

It all makes sense if you squint a little and don't think too hard. [*Anon.; quoted by David Maier in his book The Theory of Relational Databases (Computer Science Press, 1983).*]

Everything should be made as simple as possible—but no simpler [*Albert Einstein, attrib.*].

The point of this last one is that nulls, at least as usually understood, represent a grossly oversimplistic approach to a very complex problem. Oversimplifying can be harmful to your health! Which brings me nicely to the next part of this presentation.

THE ROLE OF SIMPLICITY

One of the really great things about the relational model is its simplicity. Simplicity is so important! (I'm talking about genuine simplicity here, not *over*simplification, of course.) Here are some beautiful quotes, all of them having to do with the role simplicity has to play in science; and it seems to me that we as database professionals—and other computer professionals, and scientists in general, come to that—could do a lot worse than take them to heart. Most of them need no further commentary from me, I think. First Einstein again:

Most of the fundamental ideas of science are essentially simple, and may, as a rule, be expressed in a language comprehensible to everyone [*Albert Einstein*].

---

[3] See Chapter 1 of the present book.

(This is one reason why I remain unconvinced about parts of modern physics, by the way, such as superstring theory.[4] Do *you* understand it? I've tried.)

For what is clear and easily comprehended attracts; the complicated repels [*David Hilbert, originator of that famous list of 23 math problems (1900), which in some ways set the agenda for mathematical research in the 20th century*].

Sometimes one has to say difficult things, but one ought to say them as simply as one knows how [*G. H. Hardy, author of that wonderful book A Mathematician's Apology*].

Even for the physicist, the description in plain language will be a criterion of the degree of understanding that has been reached. [*Werner Heisenberg; of course, he was a little uncertain on this point, ha ha.*]

If you cannot—in the long run—tell everyone what you have been doing, your doing has been worthless [*Erwin Schrödinger; though he couldn't even tell anyone whether his cat was alive or dead*].

By the way—talking of simplicity—here's something I enjoyed greatly when I first came across it:

adjs. **P-Celtic** (*or* **-Keltic**)*,* **Q-Celtic** (*or* **-Keltic**), pertaining respectively to one of the Celtic languages in which Indo-Germanic **qu** became **p** and to one in which **qu** became **q**, later **k** (written **c**) [*Chambers Twentieth Century Dictionary*].

And you thought SQL was complicated!
And talking of SQL—must we?—here's a quote I think is highly relevant:

The sky is darkening with chickens coming home to roost [*Alan Bennett*].

As Hugh Darwen has written:

"The chickens have come home to roost" is a common metaphor for problems that could and should have been foreseen but have been lying dormant, and therefore ... conveniently disregarded, waiting for circumstances to arise in which they are finally shown to all and sundry for what they are. It's perhaps a slightly

---

[4] Maybe I mean cosmology, not physics. I'm not entirely sure where the dividing line is.

less obnoxious way of saying "I told you so right back in [*whenever*]—now do you see how right I was?" [*from The Third Manifesto: Making It Happen, a presentation by Hugh Darwen*].

Actually, Hugh says *pigeons*, not *chickens*, but it's my belief that *chickens* is the right word:

Curses, like chickens, come home to roost [*Robert Southey*].

Indeed, many of the mistakes that were made in the original design of SQL are now coming home to roost, and causing troubles of various kinds. Here are some SQL chickens (and I hope it goes without saying that this list is a long way from complete):

- Duplicate rows (of course!)

- Nulls (of course!)

- SELECT – FROM – WHERE template

  The point here is that the template is much too rigid. I could go into details if there's time, but basically the template is a Procrustean bed—it makes the transparently false assumption that all queries can be formulated in terms of a cartesian product, followed by a restriction, followed by a projection.

- Columns with no name

  Columns with no name are a pain—almost a contradiction in terms, but SQL does allow them—because if they have no name there's no way to refer to them (obviously).

- Scalar subqueries

  And the point here is that in SQL we now need to have this very same syntactic construct, in the very same syntactic context, sometimes stand for a scalar and sometimes for a table.

- WITHOUT CHECK OPTION

  I've written at length elsewhere on this particular problem—see Chapters 2 ("Assignment") and 3 ("Naming") of my book *Stating the Obvious, and Other Database Writings* (Technics Publications, 2020).

- Extreme redundancy (I'll have more to say on this one later)

To be continued.

Chapter 13

Database Graffiti

Part 2

For a description of the background to this chapter, please see the preamble to Chapter 12. This version copyright © 2022 C. J. Date.

THE JOY OF SELF-REFERENCE

Now I'm going to shift gears somewhat ... A little light relief, in fact (?). That old chestnut definition of recursion I quoted in the previous chapter ("recursion: *see* recursion") is, of course, an example of self-referencing. Douglas Hofstadter in his wonderful book *Gödel, Escher, Bach* made tremendous play with the idea of self-referencing, as I'm sure you know. And, of course, computing in general, and database technology in particular, are full of situations that involve some kind of self-referencing. So here are some nice examples (general ones, that is, they're not computer specific). My first one I already mentioned in the previous chapter:

> The only thing we learn from history is that we learn nothing from history.

This one nicely illustrates the point that self-reference often leads to paradox. (If the statement is true, then we learn nothing from history, so there's no "only thing" that we do learn, so the statement is false. Right?)

Here's another nice one. It's from *The Haldeman Diaries: Inside the Nixon White House*—a pretty turgid book, by the way, but it does contain a few nuggets like this one:

[Secretary of State Bill] Rogers said his answer to [the] criticism that we have no planned strategy is that we do have one and that it is that we will not tell anyone what it is.

And here are a bunch more:

Ignore this notice [*anon.*].

Rule 6: There is no Rule 6 [*from the Monty Python "Bruce"s sketch*].

I am *not* in denial! [*A personal favorite.*]

Question 2: What's the answer to Question 2? [*anon.*]

This last one reminds me of the—probably apocryphal—story of the Oxford University final examination in philosophy that included the following question:

Is this a question?

To which one student replied (and I hope he got a First):

If it is, then this is an answer.

Actually I've heard another possible answer to "Is this a question?"—viz., the following:

I don't have time to answer that.

Another clever one:

This sentence no verb [*Douglas Hofstadter*]. [1]

Finally, a more graphic example (a nice example of a pie chart):

---

[1] Over the years I've been struck by the number of people who don't seem to get this one.

Question: Is Princeton too homogeneous?

Response: NO (100%)—entire pie black [*from Princeton Engineer (September 1987), quoted by Jon Bentley in More Programming Pearls (Addison-Wesley, 1988)*].

SOME FUNDAMENTAL PRINCIPLES

Now I want to state and discuss a few important general principles. Some of them apply to databases specifically, others are of wider applicability. The first is Codd's well known *Information Principle* (at least, I hope it's well known):

> **Definition (*The Information Principle*):** All information in the database must be cast explicitly in terms of values in relations and in no other way.

Codd stated this principle in various forms and various places over the years; I even heard him describe it on occasion as *the* fundamental principle underlying the relational model. What it means is that, as far as the user is concerned, every piece of information in the database that's represented in the database at all, at any given time, must in fact be represented by some explicit *value* (basically a value at a row and column intersection in a table).[2] So there must be:

- No row ordering, top to bottom

- No column, ordering left to right

- No duplicate rows

---

[2] I say "basically" here because, although it's certainly true that what occurs at a row and column intersection is a value, rows are values too, and so are the tables that contain them.

- No nulls[3]

- No pointers[4]

- No hidden "row IDs"

- No indexes or other physical access paths

And so on. In a word: *No data constructs except relations.*

This next one is related to *The Information Principle*. I love the name!

> **Definition (*The Principle of Identity of Indiscernibles*):** Two entities *A* and *B* that can't be distinguished from one another in any way whatsoever are in fact one and the same entity.

Of course, nobody knows exactly what an "entity" is, right? I mean, if you look up "entity" in the dictionary, it says something like "a person, place, or thing." And then, if you look up "thing," it says "an entity" (!). The concept of an entity is the given, the axiom, the foundation on which we build everything else, and it's essentially and necessarily undefined. However, there's one thing about entities that we can—and must!—agree on, and that's as follows: If we have two entities (two hands, two computers, two desks, two rooms, two whatevers), then there must be some way to tell them apart. For if there isn't—if there's absolutely no way whatsoever to tell them apart—then we don't have two entities, we only have one. That's *The Principle of Identity of Indiscernibles*.

By the way, I'm not using the term *entity* here in any loaded kind of way here; I mean, I'm not endorsing "the entity / relationship model" or anything like that. You could replace the term *entity* by the term *thing* if you prefer. Or

---

[3] I disagree with Codd here, strongly. Though I have to say I really don't understand Codd's position on this matter, since he certainly agrees that (whateve else they might be) nulls aren't values.

[4] By pointers here, I mean the kinds of pointers that SQL allows, which is to say pointers to rows—because (as I've explained in numerous other writings) the rows in question have to be row *variables* specifically, and row variables constitute a major violation of *The Information Principle.*

object—but that would get us into another huge chunk of undesirable territory ... Let's not go there.

As a matter of fact, the principle we're talking about here is an old *philosophical* principle. It's the basic reason why relations don't contain duplicate rows and (more generally) why sets don't contain duplicate members. By the way, Codd has a very nice line on duplicates:

> If something is true, saying it twice doesn't make it more true [*E. F. Codd*].[5]

For example, the appearance of the row (E1,50K) in the EMPLOYEES relation tells us that it's a "true fact" that employee E1 earns $50,000. If the row appeared twice, it would just be telling us that true fact twice—i.e., the same thing twice.

Another way of stating the same principle is that if *A* and *B* are *not* one and the same, then they must be *distinguishable*—i.e., they must be *uniquely identifiable* in some way. This is the basic reason why the relational model includes the notion of *keys*—keys provide the necessary unique identification functionality in the relational model.

A couple of corollaries:

- ■ An entity without *id*entity is a contradiction in terms; in fact, an entity without identity *doesn't even exist,* by definition. Note that we couldn't even talk sensibly about an entity if it had no identity.

- ■ In a relational database, we never record information about something we can't identify.

By the way, I've seen *The Principle of Identity of Indiscernibles* stated in an object context like this:

> Objects in the real world have only one thing in common—they're all different [*anon.; quoted by Antero Taivalsaari in "Classes versus Prototypes: Some Philosophical and Historical Observations," Journal of Object Oriented Programming (November / December 1997)*].

Very nice!

---

[5] But as an attendee on one of my seminars once muttered, sotto voce, when I recited this line: *You can say that again.*

———— ♦ ♦ ♦ ♦ ♦ ————

Moving on: This next one is again related to the previous one. It's one of my own (I haven't seen it formally stated anywhere), but I do think it's important. I call it *The Naming Principle*:[6]

> **Definition (*The Naming Principle*):** Everything we need to talk about must have a name.

Seems pretty obvious, right? In fact, it's really the point I was discussing a moment ago, when I said entities have identity—we can't even talk sensibly about things that have no name. But there's more that can usefully be said.

Let's see what happens if the principle is violated. Here's an example. In the Persistent Stored Modules feature (PSM) of the SQL standard, there are things called *exception handlers*. For example:

```
DECLARE HANDLER FOR SQLSTATE '22012' /* zerodivide */
        BEGIN ... END ;
```

Note that this "handler" has no name (and in fact can't have a name). So what does the PSM specification do in its explanation of handlers? It says this (very slightly paraphrased):

When the handler *H* associated with the handler declaration is created ...

In other words, it invents a name! And look at the awful circumlocution involved, too—"the handler associated with the handler declaration"—which is caused precisely by the fact that the handler doesn't have a name as far as PSM is concerned.

In fact, in that book *A Guide to the SQL Standard* I mentioned before (in the previous chapter), Hugh Darwen and I do pretty much the same thing; that is, our text discussing handlers begins "Let *H* be a handler" ... And notice too what I did when I introduced the foregoing example—I said "there are *things called* exception handlers." In other words, I was applying *The Naming Principle* right there.

---

[6] The material of this subsection is discussed at much greater length in Chapter 3 ("Naming") of my book *Stating the Obvious, and Other Database Writings* (Technics Publications, 2020).

Similar remarks apply to objects (objects as in OO, I mean). Without getting into too much detail, I'll just say this: Objects are basically variables that have no name—which is why they have to be referenced by object IDs, or in other words by *addresses* (and by the way, that's why that OO stuff is all pointers). Those object IDs are basically just *invented names*—and highly inconvenient ones at that, in my opinion. All of which goes some way toward explaining why we prohibit object IDs, as indeed we do, in *The Third Manifesto*.

Analogous remarks apply to methods (at least methods in Smalltalk, though possibly not in other object languages). Again, it's hard to talk about things that have no names ... so what typically happens is that people in fact talk, sloppily, about (e.g.) "the DETECT method," whereas in actuality there's no such thing— DETECT is really just the name of a parameter, a parameter to a method that has no actual name of its own.

As we've just seen, therefore, parameters, at least, do have names in Smalltalk—but there's one important exception: *receiver* parameters. Receiver parameters *don't* have names. And this fact accounts for that funny "selfish methods" stuff in Smalltalk concerning the construct SELF. As Bruce Lindsay says, "object systems are obsessed with self."

Yet another example: SQL permits columns in derived tables to have no name—and I hope we all understand what problems *that* causes! Columns with no name are a pain, because you can't refer to them in other SQL expressions. (I touched on this one in Chapter 12 as well—it was one of my SQL chickens.)

By the way: Since *The Naming Principle* itself is something we need to talk about, it too must have a name, of course—which it does: It's called *The Naming Principle*.

And by the way again: I'd like to insist (though this is more of a psychological issue than a logical one) that names always be apt—i.e., good ones, and appropriate The SQL standard violates this one all over the place with its syntax category names, which are often truly dreadful. Did you know, for example, that in SQL the syntactic category *<qualified identifier>* means, quite literally, an *un*qualified identifier? Unbelievable.

Another example of inappropriate naming: In the world of objects and inheritance, there's something called *specialization by constraint*. For the longest time, I thought this meant what it sounds like it *ought* to mean—namely, that if a certain constraint was satisfied, you got automatic specialization. For example, if *R* is a rectangle (i.e., if it's of type RECTANGLE), and it satisfies the constraint that its sides are all equal, then *R* is "specialized" to a square (i.e., to type SQUARE). Only comparatively recently did I discover that it actually means the exact opposite—namely, that if you had the specialization, then you had to satisfy the constraint! (If *S* is a square, its sides must be equal.) In other words, "S by C" means the *type* implies the *constraint*, not the *constraint* implies the *type*. Or in plain English, it just means you mustn't violate certain integrity constraints.

Bad terminology is the very devil.

————— ◆ ◆ ◆ ◆ —————

Moving on again, the next principle is:

> **Definition (*The Principle of Interchangeability*):** There must be no arbitrary distinctions between base and derived relations.[7]

The fundamental point here is this: The question as to which relations are base and which derived is, to a very large degree, arbitrary. For example, consider suppliers, from the usual suppliers-and-parts database, and the following relations:

```
S { SNO , SNAME , STATUS , CITY }
```

vs.

```
SS { SNO , SNAME }

ST { SNO , STATUS }

SC { SNO , CITY }
```

Here S could be a base relation and SS, ST, and SC views, derived from S via projection—or SS, ST, and SC could be base relations and S could be a view, derived by joining those base relations together.

Another example:

```
S { SNO , SNAME , STATUS , CITY }
```

vs.

---

[7] This principle, and this whole subsection, should really be expressed in terms of relvars, not relations—but relvars vs. relations was another big issue I didn't want to get into when I wrote the original script for the presentation on which these chapters are based.

```
EUROPEANS { SNO , SNAME , STATUS , CITY }

AMERICANS { SNO , SNAME , STATUS , CITY }
```

Here again S could be a base relation and EUROPEANS and AMERICANS views, derived from S via restriction—or EUROPEANS and AMERICANS could be base relations and S could be a view, derived by "unioning" those two base relations together.

In all such cases, the only requirement is that the set of *expressible* relations—i.e., the universe of all information that can be obtained from the database—mustn't change. Database design disciplines such as normalization can help in choosing a "good" set of base relations (though in fact normalization per se doesn't help at all with the examples I just gave).[8]

It follows that we must have NO arbitrary and unnecessary distinctions between base and derived relations—with respect to (e.g.):

■ Having keys or not
  (I disagree with Codd here—*all* relations have keys)

■ Integrity in general, in fact
  (*all* relations are subject to constraints—another disagreement with Codd)

■ Entity integrity
  (actually I don't believe in this rule at all—yet another disagreement with Codd)

■ Row IDs
  (row IDs might exist under the covers for base relations and not views, but the distinction mustn't show up at the logical level)

In particular, the updatability of a given set of data must *not* depend on arbitrary decisions as to how the database is designed, in other words, we *must* be able to update views!

---

[8] This remark in parentheses was kind of true when I first wrote it but is kind of not true now ... The new (or comparatively new) sixth normal form might help with the first example, and the new (or comparatively new) *Principle of Orthogonal Design*—which can be seen as suggesting another kind of normalization, in a way—might help with the second.

So: The user interacts with an "expressible" database (possibly the "real" database)—where the "real" database is all of the base relations, but an "expressible" database is some mixture of base relations and views (in general). Now, we can assume that none of the relations in any given database is derived from the rest (because any such relations could be dropped without loss of information). Hence, *from the user's point of view*, those relations are all base relations, by definition!—they're all independent of one another. And similarly for the database itself—i.e., the choice of which database is the "real" one is arbitrary, just so long as the choices are all information equivalent. In fact, that's another fundamental principle! I call it *The Principle of Database Relativity.*

———— ◆◆◆◆◆ ————

The next few principles are all interrelated, in a way. Like *The Naming Principle* and *The Principle of Interchangeability* (and *The Principle of Database Relativity*, come to that), they're all my own invention (Lewis Carroll is one of my literary heroes):

> **Definition (*The Principle of Commensurate Difficulty*):** If a construct (e.g., a given theory or a given product) seems to be difficult to explain / hard to understand / confusing (etc.), it's probably because it *is* difficult to explain / hard to understand / confusing (etc.)—and in fact very likely confused as well.

The point here is that some systems / ideas / etc. do seem to be very difficult to "get your head around" ... and it's my thesis that *it's not your fault!* Most likely, the systems / ideas / etc. really *are* difficult. Some examples:

- OS/360 (MVS etc.)

- IMS

- IDMS and (especially) IDMS/R

- Object databases

- SQL!

■ *Your choice here*

One of the reasons we get into the "commensurate difficulty" mess is because some people like to follow a different principle, one that I call:

> **Definition (*The Principle of Spurious Generality*):** Lots of bells and whistles are good. Lots of alternatives are good. Etc.

Application of this principle leads to systems that are supposedly more "general" but in fact aren't so (or aren't significantly so); the tiny increase in generality, if any, is more than offset by the accompanying increase in complexity. I think we can all provide examples! E.g. (basically the same list as before, but with a little added emphasis):

■ OS/360 (MVS etc.)

■ IMS

■ IDMS and (especially) IDMS/R

■ Object databases

■ **SQL !!!**

■ *Your choice here*

Out of this list, I want to elaborate briefly on object databases and SQL. First, object databases. The basic point here is that the "object model" (if I might be permitted to use such a term) says we can put anything we like in the database—any data structure we can create with the usual programming language mechanisms. The usual jingle, or mantra, is *persistence orthogonal to type*. So we can have lists in the database, arrays in the database, stacks in the database, etc., etc. This is spurious generality!—and I reject it (i.e., I reject the jingle). As I once heard Codd say at a conference, as part of a panel discussion:

> If you tell me you have 50 different ways of representing data in your system (i.e., at the logical level), then I'll tell you that you have 49 too many [*E. F. Codd*].

By the way, one consequence of this "anything goes" approach in the object world is that—contrary to conventional wisdom—object database systems might very well provide less data independence than relational ones. For example, suppose the "object" in question is the collection of employees in a given department, and suppose the implementation of that object is changed from an array to a linked list. What are the implications for existing code that accesses that object? (*Answer:* It breaks.)

What about SQL? Well, I fear SQL can be held up as An Awful Warning to us all on this score (spurious generality, I mean). In an attempt—I would say, a spurious attempt—to be *general*, SQL has become an extremely *redundant* language. I mean, for all but the most trivial of queries, SQL gives us many different ways of formulating the query (and some of the differences are quite radical). In my seminars—this was in the days before SQL:1992—I used to give a very simple example ("Get names of suppliers who supply part P2") and showed that it could be expressed in at least eight different ways, all of them at least superficially distinct: one using a join, one using EXISTS, one using GROUP BY, one using COUNT, etc., etc. This redundancy does *not* make SQL more general; it just makes it more complicated.

What about SQL after 1992? Well, I subsequently wrote a paper—I called it "Fifty Ways to Quote Your Query"—that shows that, in SQL:1992, the number of formulations of this query is quite literally infinite!—modulo only the size of the machine, etc.[9] (and we're not exactly dealing with a very complicated query here).

Why is this state of affairs undesirable?

- Well, first, of course, such redundancy makes the language much bigger than it needs to be, with obvious negative implications for documentation, implementation, teaching, learning, and so on. The SQL:1992 specification was some 638 pages long—and that's before SQL/CLI, SQL/PSM, and various technical corrigenda were added in. This figure does *not* impress me. Six hundred pages of definition means errors, contradictions, inconsistencies, etc., are all 100% guaranteed. By contrast, if you showed me a language specification of *six* pages, now that *would* impress me.

---

[9] I subsequently incorporated that paper into Chapter 4 ("Redundancy in SQL") of my book *Stating the Obvious, and Other Database Writings* (Technics Publications, 2020).

■ In particular, the fact that a given query can be formulated in so many different ways has the serious negative consequence that users will often have to spend time and effort trying to find the "best" formulation (i.e., the formulation that performs best), which—*grrr*—was exactly one of the things the relational model was trying to avoid in the first place. (One of the many ways in which SQL missed the relational boat, in fact.)

■ Of course, this latter criticism wouldn't be valid if all formulations performed equally well, but that seems unlikely (it's doubtful whether the optimizer will be that good). Indeed, it's worth stressing that the redundancies make SQL harder to implement (especially to optimize), as well as harder to teach, learn, remember, and use. And this situation is really rather strange, given that the people responsible for the design of SQL (I mean the people on the SQL standards committee) are, first and foremost, the SQL vendors—i.e., precisely the ones who have to do the implementing.

By the way: I'm not saying we can design languages such that there's always exactly One True Way (as Don Chamberlin puts it) to formulate any given query. That goal is probably unachievable. But I do think it's worth striving for as an ideal. I think we should try to design the language in such a way as to exclude features with overlapping functionality (except where a feature is expressly defined to be shorthand for some other combination of features). And I also think it's worth striving to make sure, to the greatest extent possible, that alternative formulations can be transformed into one another as easily as possible. To the extent this goal is met, the language becomes easier to define, easier to document, easier to teach, easier to learn, easier to remember, easier to use, and—last but not least—easier to implement.

Needless to say, the foregoing is *not* the way SQL was designed, or developed. I'll say a bit more on this issue in a moment.

You must understand too that these redundancy problems aren't easy to fix. What Hugh Darwen calls *The Shackle of Compatibility* means that, once a feature has been included in a language, it can never be taken out again—because, of course, existing programs will fail if it is. That's why it's so important to get languages right first time! It's also one reason why language design is hard.

To summarize, then, regarding spurious generality:

- Does it buy additional functionality? *Obviously no.*

- Does it buy additional usability? *This one is debatable*—if the redundancy is properly defined as a shorthand, it might. For example, we might define lists and list operators as shorthands for certain combinations of relations and relational operators. And, of course, lists might well be more usable— more user friendly, perhaps—than pure relations in some cases. Note, however, that what I haven't done here is clutter up my core or kernel model with lists (making life more complicated for everybody); I've merely defined them as a shorthand (making life simpler for some people).

But, you see, if the redundancy is properly defined as a shorthand, then there's no spurious generality!

I remark in passing that most of the redundancies in SQL were *not* properly defined as shorthands (JOIN is perhaps an exception, maybe INTERSECT and EXCEPT too)—with the result that the language is *extremely messy.* In fact, I think it's the worst computer language ever designed. (*Question:* What's the second worst? *Answer:* IBM System/360 JCL.)

FYI, here are some (pretty major!) SQL features that are redundant in SQL today:

a. EXISTS

In SQL, the expression

```
EXISTS ( SELECT * FROM T ) ≡
```

is logically equivalent to the following expression:

```
( SELECT COUNT(*) FROM T ) ≠ 0
```

Actually I wouldn't want to get rid of EXISTS—though it's worth mentioning in passing that it doesn't really do the job it was meant to do, because it isn't a faithful representation of the existential quantifier of three-valued logic.

b. Correlation names

Correlation names are redundant now that SQL has a "proper" column rename operator. To put it another way: SQL now includes the entire relational algebra as a proper subset.[10] And the relational algebra has no correlation names. But there's nothing useful—nothing relationally useful, anyway—that can be done with correlation names that can't be done with the relational algebra. QED.

c. GROUP BY

To show the redundancy of GROUP BY here would take us too far afield, unfortunately; I'll just have to ask you to trust me. The same goes for the next item, HAVING.

d. HAVING

e. IN subquery

Huge irony here!—since IN with a subquery was the original justification for the SQL language in the first place! I mean, the "structured" in the name "Structured Query Language" referred *precisely* to the "IN subquery" construct.

f. JOIN

I don't count outer join here, of course, because I reject everything to do with nulls anyway. Apart from its outer flavors, then, I should at least say that I think JOIN (unlike GROUP BY etc.) *is* properly defined as a shorthand, so I don't actually object to this particular redundancy too much. The same goes for INTERSECT and EXCEPT, I believe (next item in the list).

g. INTERSECT and EXCEPT

---

[10] Except that it has no support for relations of degree zero.

Were you surprised by anything in this list? There's obviously another presentation here! Let me just say that—precisely because the redundancies were (mostly) not originally meant to be redundant—saying just what it is that might be equivalent to, say, GROUP BY can certainly be done, but the process is pretty messy. Life is therefore harder for the optimizer! (as well as for users); indeed, numerous *incorrect* transformations have appeared in the literature. I can cite chapter and verse if need be.

■ Does it buy better performance? *Yes, possibly*—but performance shouldn't be the driving force (performance is, or should be, an implementation matter merely, not a model concern).

■ Does it buy additional complexity for the user? *Obviously yes*.

■ Does it buy additional complexity for the DBMS? *Obviously yes*.

——— ◆ ◆ ◆ ◆ ———

The opposite of *The Principle of Spurious Generality* is:

Definition (*The Principle of Cautious Design*): Given a design choice between Option *A* and Option *B* (where *A* is upward compatible with *B*), if the full implications of Option *B* are not yet known, then go with Option *A*.

If we're forced at some future time to "open up" our design to permit Option *B*, then nothing we'll have done in the past will be incompatible with that opening up. If, on the other hand, we go with Option *B* initially, and it subsequently becomes apparent that this was a bad decision, we can never close our design down again to go back to Option *A*. In other words, we should try to avoid situations in which the model—or the language, or the DBMS, or the database, or whatever else it is we're designing—provides certain options that users have to be explicitly told not to exercise.

A good example of *failure* to apply *The Principle of Cautious Design* is duplicate rows in SQL. On Day 1 in the design of SQL, the designers had a choice: No duplicate rows (Option *A*) vs. yes duplicate rows (Option *B*). *A* was upward compatible with *B*. And they made the wrong choice, of course. As a consequence, people like me have to go around telling users not to use that part of SQL that permits duplicate rows. (I guess I should be thankful, though, because it does at least mean job security.)

A good example of *successful* application of *The Principle of Cautious Design* occurs in connection with foreign keys. The original relational model insisted that foreign keys refer specifically to primary keys, not just to any old key. And I used to believe in this rule, and went around teaching it. More recently, however, I've come to believe that the rule is too restrictive, and that there are some situations—perhaps fairly unusual ones, but realistic ones nevertheless—in which a foreign key should be allowed to refer to a key that's not a primary key. But all databases that abided by the original tighter rule are still valid under this relaxed version of the rule, and they still work just fine, of course.

To sum up, *The Principle of Cautious Design* says: Stay with the simple design for as long as possible; go to the more complex design only if and when necessary. This approach guarantees maximum simplicity for maximum time, and (more important) guarantees that extensions are made in an evolutionary, not a revolutionary, manner.

Note finally that *The Principle of Cautious Design* can be used to help refute the opposite point of view!—namely, the idea that the formal system in question should provide a plethora of essentially equivalent options and alternatives in the interests of "flexibility" and "generality." This latter point of view is, of course, *The Principle Of Spurious Generality*, and I've already talked about that one.

My last general principle (acknowledgments to Hugh Darwen for the naming of this one) is:

Definition (*The Principle of Cessation of Excavation*): When you find you're digging yourself into a pit, the first thing to do is *stop digging*.

Duplicate rows and nulls are both SQL pits ... That's why, in the work David McGoveran and I did on view updating, we stated right up front that we wouldn't even consider the possibility that the views in question involved any duplicates or any nulls. We wanted rules that worked for relations, not for kludges (I'm never quite sure how to spell that word, but you know what I mean). And I'd fight to keep it that way, even if our mechanisms were to be picked up and adopted for SQL ... In other words, if the SQL standards folks did decide to adopt our ideas (ha!), I'd vote for putting in a rule right up front that says "By the way, this mechanism doesn't work if you have duplicates or nulls." Don't let's mess up a clean, sound, logical scheme by trying to "extend" it to handle the kludge cases.

By the way, there's another general and related point here: Even if you decide—very sensibly, in my opinion—never to have duplicates or nulls in *your* databases, you're still paying all kinds of prices for the fact that you're *allowed* to have those silly things. This is yet another point I could get quite eloquent on if I had more time.

To be continued.

Chapter 14

Database Graffiti

Part 3

For a description of the background to this chapter, please see the preamble to Chapter 12. This version copyright © 2022 C. J. Date.

RELATIONAL DATABASE: FURTHER MISCONCEPTIONS NUMBER 4

Another shift of gears ... Now I want to talk about a few what I call "relational misconceptions." I should begin by explaining that, over the years, I've published a series of papers on this general topic:

- "Some Relational Myths Exploded: An Examination of Some Popular Misconceptions Concerning Relational Database Management Systems" (1984)

- "Relational Database: Further Misconceptions Number One" (1986) and "Relational Database: Further Misconceptions Number Two" (1986), combined into "Further Relational Myths" (1990)

- "Relational Database: Further Misconceptions Number Three" (1992)

The generic abstract for those papers looks like this:

> Relational database management is one of the key technologies for the 1980s [*and beyond, let me now stress!*], yet the field of relational technology still suffers from a great deal of misunderstanding and misrepresentation. Misconceptions abound. The purpose of [these papers] is to identify some of those misconceptions.

And in the body of those papers I documented a few—*very* few!—of the many misconceptions regarding relational technology that had found their way into print at one time or another, and tried to respond to them by explaining just what the errors were and why they were errors.

In what follows, I want to quote some more recent statements of the same general nature (so this presentation, or at least this part of the presentation, can be seen as a continuation of that earlier series of papers). But I don't think it's worth trying to respond to the mistakes here; I think the errors are mostly so obvious, or so egregious, that any such responses would be superfluous. Let the quotes speak for themselves! (But don't you think it's sad that some people who really ought to know better *still* don't understand—in this day and age—what relational technology is all about?)

Here goes, then:

> **Relational data model:** A scheme for defining databases in which data elements are organized into relations, typically viewed as rows in tables [*David A. Taylor: Object-Oriented Technology: A Manager's Guide (Addison-Wesley, 1990)*].

Never mind the (many) inaccuracies—you mean that's *it*? What about the operators? What about integrity? declarative query? views? the set level nature? optimization? etc., etc., etc.

And from the same source:

> A newer form of database manager, the *relational model*, ... [removes] the information about complex relationships from the database ... Although the relational model is much more flexible than its predecessors, it pays a price for this flexibility. The information about complex relationships that was removed from the database must be expressed as procedures in every program that accesses the database, a clear violation of the independence required for modularity.

Well, I'm sorry, but I simply must say something about this one (it's wrong on so many levels at once):

■ First, the relational model is *not* a database manager.

■ Second, information regarding "complex relationships" is categorically *not* "removed from the database"—in fact, it's more explicit in a relational database than in a typical object database (I challenge anyone to prove me wrong on this one).

■ Third, any "procedures" we might have to write can certainly be shared among applications, just as they are in an object system.

■ Last, those "procedures" are 4GL code, not 3GL code; i.e., they're declarative, not procedural—they're not really "procedures" in the old sense (or the object sense?) at all. Not to mention the fact that they're optimized by the system instead of the user.

My next quote (from a different source now) is rather on the lengthy side:

> Relational databases can handle most varieties of structured data, but when it comes to text, compound documents, vector graphics, bit-mapped images, and so on, relational technology is out of its depth ... Those of you who attended training sessions on the relational theory of data can be forgiven for wondering why relational databases cannot adequately handle such data. After all, your instructor probably told you that the relational view was not only mathematically correct, provably correct, or something similar, but also far more flexible than anything that preceded it. That explanation is fairly simple and perhaps a little embarrassing for the computer world, because **the relational theory of data is wrong**. Data cannot always be represented in terms of entities, attributes, and relationships [*Robin Bloor: "The End of Relational?", DBMS 5, No. 7 (July 1992), boldface added*].

Gosh! ... So the relational theory of data is wrong, eh? Maybe Bloor thinks predicate logic is wrong, too? After all, the relational model is essentially just an applied form of predicate logic. If Bloor thinks he's found a bug in predicate logic, I look forward very much to hearing about it ASAP. I expect a lot of logicians and mathematicians would be pretty interested, too.

By the way, I'd also love to see some data that can't be represented "in terms of entities, attributes, and relationships."

There's quite a bit more from the same source, unfortunately:

> So what is going on with normalization? By physically storing data as two-dimensional tables, relational databases encourage you to store your data in an

atomic manner. This means that every time you wish to process an object, you must first assemble it ... It is as though you took your car apart to put it into the garage and had to reassemble it before driving it out.

I am *so* tired of this stupid car analogy ... I'm not sure who came up with it originally (I do know it wasn't Bloor), but now it crops up all over the place. It stems from a failure to understand the relational model, of course, and in particular a failure to understand the true nature of domains[1]—though in a way I can sympathize with this latter failure somewhat, since SQL has never supported domains properly. But what we really have here is a classic example of the relational model being criticized for not having been implemented! See my various presentations on this subject (especially those having to do with *The Third Manifesto*).

Bloor continues:

In order to support this form of storage, relational databases provide performance-hungry mechanisms—foreign keys that increase data volumes and disk I/O, and optimizers that knit together the data that may never need to have been stored separately. Some databases [*sic*] even allow you to configure two [stored] tables to share the same ... [disk] page in an attempt to provide a back-door way of implementing an NF² model—a late, inefficient, and untidy mechanism that [*text missing?*] the promoters of the relational way have got it wrong.

This guy is *really* confused ... By the way, note too that here we run into one of my pet peeves: the "database vs. DBMS" terminology issue. The point is: If we call the DBMS a database, then what do we call the database? Very common offense!

Bloor goes on:

I do not want to go too far in my criticism. Normalization is an excellent technique for analyzing data, even if it is an abysmal technique for physically designing databases.

By "physically designing databases," I presume he means "designing physical databases."[2] Anyway, his remarks are quite absurd. Normalization was

---

[1] These days I hugely prefer the term *type* over the term *domain*.

[2] It has belatedly occurred to me that what he might have meant was "actually designing databases." But if so, it's not what he said.

never intended as a basis for physical design. (Though in fairness perhaps I should say that the problem here is—again—partly caused by the SQL vendors, who failed to give us as much physical data independence in their products as they should have done. As a result, normalizing at the logical level, where it belongs, often does have the side effect of normalizing at the physical level too.) One final quote from the same source:

> Although it is now certain that the next generation of databases will be object databases [*oh really?*], we cannot predict with any confidence which the dominant products will be ... One thing we can be sure of: They won't be relational at the physical level.

By the way, I should tell you that I've crossed swords with Mr Bloor before, in one of my earlier "relational misconceptions" articles. He was claiming in 1990 that SQL products lost updates, and further that the reason they did so was because of a flaw in SQL (i.e., nonSQL products didn't have the problem, or so he said). The claim was utter nonsense, of course. It was also very badly expressed! For example:

> [Cursors] may be implemented as pointers or as direct copies of data ... where the cursor is more complex it is likely that the cursor will be held as an actual copy of information from the buffer [*Robin Bloor: "SQL Compromises Integrity," Daemon 1, No. 1, ButlerBloor Ltd., Milton Keynes, England, June 1990*].

I'm tempted to offer a small prize to whoever can find the most errors in this quote. But it's so galling—the sloppiness of expression, I mean. As I wrote at the time:

> I have two broad problems with [Bloor's article]: its overall message on the one hand, and the quite extraordinarily imprecise language in which that message is expressed on the other ... It is very distressing to find such sloppiness in publications dealing with relational technology of all things, given that one of the objectives of the relational model was precisely to introduce some sorely needed precision and clarity of thinking into the database field [*from my paper Relational Database: Further Misconceptions Number Three*].

Anyway, back to the stuff about the relational model being wrong etc.: Not very surprisingly, Ted Codd responded to Bloor's article (in the October 1992 issue of *DBMS*). He referred to "the two mysterious assertions" in Bloor's final paragraph ("Although it is now certain ... physical level"), and asked (very reasonably, in my opinion):

- Where are "object databases" precisely defined?

- What is the meaning of "relational at the physical level"?

Bloor replied a month later (*DBMS*, November 1992), in an article entitled "In Response to Dr Codd." As far as I can see, he didn't answer either of Codd's questions. But he did say:

> In [my original] article I commented on the diminishing influence of the relational model of data in commercial databases ...

Words fail me. What can I say? (Actually he might be right to say the relational model's commercial influence is diminishing ... but if he is, it's the industry's loss, and it's partly the fault of certain "experts" who ought not to be working in a field they don't seem to have even the most elementary understanding of. Naming no names.)

Let's move on ... Here's another mind-boggler (again rather lengthy):

> As a designer of commercial manufacturing applications on IBM mainframes in the late 1960s and early 1970s, I can categorically state that relational databases set the commercial data processing industry back at least ten years and wasted many of the billions of dollars that were spent on data processing ... Why were relational databases such a Procrustean bed? Because organizations, budgets, products, etc., are hierarchical; hierarchies require transitive closures for their [explosion] and transitive closures cannot be expressed within the classical Codd model using only a finite [*sic!*] number of joins.
>
> Computing history will consider the past 20 years as a kind of Dark Ages of commercial data processing in which the religious zealots of the Church of Relationalism managed to hold back progress until a Renaissance rediscovered the Greece and Rome of pointer-based databases. Database research has produced a number of good results, but the relational database is not one of them [*Henry G. Baker, "Relational Databases," CACM 35, No. 4 (April 1992)*].

This one is simply staggering ... Let me just say that I think it's pretty appalling that such nonsense should appear in *Communications of the ACM*, of all places—i.e., in a reputable, high quality *technical* journal! Looks like they need some good technical editorship.

My next one is a bit of a cheat—I mean, it's not a new one, I included it in article "Relational Database: Further Misconceptions Number Three"—but I have my reasons for wanting to repeat it here:

> One of the great mystiques proclaimed by the relational theorists is that relational theory has a firm mathematical foundation and that is supposed to give relational systems a long term basis for stability. If we are to accept the fact that a nonprocedural [language] is the only means to manipulate relational data, then relational theory is at odds with queueing theory, which also has a firm mathematical foundation. An interesting question then becomes, which is more relevant in the real world—queueing theory or relational theory? Queueing theory is a daily fact of life—on the crowded freeways, in the supermarket, at the lunch counter, in the bank, in the bathroom in the morning, and so forth. Applied queueing theory is observable 100 times a day in the life of modern man [*sic*]. Where then is relational theory observable and relevant? [*from William H. Inmon: "Why Large On-Line Relational Systems Don't (and May Not Ever) Yield Good Performance," in System Development 6, No. 2 (April 1986)*].

There are, of course, many things wrong with this extract, but I'd just like to respond to one of them: the one about relational theory being "at odds with queuing theory." First, the point isn't demonstrated at all in Inmon's paper. Second (and much more important), it's a complete red herring! (Which do you prefer, Thursdays or porridge? The comparison is about as meaningful.)

I might add that *queueing* is a "daily fact of life," but queuing theory (regrettably) isn't; indeed, if it were, we might see less queueing (and I could tell an anecdote or two here too, if we had time).

Further, relational theory certainly is "observable and relevant," because it consists (in large part) of elements from set theory and predicate logic, which form the basis of much of mathematics (or is Inmon arguing that mathematics is not observable and relevant?). As a matter of fact, a knowledge of predicate logic enables us to pinpoint the logical errors in arguments such as Inmon's, which I think makes it very relevant indeed.

In fact, the entire extract is an illustration of what's sometimes known as *ignoratio elenchi*—the fallacy of arguing to the wrong point.

And finally, my favorite "misconception" quote. This one comes from a certain product ad:

> [Product X] is a relational database management system that literally redefines the meaning of relational.

I've concealed the product name in order to protect the guilty. "Redefines the meaning of relational" indeed.

SOME *GOOD* QUOTES

After that rather depressing collection of nonsense, let's look at some *good* quotes ... First, a few from Ted Codd:

How about recently?

You have to hand it to Ted. "How About Recently?" was the title of a paper he wrote back in the 1970s describing a prototype system he was working on called Rendezvous. Rendezvous was a natural language front end to a relational DBMS. Now, most people writing such a paper would give it a title like "Experiments with a Natural Language Front End Query Generator to a Relational Database Management System" (or some such)—but Ted called it "How About Recently?" And the reason he did so was because that was a query a user actually asked. You see, the way Rendezvous worked was this: The user posed a natural language query (the natural language in question was English in the prototype), and the system then took whatever portions of the query it could understand and translated them into fragments of relational calculus; but when it found a portion it didn't understand, then it would engage in a dialog with the user. For instance:

User: How many London parts are there? [*The database was suppliers and parts, of course.*]

System: The word "London" is unfamiliar. Is it one of the following:

1	part number	4	part weight
2	part name	5	part city
3	part color	6	none of the above

Select by number the closest catalog item.

User: 5

Once *Rendezvous* had completed its internal relational calculus formulation, it then translated it back into English for approval by the user:

System: This is what the system understands your query to be:

Count the number of parts stored in London.

Is the system's understanding

1 correct and complete
2 not yet complete
3 incorrect

Select exactly one item by number.

User: 1

At this point the user had the option of trying again to get the system to understand the query properly, if it isn't yet "correct and complete." In the example, of course, everything's fine, so the system can go ahead and execute the relational calculus version:[3]

System: The answer to your query is:

There are 3 parts stored in London.

You get the general idea. Now, it's true that the dialogs tended to have a rather plodding quality, but overall the system seemed to work pretty well (at least it was pretty robust). Anyway, back to "How About Recently?" ... In his paper, Ted gives an example like this. The user says: "Tell me about shipments of pipes by Los Angeles suppliers in 1991." And the system responds. Then the user says "How about recently?" ...

■ From the system's point of view, this natural language query is completely meaningless (it understands absolutely nothing here at all).

---

[3] By the way, isn't it interesting that Rendezvous used relational calculus, not SQL, as its target language? I wonder why that was. (Well, no, I don't, of course.)

- So it proceeds to indulge in an *incredibly tedious* dialog with the user (it goes on for several pages in the paper).

- And at the end of the whole process it says:

There is no data in the database that satisfies your request.

Serves the user right, in my opinion.

Here's another Ted Codd story: In 1971-1972 I was still in England, working for IBM U.K., and active in a British Computer Society Working Group on database management. We (i.e., the BCS group) decided to run a one day conference devoted to relational databases—it must have been one of the very first conferences, if not *the* first, to be devoted to the topic, as a matter of fact— and we invited Ted to come and be our star speaker. Well, IBM U.K. management was very concerned about the possible impact of this conference on its efforts to sell IMS in the U.K. (the truth is, they'd been getting some failures in this connection, and they were looking for scapegoats). So, after much transatlantic correspondence, they went so far as to take Ted and myself out to dinner the night before the conference in order to shape our heads—i.e., to warn us to be careful over what we might say the next day. (I was one of the speakers too, of course.)

Well, during Ted's talk the inevitable question came up: "What are the implications of all these relational ideas of yours for IMS?"

People had been waiting all day for this question, of course. The audience held its breath ... You could have heard a pin drop. And Ted looked rather severely at the questioner—and took off his glasses—and put them back on again—and then said:

I did not fly 6000 miles across the Atlantic to talk about IMS.

As I recall, this response drew a round of applause.

While I'm on the topic of Ted at conferences, I remember a conference in Miami Beach in 1972 (I think it was) where we were on a panel together ... An audience member asked a question, and Ted said "I just happen to have a slide here that will answer your question," and he pulled it out of his case and showed it like this (just the top three lines):

blah blah blah blah blah ...
blah blah blah blah blah ...
blah blah blah blah blah ...

Then in answer to another question he showed a bit more of the slide (another three lines):

blah blah blah blah blah ...
blah blah blah blah blah ...
blah blah blah blah blah ...

And so on and so on, until ultimately he'd shown every part of the slide except the last line, which said:

*** IBM Confidential ***

I have many more Ted Codd stories, but I think we should move on. Here are some more excellent quotes. This one and the next are due to Hugh Darwen:

Types are to tables as nouns are to sentences.

For example, consider the employees table, wth two columns ENO and SALARY, of types "employee number" and "money," respectively. The sentence corresponding to that table is "ENO earns SALARY," and the nouns in that sentence are ENO and SALARY, corresponding as I say to those types "employee number" and "money."

This is really a great observation, but it needs more time than I have now to deal with it properly. My presentations on *The Third Manifesto* cover it and explain it in depth. For now, let me just recommend that you ponder it and take it to heart (if indeed you haven't already done so).

Here's Hugh Darwen again, this time talking about OO:

What problem, that I never knew I had, does all this strange talk of methods ... purport to solve? Let's identify very precisely the problems that methods solve ... Having done that, let's be sure that the methods solution really is better than any old-fashioned solution ... And then let's keep methods just in those places. [*"The Madness of Methods," private communication.*]

Here's another nice one:

It's little wonder that so many students develop a disdain for theory. They think that all the confusion they experience is because of the presence of this dreaded thing known as theory. How could they possibly know that [their] confusion arises [precisely because of] the absence of theory! [*Gene Hackett, private communication.*]

I've been saying for years that *theory is practical!* The crucial point is, theory—at least, relational theory—is *not* just theory for its own sake; the purpose of that theory is so that we can build systems that are *100% practical.* Every last detail of the theory is there for solid *practical* reasons (yet another issue discussed at length in many of my seminars).

Regarding "theory is practical," by the way, here's another nice quote:

Those who are enamored of practice without theory are like a pilot who goes into a ship without rudder or compass and never has any certainty where he [*sic*] is going. Practice should always be based upon a sound knowledge of theory.

This one is from Leonardo da Vinci (1452-1519), no less—the *Notebooks.*

I'll close this section with a few more good quotes, some but not all of which are directly database related:

The database is not the database—the log is the database, and the database is just an optimized access path to the most recent version of the log. [*Anon.*]

This observation is highly relevant to the current work on "temporal databases" (keeping historical records in particular).

On a clean disk you can seek forever [*Tom Steel*].

The three rules of programming: [4]

1. Never interfere with a working program (perhaps better known in the form "If it ain't broke, don't fix it").

2. All programs contain at least one bug.

---

[4] These rules are reminiscent of the three laws of thermodynamics: 1. You can't win, you can only break even. 2. You can only break even at absolute zero. 3. You can't achieve absolute zero.

3. All programs can be reduced by at least one instruction.

Which reminds me of the old junior programming manager story: "Come on team, I want you to get this program coded *really quickly*, so we have plenty of time for debugging."

The next one is from the IBM "FS" (Future System) functional specification (S/3.7 – FS-0010):

WORLD TRADE REQUIREMENT: Language

Text on Lights, Keys, etc. will be released in U.K. English, French, German, Italian, Spanish and Japanese in addition to English.

Some people think this is funny.

BOOKS AND BOOK REVIEWS

I'm shifting gears again ... In the previous chapter, I talked about *referencing* (actually self-referencing, mostly). The concept of referencing is very important in database circles, of course, especially in the context of foreign keys and referential integrity. And in connection with these notions, I want to mention a great typo I came across a few years back. It was in a White Paper that described a then new DBMS product (it might have been DEC's Rdb/VMS). Anyway, the White Paper had the term "referential integrity" set throughout as *reverential* integrity. Very nice.

Another nice one: A certain review, again from a few years back (it was in *Computerworld*, in fact), of a book by James Martin titled *System Design from Provably Correct Constructs* (Prentice-Hall, 1985) was headed "How to Write Programs that are *Probably* Correct" (emphasis added). Again, very nice! (Actually, I think we all know how to write programs that are *probably* correct.)

While I'm on the topic of book reviews, I can't resist mentioning one of the best I know:

The covers of this book are too far apart [*Ambrose Bierce, review, quoted by Matthew Parris in Scorn with Added Vitriol, Hamish Hamilton Ltd. (1995)*].

And another:

> This is not a [book] to be tossed aside lightly. It should be thrown with great force. [*Dorothy Parker, of course.*]

I can think of several database books to which the foregoing remarks apply only too well. Though I suppose I'd better be careful what I say here, having published a few books on the subject myself (and some of them having the covers very far apart indeed) ... But there's one particular database book I really must beat up on. In a field that's filled with really bad books, this one stands out as one of the all time worst. It's by a well-known database "expert" who used to specialize in IMS ... in fact, he spent a lot of time in the 70s and 80s rubbishing the whole relational idea, most especially as it was realized in IBM's DB2 product (since it looked as if DB2 and IMS were going to become head to head competitors, as indeed they did) ... then overnight he became a *relational* expert (!) and started publishing books on DB2, etc. I'm not going to name the author here, but in his book on DB2, on page 91, we find the following truly amazing text:

> Consider a data relationship in which a part can have multiple suppliers and vice versa ... There are two base tables: a part table and a supplier table. Then there is a cross-reference table from part to supplier **and another cross-reference table from supplier to part** [*boldface added*].

As you can see, this quote betrays a really deep understanding of relational technology ... Can you imagine being given advice by this "expert"? Can you imagine the quality of that advice? Unbelievable. Trees should not be destroyed to make books like this one. (In fact, I believe it was in connection with this book that Chris Loosley, reviewing it for *InfoDB*, recommended that purchasers write to the publisher and demand their money back.)

By the way, I do have several pieces of serious advice for people who want to write well and to the point (on database matters or anything else):

> Read over your compositions, and where ever you meet with a passage which you think is particularly fine, strike it out. [*Dr Johnson again.*]

Perfect. No further comment needed from me.

> Delete the adverbs. [*Evelyn Waugh—but I've lost the source, and these are probably not his exact words.*]

I'm guilty of violating this one myself!—I sprinkle adverbs all over the place, even though I know they tend to fuzz up the message and make for soggy writing. It's a bad habit.

> Always consider deleting the first paragraph. [*James Reeves—I think!—I got this one from Hugh Darwen.*]

This is a nice one! The first paragraph is *so* hard to write, and people often make a hash of it. Good opening paragraphs, and sentences, tend to be memorable ones. For example, do you recognize these? (I love this kind of stuff.)

- This is the most beautiful place on earth.

- Call me Ishmael.

- Stately, plump Buck Mulligan came from the stairhead, bearing a bowl of lather on which a mirror and a razor lay crossed.

- It was a bright cold day in April, and the clocks were striking thirteen.

- It is a truth universally acknowledged, that a single man in possession of a good fortune must be in want of a wife.

- It was love at first sight.

- I have walked by stalls in the market-place where books, dog-eared and faded from their purple, have burst with a white hosanna.

- There were 117 psychoanalysts on the Pan Am flight to Vienna and I'd been treated by at least six of them. And married a seventh.

- All this happened, more or less.

MISCELLANY

A few miscellaneous items (include these only if there's time) ... First another quote from *The Haldeman Diaries: Inside the Nixon White House*:

[Nixon was] impressed by a long ... memo, [the] gist of which is the lack of real intellectuals in the Administration. [He] agrees, and wants [us] to recruit in this direction ... Main problem is most intellectuals are not on our side.

You can't make this stuff up! By the way, it's interesting to note that this one postdates by several years Alan Bennett's line (in his play *Forty Years On*) to the effect that the only thing wrong with intelligent people is that they're all left wing. (The actual quote is: *Why is it always the intelligent people who are socialists?*)

Talking of politics reminds of another nice one:

Will the last one to leave the country please switch off the politicians?

And now a few random quotes:

■ Story told of a certain well known personality I won't name here: Apparently the person in question once asked a colleague, somewhat plaintively: "Hey, why do people take such an instant dislike to me?" Back came the reply, quick as a flash: "Because it saves time."

■ "You are a famously deep thinker; you are 69 years old; yet your face is free of wrinkles" [*said to T. H. Huxley by a friend. Huxley replied:*] "Yes, it is true that I think a lot, but I am seldom puzzled" [*quoted by Stan Kelly-Bootle in Software Development 4, No. 5, May 1996*].

■ Somebody once asked Professor Murray (Regius Professor of Greek at Cambridge University): "Are you interested in incest?"—to which he replied, rather brusquely: "Only in a very general kind of way."

■ Do you know the proof that all odd numbers are prime?

statistician	59 23 87 ...
physicist	1 3 5 7 9 (experimental error) 11 13 ...
engineer	1 3 5 7 9 11 13 ...
mathematician	1 3 ... (induction)
computer scientist	1 1 1 ...

Or the proof that all numbers are small? (*Easy!* One is small; adding one to a small number yields a small number; the result follows by induction.)

■ My favorite "damning with faint praise" review:

Possibly the most significant disc of early 20th century Scottish music to appear this decade [*review of Sir John Blackwood McEwen, Three Border Ballads, London Philharmonic Orchestra, conductor Alasdair Mitchell, Chandos CHAN8241*].

THE GREAT DATABASE LIMERICK COMPETITION

I'll close by announcing—actually not for the first time—*The Great Database Limerick Competition!* Your task is to complete a limerick using one of the following as the opening line or lines. I might award a small prize for the best entry, if the quality of entries warrants it.

1. The last DB2 ever sold

2. The debate between Bachman and Codd

   This one refers to the famous "Great Debate" (*Data Models: Data Structure Set vs. Relational*), held at the ACM SIGMOD Workshop on Data Description, Access, and Control in Ann Arbor, Michigan, May 1st-3rd, 1974. Charlie Bachman was pushing the CODASYL stuff and Ted Codd was evangelizing for The New Way (i.e., relations, of course).

3. What database language can equal
   The query expressions of SQL

   In this last one, you can replace "The query expressions" by "The glory and grandeur," or "The flaws and the failures," or indeed anything else that makes sense (and scans!).

Alternatively, I'd like to encourage you to try your hand at producing some wholly original limericks of your own, or any other poetic compositions on the same general subject. I look forward to seeing what you might come up with. The judge's decision is final!

CONCLUDING REMARKS

I'd like to close by acknowledging the many people, far too many to mention individually, who've drawn my attention over the years to one or other of the items included in this presentation. In particular, I should say that the opening lines of the third limerick ("What database language can equal," etc.) are due to an old friend and ex-colleague of mine, the late Bob Engles of IBM. I must also thank Hugh Darwen for letting me use his coinage "The Askew Wall" in my subtitle ("Scribbles from the Askew Wall"). Finally, I'd also like to request any further database quotations, anecdotes, etc., that you might be aware of and think I might like to add to my collection. Thanks in advance!—and thanks very much for listening.

Postscript

I first proposed The Great International Database Limerick Competition in 1996 or so. The idea was, I provided the first line or two, and you were invited to complete the verse. Here are some of my own attempts:

What database language can equal
The flaws and the failures of SQL?
    Well designed it is not
    And your brain it will rot
If you try to use it to speak well.

———— ♦♦♦♦♦ ————

What database language *should* equal
The mumblings and bumblings of SQL?
    It's such a great shame
    That we ruined the game
Before ever we managed to speak well.

———— ♦♦♦♦♦ ————

What database language can equal
The juggernaut progress of SQL?
    It's so vast (though it's vague)
    Like a hideous plague
It shapes all thought to its oblique will.

——— ♦♦♦♦♦ ———

The last DB2 ever sold
Was a hard thing to love, truth be told
    But at least it was blue—
    Although it is true
That blue no longer means gold.

——— ♦♦♦♦♦ ———

This one is unfortunately much closer to the truth now than when I wrote it:

The last DB2 ever sold
Was a horrible sight to behold
    With its S-Q-L-4
    And objects galore
And tables quite out in the cold.

——— ♦♦♦♦♦ ———

The same goes for this one:

The last DB2 ever sold
Was not very nice, truth be told
    "Relational," ye-es ...
    But old IMS
Was not so complex to behold.

——— ♦♦♦♦♦ ———

The last IMS ever sold
Was an ugly thing to behold
    With its marketing stance
    Based on paired virtual aunts
And get next within uncle, with hold.

———— ♦♦♦♦♦ ————

The debate between Bachman and Codd
Was a highlight of that year's SIGMOD
    And when everyone said
    That tabular Ted
Was the winner, none thought it odd.

———— ♦♦♦♦♦ ————

The debate between Bachman and Codd
To some seemed decidedly odd
    Tables or nets?
    None would place bets
Till a voice cried **IT'S TABLES**, by God!

———— ♦♦♦♦♦ ————

This was the winning entry (by me) in another "technical" limerick competition:

The COBOL Committee has spoken!
And spoken, and spoken, and spoken;
    And spoken. And spoken.
    And spoken—and spoken—
And spoken ... and spoken ... and spoken ...

———— ♦♦♦♦♦ ————

An attendee at one of my seminars produced this one:

> Wise sage Mr Date said to me
> "What you think to be true may not be
>   Of null: It's too vague—
>   Avoid like the plague—
> And NOT is not not, don't you see?"

——— ♦♦♦♦ ———

Index

For alphabetization purposes, (a) differences in fonts and case are ignored; (b) quotation marks are ignored; (c) other punctuation symbols—hyphens, underscores, parentheses, etc.—are treated as blanks; (d) numerals precede letters; (e) blanks precede everything else.